RISK AND DECISIONS

RISK AND DECISIONS

Edited by

W. T. Singleton

The University of Aston in Birmingham

and

Jan Hovden

Scientific and Industrial Research Foundation,
SINTEF, Trondheim, Norway

JOHN WILEY & SONS
Chichester · New York · Brisbane · Toronto · Singapore

Library of Congress Cataloging-in-Publication Data:

Risk and decisions.

   Includes bibliographies and indexes.
   1. Risk management.   2. Risk.   3. Decision-making.
I. Singleton, W. T. (William Thomas)   II. Hovden, Jan.
HD61.R564 1987   658.4'03   86-15664
ISBN 0 471 91208 5

British Library Cataloguing in Publication Data:

Risk and decisions.
  1. Risk-taking (Psychology)
  I. Singleton, W. T.   II. Hovden, Jan
  363.1   BF637.R57

ISBN 0 471 91208 5

Typeset by Activity, Salisbury, Wilts
Printed and bound in Great Britain

Table of Contents

Section A. Concepts and Measures

Section B. Risk and Behaviour

List of Contributors

E. N. Bjordal
Head of Technical Safety, Norsk Hydro A/S, P.O. Box 490, 1301 Sandvika, Norway

B. Brehmer
University of Uppsala, The Psychological Institution, PLO. Box 277, S-75104 Uppsala, Sweden

J. Døderlein
Director,
The Royal Norwegian Council for Scientific and Industrial Research, P.O. Box 70—Tasen, 0801 Oslo 8, Norway

I. Glendon
Dept. of Applied Psychology, University of Aston, Gosta Green, Birmingham, England

A. R. Hale
Technisch Hogeschool Delft, Veiligheidskunde/Safety Science Group, Postbus 5050, NL 2600 GB Delft, Netherlands

A. Hedge
Dept. of Applied Psychology, University of Aston, Gosta Green, Birmingham, England

O. H. Hellesøy
Dept. of Social Psychology, University of Bergen, P.O. Box 25 5014 Bergen—U, Norway

J. Hovden
Senior Scientist,
SINTEF, Division of Safety and Reliability, 7034 Trondheim, Norway

E. Iversen
Dept. of Social Psychology, University of Bergen, P.O. Box 25, 5014 Bergen—U, Norway

T. J. Larsson
Institute for Human Safety and Accident Research, S-11621 Stockholm, Sweden

J. Marek
Dept. of Social Psychology, University of Bergen, P.O. Box 25, 5014 Bergen—U, Norway

M. R. H. Page
Hilperton Grange, Nr. Trowbridge, Wiltshire, BA14 7QY, England

J. Rasmussen
RISØ National Laboratory, DK 4000 Roskilde, Denmark

F. J. C. Roe
19 Marryat Road, Wimbledon Common, London, SW19 5BB, England

T. Sande
Research Coordinator,
A/S Norske Shell, P.O. Box 10, 4033 Forus, Norway

W. T. Singleton
Dept. of Applied Psychology, University of Aston, Gosta Green, Birmingham, England

E. Spjøtvoll
Dept. of Mathematical Statistics, Norwegian Institute of Technology, 7034 Trondheim, Norway

Preface

The origins of this book can be traced back about seven years when one of us (J. H.) called to see the other at the Applied Psychology Department, University of Aston in Birmingham. J. H. was already working on the philosophy of risk supported by the Norwegian Risk Research Committee. This was the first of many meetings in several countries: Norway, Sweden, Finland, England and Scotland where the topic was discussed in formal and informal meetings to do with occupational safety and accidents. This orientation remains in the book, there is some general consideration of risk and decisions in their total context but the emphasis is on risks to health and decisions to do with work and technology.

We began to suspect that one of the basic features underlying the confusion in this whole field of Safety/Risk/Decision-making was that the people involved: research workers, safety specialists, policy-makers and other practitioners were using words and concepts for which there weren't any agreed and accepted definitions and they could well be using them differently. Anyway, it seemed to us that it would be a good idea to try to clarify at least a little bit further what all the professionals involved mean by the term 'risk'. From these discussions the idea gradually emerged that we ought to have a seminar specifically devoted to the concept of 'risk' itself.

The proposition was put to the Risk Research Committee and we were pleased to get a very positive reaction not only from the Committee but also from its parent organization, the Royal Norwegian Council for Scientific and Industrial Research (see Introduction). The director, Jan Døderlein, took a personal interest and was able to participate in the seminar. The Risk Research Committee provided the financial support, the encouragement and also the guidance of one of their members, Julius Marek, Professor of Social Psychology, University of Bergen.

The objectives, structure, content and organization of the Seminar was determined by an organizing committee of three, Julius Marek and ourselves. It was unfortunate that, although Julius Marek made this significant contribution to the organizing committee and to the seminar itself, he was not able, because of the pressure of other duties, to act as one of the editors.

Thus the strategy of the meeting was the encouragement of close interdisciplinary international communication around the theme of risk. The meeting itself was also supported by the Norwegian Society of Chartered Engineers, in particular we would like to thank their conference manager, S. G. Nyblin who acted very efficiently as our seminar manager.

Our objective was a very ambitious one in that we wished to clarify the meaning of 'risk'. The answer must be simultaneously recondite and pragmatic. We needed to be recondite in that the term 'risk' is already abstract and we had to try to match this level of abstraction to retain useful generality. We needed to be pragmatic in that our objective was to say something which will make sense to the range of people who use this term in their diverse problem solving roles.

It sometimes helps to separate the issue into a series of questions. The sort of questions we had in mind were:

1. When different professionals use the term 'risk', are their apparent differences of approach due merely to the different jargons which they use or are the jargons obscuring more fundamental differences in meaning? Are these fundamental differences to do with objectives and values?

2. Is 'risk' essentially a statistical concept in that the best we can ever do is describe what happens in homogeneous populations or can we sometimes say something about individuals or instances?

3. In moving from evidence (the past) to prediction (the future) what are the positive (logically coherent) rules and what are the negative rules (avoidance of common mistakes)?

4. When there is inadequate evidence, how do experts and laymen form opinions? Are there qualitative differences between expert and lay methods or is it just differences of weighting and emphasis? What are the rules for testing whether or not opinions have any validity?

5. Are there standard biases which enter into decision-making by experts, by laymen or by groups?

6. What factors other than probabilities do individuals use in formulating opinions involving risks?

7. Is life-expectancy the ultimate criterion?

These are recondite questions difficult to digest; to conclude, we add some flavour which hopefully will aid digestion in the form of a few pragmatic statements.

— In our society we are in difficulties about 'risk' because technology is continuously changing the frame of reference. The present is too different from the past and different again from the future.

— There is, however, a constant and dominant factor in human nature and human behaviour. Technology does not intrude into ethics, except perhaps for a few engineers and scientists.

— The history of human behaviour studies includes a series of concepts which have been taken aboard because they seemed real, important and interesting and then abandoned at least temporarily because they were far too difficult to cope with. For example; instinct, set and fatigue. Risk may be one of these.

— However, the fact that a topic is difficult to treat in the laboratory is not sufficient reason for rejecting it. The way forward might lie in field methodology rather than laboratory methodology.

— The process is usually easier to define than the product. If useful ways of exploring risk can be clarified, even without completely describing the topic of risk itself, then that is progress.

The discussions reported after each section were produced by the editors, partly on the basis of records of the actual discussions at the seminar and partly on the basis of their own continued deliberations thereafter. It seemed more appropriate to try to integrate these discussions into a continuous commentary rather than ascribing particular comments to particular contributors. The editors would like to acknowledge the stimulation of the extensive discussion periods during the seminar and to thank all those present for their individual insights and contributions.

W. T. SINGLETON,
Occupational Health and Ergonomics Unit
Institute for Social and Preventative Medicine, University of Geneva.

J. HOVDEN,
Scientific and Industrial Research Foundation, SINTEF
Norwegian Institute of Technology, Trondheim.

September 1985

Risk and Decisions
Edited by W. T. Singleton and J. Hovden
© 1987 John Wiley & Sons Ltd.

Introduction

JAN M. DØDERLEIN
Royal Norwegian Council for Scientific and Industrial Research

WHY RISK RESEARCH?

In introducing this seminar, I choose to point to some ethical, political and scientific problems of risk which I think merit particular attention at this time, generally leaving the problems open for discussions without proposed solutions. It is my hope and my expectation that the seminar will further our understanding of these problems.

Before pointing to the problems I will, however, comment on why the Risk Research Committee has the full support of its parent organization, the Royal Norwegian Council for Scientific and Industrial Research (NTNF) in sponsoring the seminar. The prime objective of NTNF is to create, support and assist research and development furthering the competitiveness of Norwegian companies in the international market place, and for improving the quality of life in Norway. Clearly the understanding of accident risks and its management are important in meeting these objectives. Among the reasons for this let me emphasize three: improvements in the standard and quality of living brings new and previously marginal risks into the focus of attention, justifiably or not—partly as a consequence of this, stringent new laws and regulations on environmental protection and product control have emerged—new technologies are mistakenly assumed to introduce new and/or increased risks to life and material property.

Why has NTNF chosen to create a separate advisory body, the Risk Research Committee for planning and coordinating risk research, when we know that risk research (and risk management) must be closely integrated in the various fields of human activity, e.g., air transport risk in the airline industry, off-shore risks in the offshore industry? There are three main reasons for our choice: NTNF tried for some years to integrate the appropriate risk research into its various areas of discipline- or business-oriented research, into

1

marine research, off-shore research, information technology research, environmental research and so on. In spite of some minor successes, we felt that risk
research often was given a too low priority, and was not always well focused in
each area: an important national goal in risk management should be to increase
and deploy resources for risk reduction according to a set of reasonable
national objectives, across the full spectrum of societal activities. This
obviously necessitates clarification of objectives and comparison of risks from a
national perspective: risk (or better, safety) research and management has
developed rapidly into a multidisciplinary semiscientific field over the past 20
years, with its own paradigms and methods.

Consequently, we felt the need to create a focused, nationally-oriented
multidisciplinary unit to pursue aspects of risk research which go beyond the
more detailed work related to specific applications in industry and government. Embedded in these remarks you will find some of the objectives and
expectations that have led NTNF to support the Risk Research Committee in
sponsoring this seminar.

COMMENTS ON THE OBJECTIVES OF THE SEMINAR

I feel strongly that all research takes as its starting point more or less precise
problem definitions, and that problems always arise out of the expectations of
individuals or organizations. This prompts some philosophical comments on
risk research objectives and problems.

To my mind risk research should encompass all the factors in Fig. I.1 and
their interrelations.

In a risk/safety context I take efficient minimization of accident losses (in
terms of lives, health, environmental protection and material goods) as a prime
expectation of individuals and organizations. Effective risk management is
limited by general boundary conditions on ways and means of risk minimization: general expectations within individuals and organizations, the laws of
nature and available technology and political and legal constraints. The overall
risk research objectives are to devise and bring to application the appropriate
requirements and tools to achieve selected risk reduction and to point to
changes in boundary conditions 'contributing to a rational handling of risk
problems by society'.

In doing this work a very important aspect to me personally is this: most
decision-makers in society daily make what are apparently nonrisk related
decisions which are nevertheless changing societal, organizational and individual risk profiles, without being aware of the risk implications of these
decisions.

My humble request to this seminar is that work towards alerting decision-
makers to this state of affairs should be promoted as an important task also for
risk researchers. Making this request I run the risk of promoting a confusion of

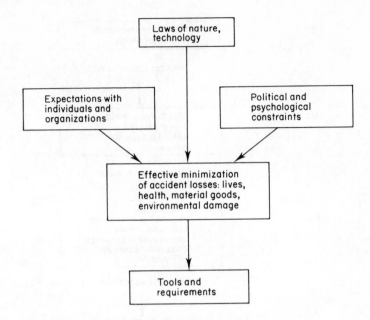

Fig. I.1. Risk research aspects.

roles and responsibilities between risk researchers and political decision-makers. To avoid this I would like to clarify my view on distribution of responsibilities and tasks between the various bodies involved (Fig. I.2).

An additional aspect of Fig. I.2 merits separate mention. It is well known that new public institutions for coping with risk management (laws, regulations, agencies, etc.) are being created at a very high rate (e.g., Rowe, 1986). Perhaps we as risk researchers have a duty to make the regulators think through the consequences of this, and perhaps preferably in the light of the following wise words by F. A. Hayek: '*Nations stumble upon institutions, which are indeed the result of human action, but not the result of human design.*'

SOME KEY PROBLEMS OF RISK

I will give brief comments on some of the problems of risk that I consider particularly urgent, classified into four main problem areas: what is risk, two epistemological problems, finding risk facts, and fundamental risk-policy principles.

What is risk?

Trying to define the concept of risk has so far proven to be an almost useless exercise. Clearly there are many different and several useful concepts in use. I

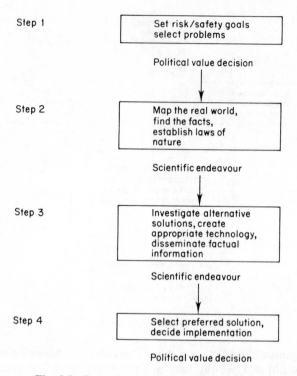

Step 1

Set risk/safety goals
select problems

Political value decision

Step 2

Map the real world,
find the facts,
establish laws of
nature

Scientific endeavour

Step 3

Investigate alternative
solutions, create
appropriate technology,
disseminate factual
information

Scientific endeavour

Step 4

Select preferred solution,
decide implementation

Political value decision

Fig. I.2. Role distribution in safety decisions.

think that we should be pragmatic about questions of definition; several implicit and problem-oriented definitions are acceptable as long as they are useful; and that we should not spend time arguing about definitions without reference to their practical usefulness within a reasonable requirement as to precision. I fully support the point that Tom Singleton has made at the seminar: 'It is progress if useful ways of exploring risk can be clarified without describing the topic itself.'

Two epistemological problems

The application of the concept of 'probability' in various sciences ranging from logic to psychology, has for several decades been the subject of heated controversy between the objectivists (e.g., frequentcists) and the subjectivists (e.g., the Bayesians). In his paper to this seminar Spjøtvoll (1986) comments on the controversy and takes a middle position.

I suggest that this controversy can be shown to be based on misunderstandings and a certain unwillingness to be pragmatic in questions of definition, if it is analysed on the basis of Popper's epistemology (Popper, 1982a), including his propensity interpretation of probability (Popper, 1982b). As an example, consider Spjøtvoll's distinction that 'the (subjectivist) has been able to come up with an estimate of the (prior) unknown probability, the (objectivist) has not'. As I interpret Popper, this distinction is not true since the objectivist can come up with any hypothesis on prior probability in any way he/she chooses without becoming a subjectivist in the process. How he/she gets the hypotheses is irrelevant for the scientific endeavour as long as the hypotheses are useful and falsifiable.

The overall controversy, of course, encompasses more disagreements than this example, but still I think it points to a general direction for controversy resolution. Subjectivists' methodology can be useful for generation of hypotheses and trial data. The (objective) propensity interpretation assumes probabilities to be real properties of real physical systems, and these probabilities fulfil the various axiom systems for probability calculi, while subjective probabilities do not. I believe that the controversy should and can be resolved by accepting probabilities as objective while at the same time accepting appropriate subjectivist methodologies as useful tools for generating ideas, hypotheses and input data for objectivist probability studies. Perhaps the (Utopian?) possibility of using a different word for subjectivist 'probability' could be explored.

A second problem that has been much discussed is the 'zero-infinity' problem: how do we handle (in theory and in practice) risk problems where the probability for the relevant event approaches zero while the consequences approach infinity? Again, I suggest that this problem can be shown to be a nonproblem if approached on the basis of the propensity interpretation of probability.

Finding risk facts

Reasonably accurate and well-defined empirical statistical data bases are prerequisites both for risk management in general and for progress in most of the problem areas taken up in this seminar, including the fundamental risk policy questions taken up below. On a practical level, I believe that much of the success of the airlines in risk management is due to the meticulous and longer-term establishment of data bases on accidents and near accidents. In most other areas of human activity, data bases for risk studies are fragmented and generally inadequate in accident data definition, data collection, data handling and data accuracy. Data collection and handling often seems haphazard, uncoordinated and short term. Perhaps even more important, data requirements are often not defined on the basis of the specific risk management uses to which the data will be put. Finally, data from different areas of activity (and from different countries) usually are incommensurable and integral or international comparisons become very uncertain, if not impossible.

Fundamental risk policy principles

Decision processes and criteria by society and by organizations on risk questions are very complex and we know far too little about them. How and why do we decide to set up new regulatory agencies, create new laws and regulations etc.? Perhaps particularly complex is the question of how we implicitly decide what risks are deemed acceptable by our decisions on risk reduction resource allocation.

I postulate that it is an important task for risk research to assist our decision-makers in making risk decision criteria and processes as clear, conscious and deliberate as possible. As a practical basis for this task, I suggest that we need to continue to think through and discuss with the decision-makers some basic principles of risk policy. Because of the complexity of the problem, I think substantial oversimplifications are required, at least as a starting point.

Let me start with two facts which I think are fundamental to any decision on risk reduction:

— all risks can be reduced provided that sufficient resources are employed (law of nature);
— resources available for risk reduction are limited (law of society and organizations, equivalent to 'some level of risk is acceptable').

With these facts in mind, I think it may be instructive to consider if and how a weighted combination of the following three risk reduction principles could and should influence our risk decisions.

Risk democracy:

Risk should be as evenly distributed over the population as possible. This is, in principle, politically highly acceptable. It will lead to ineffective and inequitable allocation of available risk reduction resources.

Risk-cost effectiveness:

Risk-reduction resources should be deployed where maximum risk reduction per dollar invested is obtained. Carried to its extreme this principle is probably politically unacceptable.

Risk-benefit equity:

Risk and benefit distribution for any particular activity (or in general) should be made as equal as possible over the population. While politically attractive, even a weak application of this principle would seem difficult although there are several practical examples.

These three risk-distribution principles are probably mutually exclusive.

Cutting across the above facts and principles we have the conjecture of risk transfer: any risk reduction is accompanied by a (smaller or larger) risk increase in some other activity. While this conjecture may be of little theoretical interest, I think risk managers would do well to apply it as a check when planning practical risk-reduction measures. Clearly, the conjecture has a direct bearing on how any risk reduction relates to the principles of risk democracy, risk cost effectiveness and risk benefit equity.

Next I wish to comment on a few risk-related problems which to my mind touch on the professional ethics of risk scientists and risk managers.

Any risk decision needs to take into account quantifiable as well as nonquantifiable accident losses. All such losses are expressible in terms of:

— loss of human lives,
— reduction in life expectancy,
— loss of human health,
— material losses,
— environmental damage,
— societal disturbances.

How do we weigh these incomparable loss parameters against each other? To my mind decisions in this area should be made by our political decision system, but the basic empirical facts and consequences of alternative decisions are rarely made available as background material for decision makers (e.g., why do we make investments of about $20,000 to save one human life in some areas of activity, and $20,000,000 in other areas?).

In discussing the role of perceived risk in evaluation of decision alternatives, Brehmer (1986) refers to research indicating that the moral value of the risky activity was a more important determiner of risk acceptability than probability or value of accident consequences. This immediately gives rise to several questions:

— how many lives or dollars are we prepared to pay to give priority to morally valuable activities?
— who decides on 'morally valuable'?
— what is the moral value of sacrificing human lives for moral value?

I believe that most of us in our work tacitly assume the validity of two principles which I will state explicitly.

Firstly, I think that we feel that it is our duty to make available to the public and the politicians as much knowledge as we have on risk-related problems. Is this really a responsible philosophy, considering how little we know, and especially considering that constantly pointing out the many inescapable dangers of daily life may rob many of their peace of mind and happiness? (My answer: Yes, I think it is a necessary and responsible philosophy.)

Secondly, I think that we generally feel that the principle of risk voluntariness should obtain to a large extent: each individual should have substantial freedom to choose his/her personal risk profile. Have we as risk researchers consciously and systematically evaluated this principle, have we considered the costs and benefits of forcing people to reduce risks to themselves and others by their own actions (compare the automobile seat belt discussion)? How does the principle of risk voluntariness interact with risk-democracy, risk-cost effectiveness and risk-benefit equity?

In this section, I have touched upon numerous questions which have ethical aspects. Recently there has been a public debate in many places on the ethical and societal responsibilities of scientists in general and risk scientists in particular. There is a clear tendency to ascribe special responsibilities especially to risk scientists, responsibilities that go well beyond the responsibility of carrying out good scientific practices. Personally I feel that a scientist's ethical obligations as a scientist are closely related to and limited by the role distribution shown in Fig. I.2. In addition, I will point to a distinction which is very important to me and which is seldom brought into the discussions, the distinction between feeling an ethical responsibility in my daily work as a scientist and having or being given a responsibility. I feel very strongly responsible for my work. Having or being given responsibilities is something quite different because then I must also be given the means to fulfil these responsibilities. As you know, these means are not and should not be accorded risk scientists for the problems and questions discussed in this section. Thus for decision-makers and risk scientists alike, I should like to emphasize very strongly: *the place of facts in a world of ethical values should be set by the values, but facts cannot be changed by values*.

REFERENCES

Rowe, W. D. (1986). Contribution to discussion in this seminar.
Brehmer, B. (1986). 'The Psychology of Risk', contribution to this seminar.
Popper, K. R. (1982a). *The Open Universe*. London: Hutchinson.
Popper, K. R. (1982b). *Quantum Theory and the Schism in Physics*. London: Hutchinson.
Doderlein, J. M. (1982). 'Understanding risk management', *Risk Analysis* 3, 17–21.
Spjøtvoll, E. (1986). 'Probability: Interpretation and Estimation', contribution to this seminar.

Discussion: Introduction

The discussion was opened by W. D. Rowe who said that his own conception of risk had changed from the traditional view of potential for harm which is a function of probabilities and consequences to the more pragmatic view that risk is the down side of a gamble. Probabilities are only useful over a limited range and the magnitude of a consequence is measured in relation to the perception of the risk taken. It is not clear whether risks are increasing or the perception of risks is increasing. There was a marked increase in laws concerned with environmental protection in the 1970s. Probabilities, he thought, are of greater significance to professionals engaged in risk-analysis than they are to the public and others trying to make decisions.

Public decisions including probabilities are confounded by the dominance of value judgements in these decisions. Risk analysis has two main functions:

— regulatory analysis which may involve also computer analyses,
— management support analysis used as an aid to marketing, planning and risk management.

It was generally agreed that the average person does not collate risks systematically and in cases where the professional wishes to do so, data bases must be organized in terms of their planned use. Belief systems or values may be the basis of communication but they do not change facts. Conversely, value judgements are not resolvable scientifically. Decision-makers often change risk profiles without being aware that they are doing so. In particular, decisions involved in the progress of technology lead to increased quality of life but also to new risks which require new laws. The Doderlein emphasis on the importance of individual freedom to select a personal risk profile was supported.

Risk management is complicated not only by the difficulties of risk analysis but also by the impact of the legislature, different insurance policies and practices and the views of the law courts. Managers and other decision-makers must somehow cope with qualitative differences between parameters.

In view of the complexities already uncovered there was some pessimistic discussion as to whether, as mentioned in the preface, risk might indeed be merely a term which will eventually outlive its usefulness. It is currently fashionable because of universal concern about safety and risk but it will only survive technically if studies in this context can be demonstrated to be reliable and valid.

Section A

Concepts and Measures

Risk and Decisions
Edited by W. T. Singleton and J. Hovden
© 1987 John Wiley & Sons Ltd.

Chapter 1

Probability: Interpretation and Estimation

EMIL SPJØTVOLL
The Norwegian Institute of Technology, Trondheim

INTRODUCTION

Probability is a basic notion in the evaluation of risk. It is not synonymous with risk, as risk usually is defined to be some function of probabilities and consequences. For example, Rowe (1977) describes risk estimation as a five-step process. The first four steps involve probabilities:

— the probability of the occurrence of a hazardous event,
— the probabilities of the outcomes of this event,
— the probability of exposure to the outcomes,
— the probabilities of 'consequences'.

The present article is concerned with the concept of probability. A basic contention is that probability is a mathematical concept which follows certain mathematical rules and laws. For practical use it has to be interpreted. This can be done as 'objective' or 'subjective' probabilities. Or, equivalently, the frequency interpretation of probability and the Bayesian approach, respectively. These alternative ways of interpreting probability has caused a lot of controversy among statisticians. A recent discussion paper (Rubin, 1984) shows that the debate still goes on.

In this paper, an intermediate position is taken. After a description of the two approaches to probability, it is shown that the Bayesian results may be useful also from a frequency point of view. This is particularly the case in situations with scarcity of data. Recent, though controversial, developments with so-called Stein-estimators also give results similar to the Bayesian ones.

13

PROBABILITY AS A MATHEMATICAL CONCEPT

To solve problems involving uncertainties and random variations, mathematical concepts from the theory of probability and mathematical statistics are employed. The use of mathematics requires precisely defined concepts and operations. From these, one may, by means of mathematical methods, deduce new results and relations. To apply such results to a practical problem, one has to formulate the problem to fit the mathematical assumptions or framework. Whether the mathematical results are interesting or useful will depend on how well the basic mathematical concept represents the 'real world', and how much the practical situation has been tailored to fit the mathematical model.

The basic ingredients in the mathematical model for probability are the *sample space*, the *events*, and the *probability function*. The starting point is a sample space S of outcomes $x \in S$. The elements of S are called outcomes because they are supposed to be the possible results or outcomes of a certain statistical experiment. Thus the elements of S may be thought of as a list of possible outcomes of an experiment. An event A is a subset of S, $A \subset S$. Thus, an event consists of one or several outcomes. In more formal mathematical treatments of probability it is also necessary to define the collection C of events one wants to consider. An event would then be a member of C, i.e., $A \in C$.

It is for the events that probabilities are defined. That is, to each event is attached a real number $P(A)$, the probability of A. It is assumed that the probability function P satisfies the following axioms for probability:

(a) $0 \le P(A) \le 1$.

(b) $P(S) = 1$.

(c) If $A_1, A_2, \ldots, A_n$ is a sequence of disjoint events then

$$P(A_1, \subset A_2 \subset \ldots \subset A_n) = P(A_1) + P(A_2) + \ldots P(A_n).$$

Two or more events are disjoints if they have no elements in common. Or, in other words if no two of them can occur simultaneously.

The triplet (S, C, P) is called a *probability space*. For a real situation to be treated by probablistic methods, it has to put into this framework.

THE FREQUENCY INTERPRETATION OF PROBABILITY

For the mathematical concept of probability to be useful, it has to be related to some real world phenomena or relations. The frequency interpretation of probability is based on a sequence of independent repetitions of the same experiment. Consider a statistical experiment with probability space (S, C, P). Let the experiment be repeated n times, and let n_A be the number of times a certain event A occurs. The ratio n_A/n is called the *relative frequency* of A. Then, according to the frequency interpretation of probability, $P(A)$ is the correct assignment of probability for A, if

$$n_A/n \text{ tends to } P(A) \tag{1}$$

as n gets large.

To give a precise meaning to the statement (1) is not simple. Unfortunately, it cannot mean that n_A/n gets uniformly closer to $P(A)$ the larger n is. For example, assume that the probability of a head when tossing a coin is 1/2. Suppose that after $n = 10$ tosses one had obtained $n_A = 5$ heads. Then n_A/n equals the assumed probability. However, the next toss will give either a head or a tail, leading to n_A/n equal to 6/11 or 5/11 which is away from the assumed value.

Neither is it possible to specify a large n, so that for larger values the relative frequency is within specified limits close to the probability. Feller (1957) reports the results of $n = 10,000$ tossings of a coin. Of these 4,979 resulted in a head, giving a relative frequency 0.4979. Even such a large number of repetitions is not sufficient to claim with certainty that 1/2 is the 'true' probability. Perhaps the coin is a bit biased and the 'true' probability is closer to some other value.

In probability theory, there exists precise mathematical formulations of (1). One of these states that

$$P(\lim_{n \to \infty} n_A/n = P(A)) = 1.$$

This means that as n tends to infinity, then with probability one, the relative frequency tends to the probability. However, this is a statement within the mathematical model. It says that if relative frequencies conform to the mathematical model, they should tend to the probabilities. Thus wildly fluctuating relative frequencies would indicate that the probability model was not a good one for describing random phenomena. The experience is, however, that relative frequencies tend to stabilize with a large number of repetitions. In that manner they seem to give an operational and testable meaning to probability.

SUBJECTIVE PROBABILITY—THE BAYESIAN APPROACH

Another way of interpreting probability is to say that it represents a measure of how likely or reasonable one considers an event A. The exact value of the probability will depend upon previous experience with similar or analogous experiments, knowledge of particular aspects of the experiment at hand, symmetry arguments, etc. For example, when tossing a completely new coin like the new noncircular Norwegian 10-krone coin, one would say that the probability of head is 1/2 even if one has never tried it before. This assignment of probability would be based upon previous experience with other types of coins, and also on physical arguments related to the symmetry of the coin. The point is that one could agree on the value 1/2 without performing any new experiments.

In more complicated situations, such numerical assignment of probabilities will be more difficult. However, it is possible to start with more basic ideas not involving numerical values. Suppose that for any pair of events one is willing to state which one is more likely to occur, or that they are equally likely. Then, under certain reasonable assumptions and consistency requirements on the orderings, it can be shown (DeGroot, 1970) that there exists a probability distribution satisfying the axioms, and which corresponds to the original ordering of events. This means that $P(A) > P(B)$ if and only if A was considered to be more likely than B.

In this way, probability is a measure of the belief one has in the occurrence of an event. This is the subjective or Bayesian approach to probability. In a given situation, the assignment of particular numerical values is subjective in the sense that different persons may end up with different values. Even given the same information about the same problem two persons may interpret it differently. The view expressed in a quotation from E. T. Jaynes (Kaplan and Garrick, 1981) that '... two beings faced with the same total background of knowledge must assign the same probabilities', is either a tautology or easily disproved.

From the subjective point of view it would be perfectly possible to start out with the assumption that the probability of head for the 10-krone coin is 0.60. This could, for example, be based upon physical arguments related to the differences between the two sides of the coin. After tossing the coin a number of times, the value 0.60 would be supported or contradicted. Based on the results, however, the Bayesian would adjust the probability in the direction of the results of the experiment. Thus, the probability assigned to an event need not be a constant value, but can change with the accumulated experience.

COMPARISON OF THE TWO APPROACHES

A simple example on objective and subjective probabilities

We start this section with an example which is intended to bring out one major difference between subjective probability and the frequency interpretation of probability. The example is also related to the useful distinction made by, e.g., Doderlein (1983), between objective probability as a property of the real physical system under study, and subjective probability which in addition includes the experience, thoughts and feelings of individuals.

Suppose we are told that an urn contains either nine black and one red ball or one black and nine red ones. One ball is taken randomly from the urn. What is the probability that the ball is black? The objective probability would be 0.9 or 0.1. It is 0.9 if the urn is the one with nine black balls. If it is the other one, the probability is 0.1. This would also be the limiting relative frequencies one would observe when drawing several times from the same urn, each time putting the ball back into the urn.

Using subjective probabilities one would (or could) assign a certain probability p that the urn is of the first type. The value of p could depend upon one's knowledge of the person who has put the balls into the urn, the availability of balls of different colours, etc. If there was no information to guide the choice of p, it might be reasonable to put $p = 0.5$. Using standard probability calculations, the probability of drawing a black ball will be

$$p0.9 + (1 - p)\,0.1 = 0.1 + 0.8p. \tag{2}$$

Thus, with $p = 0.5$, one would state that the probability of drawing a black ball is 0.5. Clearly, this probability is not a property of the physical systems, but it may still be useful for certain purposes. One important point is that the Bayesian has been able to come up with an estimate for the unknown probability, the other has not. The estimate may, of course, be far from the correct value. But estimates—Bayesian or not—are rarely equal to the true value of the quantity they try to estimate. We shall continue this part of the discussion in the next Section. First, however, we need an extension, which actually is only a reformulation, of the general set-up for a probability model described earlier. Incidentally, it also sheds additional light on the Bayesian approach.

Reformulation of the probability model to include unknown parameters

Usually the probability distribution p in the general probability model depends upon some unknown parameter θ. Let θ have values in some set Ω. We write P_θ to designate the probability distribution when θ is the true value. Thus the probability space is (S, C, P_θ) for some $\theta \in \Omega$. Since P_θ has generated the observation $x \in S$, the value of x gives information about θ. In the frequency approach, methods for drawing conclusions about θ include estimation, confidence intervals and testing.

The Bayesian statistician adds something to the above formulation of the situation. Namely he tries to formalize all he knows about the parameter θ in a probability model for θ. Formally, this can be written (Ω, D, Q) where D is the collection of subset of Ω for which one wants to calculate probabilities, and Q is a probability distribution assigning probabilities to the subsets in D. The distribution Q is called the *prior distribution of* θ. The Bayesian like the nonBayesian assumes that there is some objective probability distribution P_θ which has generated the data, but when drawing conclusions from the data he also uses his prior distribution which contains what he originally believed about θ. We shall demonstrate the effects of this by means of an example.

Comparison of estimates in a binomial example

Consider an experiment where a coin with an entirely new design is tossed n times. Let X be the number of heads in the n tosses, and let the probability of head be θ. Assuming independence between the tosses, the probability distribution of X is the binomial distribution

$$P_\theta(x) = (n)\theta^x(1 - \theta)^{n-x} \qquad x = 0,\ldots,n. \qquad (3)$$

A natural estimate of θ is

$$\hat{\theta} = X/n.$$

The estimate is unbiased, i.e.,

$$E(\hat{\theta}) = \theta,$$

and the variance equals

$$\text{Var } \hat{\theta} = \theta(1 - \theta)/n. \qquad (4)$$

In addition to the above assumption a Bayesian would specify a prior distribution for 0. Suppose that his prior is a beta distribution with parameters a and b.

$$q(\theta) = \frac{\Gamma(a + b)}{\Gamma(a)\Gamma(b)} \theta^{a-1}(1 - \theta)^{b-1} \qquad 0 \leq \theta \leq 1. \qquad (5)$$

The mean of this distribution is

$$E(\theta) = \frac{a}{a + b}. \qquad (6)$$

This is also, in a certain sense, the Bayesian best estimate of θ before the observations are available. The variance is

$$\text{Var }(\theta) = \frac{ab}{(a + b)^2(a + b + 1)}. \qquad (7)$$

When combining the prior distribution with the distribution $P_\theta(x)$ of the observation, the Bayesian obtains the *posterior distribution* of θ. In this case, the posterior also turns out to be a beta distribution, now with parameters $a + x$ and $a + b + n$. Using a quadratic loss function, the best Bayesian estimate of θ is

$$\hat{\theta}_\beta = \frac{a + X}{a + b + n}.$$

This estimate may be written

$$\hat{\theta}_B = (1 - w_n) \frac{a}{a + b} + w_n \hat{\theta}, \qquad (8)$$

where

$$w_n = \frac{n}{a + b + n}. \qquad (9)$$

Thus, $\hat{\theta}_B$ is a mixture of the frequency estimate $\hat{\theta}$ and the estimate (6) of θ based only upon the prior distribution.

One important aspect of the formulae (8) is that as n tends to infinity, w_n tends to 1, and thus $\hat{\theta}_B$ tends to $\hat{\theta}$. Thus with many observations the two estimates are practically equal.

Next, compare the two estimates for a finite number of observations, the mean square error of $\hat{\theta}_B$ is easily found to be

$$E(\hat{\theta}_B - \theta)^2 = (1 - w_n)^2 \left(\frac{a}{a + b} - \theta \right)^2 + w_n^2 \theta (1 - \theta)/n. \qquad (10)$$

The mean square error of $\hat{\theta}$ equals its variance (4).

Now consider some definite values of a, b and θ. Let the true value of θ be 0.5. Suppose also that the Bayesian has been unfortunate in his choice of prior distribution, having chosen $a = 60$ and $b = 40$. Then from (6) his prior estimate of θ is 0.60. The standard deviation of the prior distribution is 0.049. Thus, the distribution is quite well concentrated around 0.60. The prior probability that θ is less than the true value can be calculated to approximately 0.025. Thus, the Bayesian has put very little probability near the correct value.

Table 1.1.

n	1	5	10	20	30	40	50	60	70	100	200	∞
R	0.05	0.18	0.34	0.58	0.76	0.90	1.00	1.08	1.14	1.25	1.33	1.00

Ratio, R, of mean square error for Bayesian estimate to the variance of best unbiased estimate for various sample sizes n. The case $a = 60$, $b = 40$, $\theta = 0.50$.

In Table 1.1 is shown the mean square error of the Bayesian estimate relative to the frequency estimate $\hat{\theta}$. It is seen that for $n < 50$ the Bayes estimate is the better one. For $n > 50$, the estimate $\hat{\theta}$ is better, but only slightly.

So, in this situation, even with a wrong starting point the Bayesian estimate is better for small sample sizes. The reason is that the frequency estimate $\hat{\theta}$ may fluctuate a great deal for small values of n, whereas the weighting (8) in the Bayesian estimate makes it more stable. This I believe, is also more generally the case. Subjective knowledge, if not too biased, combined with empirical data give better results than the empirical data alone.

ASSESSMENT OF SUBJECTIVE PROBABILITIES

The determination of subjective probabilities should be based upon the total knowledge available which relates to the problem or system under study. This knowledge may come from experience with similar situations, reasoning by analogy or symmetry, and from knowledge of special features of the problem at hand. The total information has to be transformed into numerical values for probabilities.

To determine the subjective probability for one particular event may not be so difficult. A possible technique of comparing with a uniformly distributed random variable is described by Lindley (1970) and Kaplan and Garrick (1981). Such a comparison is also basic in DeGroot's (1970) proof of the existence of a subjective probability distribution.

So, for each event $B \in D$ a subjective probability may be assigned. However, the probabilities so determined may not be consistent in the sense that they satisfy the axioms of a probability distribution Q. In a series of papers, Winkler (1967, 1971) has discussed procedures for an iterative determination of subjective probabilities where one adjusts the probabilities after being confronted with the inconsistencies.

A simple way to obtain consistency is to use a standard probability distribution to describe the uncertainty. An example of this is the beta distribution (5). The distribution is completely determined when the parameters a and b are specified. This can be done indirectly by using subjective estimated values for the mean (6) and the variance (7). The variance may be a difficult concept for nonstatisticians. Alternatively, one may try to infer the values of a and b from more basic probability assessments (Winkler, 1967). The PERT estimate in project planning and control (see, e.g., Hillier and Liebermann, 1974) uses the most likely value and the range to determine the parameters of the subjective distribution. If one is able to specify two percentiles, they will also determine the distribution. A recent reference using this approach is Mosleh and Apostolakis (1982).

Prominent in textbooks on Bayesian statistical inference are the so-called noninformative prior distributions. These are to be used when one has no or little information about the problem. Then the prior distribution should be chosen so that relative to the data it has very small influence on the final conclusions. For example, the noninformative prior for the binomial distribution (3) is the limit of the beta distribution (5) as a and b tend to 0. From (9) it is seen that in this case the weight $w_n = 1$, so that $\theta_B = \theta$. Thus only the data determine the value of the estimate.

In assessing a probability distribution the subjective knowledge of several experts can be used and combined in various ways. The IEEE Guide (1983) has used the Delphi method (Linstone and Turoff, 1975) where the final estimate is the geometric mean of failure rates estimated by experts, possibly weighted by how 'expert' an expert is. As demonstrated, for example, in Morgan *et al.* (1984) experts may differ widely in their views, so that it seems meaningless to form some average. In such cases, a possibility is to work out alternatives based on different subjective distributions. An excellent summary of practical problems and experiences in determining subjective probabilities are given in the review by Lichtenstein *et al.* (1982).

JAMES–STEIN ESTIMATORS

One of the strangest results in theoretical statistics is the so-called Stein's paradox when estimating the mean of several populations (Stein, 1955) Let the problem be to estimate the means $\mu_1, \ldots , \mu_p$ of p normal populations. For the estimation are available observed means $\bar{X}_1, \ldots , \bar{X}_p$, respectively. The populations are assumed to have equal variances, but may otherwise be completely unrelated. Then it can be shown that the natural estimators

$$\hat{\mu}_1 = \bar{X}_i \qquad i = 1, \ldots p, \tag{11}$$

can be improved by the James–Stein (1961) estimator

$$\hat{\mu}_i = (1 - c)\bar{X} + c\bar{X}_i \qquad i = 1, \ldots p. \tag{12}$$

Here $\bar{X}$ is the average of $\bar{X}_1, \ldots \bar{X}_p$, and c is a quantity which depends upon the observations. It is seen that the improved version pulls each natural estimator closer to the average of all estimators. Since the populations are supposed to be unrelated, this seems paradoxical. Although these results were obtained many years ago, it is only in the recent years they have found some acceptance for practical use.

The improvement of (12) over (11) as measured by the sum of the squared errors depends how different the μ_1's are. If they are close in numerical values, the improvement may be substantial.

EMPIRICAL BAYES AND BAYESIAN METHODS

The above result concerns the situation when the μ_1's are totally unrelated. In other situations the parameters may be assumed not to be totally different or they may even be assumed to come from a certain population. Under this assumption one also gets estimates of the form (12) or, similarly, (8). This is the empirical Bayes approach (Robbins, 1964). Suppose that we want to estimate the probability that a certain valve used in a large technical system closes on command. The probability may vary due to different types, environmental conditions and system configurations. Let us assume that the probabilities vary according to a beta distribution (5). If there are data available from some valves, it is possible to estimate the parameters a and b of the beta distribution. Then, using these, it can be shown that the estimator (8) would be the 'best' way to estimate the probability for a given value in a given environment. Thus, data for this particular valve are combined with the information about the population mean obtained from other valves.

Such types of estimators have also been used by actuaries in credibility theory. A review is given by, e.g., Norberg (1979). In this context, the formulae (12) could be interpreted as the premium charged to an individual in a certain group. It is a mixture of the average premium for the group based upon risk assessment for the group and the premium corresponding to the risk experience for the individual. The weight c is called the credibility factor.

It seems that the above results have some bearing on the use of subjective probabilities in conjunction with data. The Bayesian approach will pull the estimators towards a fixed value in a manner analogous to James–Stein estimators and empirical Bayes estimators. The latter two are justified from a non-Bayesian point of view. These estimators require numerical data for the modification of the natural estimators. However, without numerical information, it is not unreasonable to mimic such procedures by pulling the estimators towards an average value based on subjectively evaluated previous knowledge. This should not be less reasonable than pulling estimators towards the mean of totally unrelated populations, as is done by the James–Stein estimator.

PROBABILITY IN RISK CALCULATIONS

The presentation of results

As stated in the introduction, probability evaluations are used repeatedly in a risk calculation. In my opinion, the result of a risk study should be presented as the possible consequencies together with their probabilities of occurrence. It is not enough to calculate an expected or average consequence.

As an example, suppose one has calculated that some activity increases the number of deaths per year by one. This may correspond to very different situations depending upon the probability distribution of the number of deaths. For example, with a Poisson distribution the standard deviation would also be one. Thus, there is little variation from one year to the next. The situation is well behaved and in a certain sense under control. On the other hand, suppose one had a million deaths or none, the former with a small probability of 10^{-6}. The mean number of deaths per year is one, but the standard deviation is 1,000. This corresponds to a very unstable situation.

To calculate such probability distributions is, in principle, straightforward, if the necessary intermediate probability distributions are given. The computational work, however, may be extensive, and some form of approximation or simulation may be necessary.

It is shown earlier in this article that subjective distributions may be used even if they are biased or not well calibrated. They tend to stabilize estimates when there are few data, and lose influence when much data is available.

When several experts are used they may give widely different subjective distributions. This is not necessarily a contradiction. Even if two experts are each well calibrated in their subjective evaluations, they may differ in particular cases. Two meteorologists may give different probabilities for rain on a given day, although their probabilities on average correspond to what actually happens. From a statistical point of view, it would, in such cases, be justifiable to use some kind of an average subjective probability distribution. The effect of mixing very different distributions would show up in a less concentrated distribution for the consequences.

The 'risk' of risk estimates

A statistician uses measures of performance to evaluate standard statistical procedures. These measures of performance are the 'risk' in statistical terminology. The performance of an estimator may be measured by its bias and variance. A confidence interval is evaluated by its probability of containing the true value of the parameter of interest, and how good it is in excluding false values. Suppose that a risk analysis has ended up with a point estimate or a probability distribution for the possible consequences. In principle, given the assumptions made in the analysis, the performance of such an analysis may be evaluated in the standard way. However, one knows that many of the assumptions are very rough approximations and sometimes mere guesses.

Sensitivity studies comes naturally to mind. A statistician, however, would like to have some kind of measure characterizing the additional uncertainty in the results due to the unreliability of the assumptions. One way to do this empirically could be systematically to compare estimates from risk studies with what actually happens. This could perhaps give us some factor of optimism or pessimism to modify the average risk study.

It would be a more scientific approach, if it were possible to take explicitly into account the fact that, for some part of the system, knowledge is lacking.

Recently, an approach to formalize such situations has been suggested (Schafer, 1982). Thus one could put 30 per cent confidence in a certain subjective distribution, and the remaining 70 per cent probability corresponds to total ignorance. It remains to see how such an approach can be formalized in risk calculations and in the presentation of results.

REFERENCES

DeGroot, M. H. (1970). *Optimal Statistical Decisions*. New York: McGraw-Hill.

Doderlein, J. M. (1983). 'Understanding risk management', *Risk Analysis* **3**, 17–21.

Feller, W. (1957). *An Introduction to Probability Theory and Its Applications*, Vol. 1, 2nd Edition. New York: Wiley.

Hillier, F. S. and Lieberman, G. J. (1974). *Operations Research*, 2nd Edition. San Francisco: Holden-Day.

IEEE (1983). *Guide to the Collection and Presentation of Electrical, Electronic, Sensing Component, and Mechanical Equipment Reliability Data for Nuclear-Power Generating Stations*. Published by the Institute of Electrical and Electronics Engineering, Inc.

James, W. and Stein, C. (1961). 'Estimation with quadratic loss', *Proceedings of the Fourth Berkeley Symposium on Mathematical Statistics and Probability*, Vol. 1. Berkeley: University of California Press.

Kaplan, S. and Garrick, B. J. (1981). 'On the quantitative definition of risk', *Risk Journal* **1**, 11–27.

Lichtenstein, S., Fischhoff, B. and Philips, L. D. (1982). 'Calibration of probabilities: The state of the art to 1980', *in* D. Kahneman, P. Slovic and A. Tversky (Eds), *Judgement Under Uncertainty: Heuristics and Biases*. Cambridge: University Press.

Lindley, D. V. (1970). *Introduction to Probability and Statistics from a Bayesian Viewpoint*. Cambridge: University Press.

Linstone, H. A. and Turoff, M. (1975). *The Delphi Method: Techniques and Applications*. Massachusetts: Addison-Wesley.

Morgan, M. G., Morris, S. C., Henrion, M., Amaral, D. A. L. and Rish, W. R. (1984). 'Technical uncertainty to quantitative policy analysis—a sulfur air pollution example', *Risk Journal* **4**, 201–216.

Mosleh, A. and Apostolakis, G. (1982). 'Some properties of distributions useful in the study of rare events', *IEEE Transactions on Reliability* **31**, 87–94.

Norberg, R. (1979). 'The credibility approach to experience rating', *Scandinavian Actuarial Journal*, 181–221.

Robbins, H. (1964). 'The empirical Bayes approach to statistical problems', *Annals of Mathematical Statistics* **35**, 1–20.

Rowe, W. D. (1977). *An Anatomy of Risk*. New York: Wiley.

Rubin, D. E. (1984). Bayesianly justifiable and relevant frequency calculations for the applied statistician', *Annals of Statistics* **12**, 1151–1172.

Schafer, G. (1982). 'Belief functions and parametric models', *Journal of the Royal Statistical Society, B*, **44**, 322–352.

Stein, J. (1955). 'Inadmissability of the usual estimator for the mean of a multivariate normal distribution', *Proceedings of the Third Berkeley Symposium on Mathematical Statistics and Probability*. Berkeley: University of California Press.

Winkler, R. L. (1967). The quantification of judgement: some methodological suggestions', *Journal of the American Statistical Association* **62**, 1105–1120.

Winkler, R. L. (1971). 'Probablistic prediction: some experimental results', *Journal of the American Statistical Association* **66**, 675–685.

Risk and Decisions
Edited by W. T. Singleton and J. Hovden
© 1987 John Wiley & Sons Ltd.

Chapter 2

The Psychology of Risk

BERNDT BREHMER
Uppsala University

INTRODUCTION

There is often disagreement between experts and lay people about the level of
risk for various activities, particularly for new technologies. Such disagreements may lead to mutual distrust: experts point to misunderstanding and
misinformation about the real characteristics of a new technology on the part of
the public and consider the public irrational, while the public will note that
experts often disagree, that the risk estimates they provide are often based on
judgement rather than fact and will call them subjective and biased.

This points to two important fields for psychological research in the area of
risk: that of how people in general perceive or judge risk and how expert
judgements of risk are made. This paper will be concerned with the former
problem. Roughly speaking, psychological research on risk falls into two
categories: studies of individual differences in risk-taking and studies of how
people perceive risks. This paper will be concerned with the second kind of
approach, but a few words about the individual differences approach may
nevertheless be in order.

INDIVIDUAL DIFFERENCES

Research on individual differences in risk-taking is closely related to accident
research. The basic idea is that differences in accident rates can be explained in
terms of differences in risk-taking. This approach has not met with much
success; firstly because it has not proved possible to demonstrate reliable

25

differences in accident rates at the individual level, and secondly because it has not been possible to establish reliable individual differences in risk-taking (e.g., Slovic, 1962). This does not mean that there are no differences in risk-taking, or in attitudes to risk, but if there are such differences they are likely to be specific to certain contexts. That is, a daring mountain climber or sky diver does not have to be an avid gambler as well.

Current research in this area is concerned mainly with possible differences among groups of people. For example, one area of interest is whether the higher accident rates for young male drivers can be explained in terms of attitudes towards risk.

PERCEPTION OF RISK

The term 'perception of risk' is, of course, somewhat of a misnomer. The term perception carries the implication that there is some risk 'out there' to be picked up. But the 'objective risks' that are supposed to be perceived are of course not real objects, but only numbers that have been computed according to this or that formula. We do not perceive risks, we perceive various features of decision problems and this, in turn, leads to feelings of risk. Consequently, it makes little or no sense to ask whether risk is correctly perceived. All we can do is to compare intuitive risk estimates with risk estimates that have been obtained from various formulae.

Much of the research effort has been spent making such comparisons. This is unfortunate, because it has made psychological risk into an almost exclusively cognitive concept, where the main research question has tended to be how people compute risks intuitively and whether they compute these risks correctly, that is according to somebody's favourite formula. The motivational and emotional aspects of psychological risk have largely been ignored. This has limited psychological research on risk unduly, for it seems at least as reasonable to consider psychological risk as an emotional and motivational concept as to consider it a cognitive one. In fact, the most useful approach to psychological risk may well be to consider risk judgements as intuitive value judgements which express a diffuse negative evaluation of a decision alternative, a general feeling that this is something one does not want.

Psychological research on risk has not been directed at an analysis of the intuitive feelings of risk and their function in human decision-making. Instead psychologists have followed a psychophysical approach where various objects of interest, usually new technologies, have been 'measured' psychologically by having people make risk estimates.

DEFINITION OF RISK

The psychophysical approach to risk is hampered by the fact that there is no generally agreed definition of objective risk. Vlek and Stallen (1981) list six definitions of risk which are all common in the literature:

— risk is the probability of a loss,
— risk is the size of the possible loss,
— risk is a function, mostly the product of probability and size of loss,
— risk is equal to the variance of the probability distribution of all possible consequences of a risky course of action,
— risk is the semivariance of the distribution of all consequences, taken over negative consequences only, and with respect to some adopted reference value,
— risk is a weighted linear combination of the variance of and the expected value of the distribution of all possible consequences.

A common characteristic of these definitions is that they are context free, that is they refer only to abstract terms such as probability and loss which are designed for cross situational generality. It is an important question whether or not such a context-free approach has any psychological validity.

The plethora of definitions of risk is only one of the problems with the general psychophysical approach. Another problem is that, except in some simple situations, the various objective aspects of the risky events cannot be measured but have to come from expert judgement. The concept of 'objective risk', therefore, seems problematic at best. Because of these and other problems, most psychological work on risk is now directed at finding which factors affect risk judgements rather than at relating subjective to objective risk.

VARIETIES OF RESEARCH ON PERCEIVED RISK

It is convenient to discuss research in this area under three headings. The first group of studies concern gambles, and aims to clarify which aspects of gambles make them seem risky. The second group is concerned with judgements of risk of events with which the subjects have some personal experience, that is events that occur with some regular frequency in their daily lives, such as the probability of getting caught while speeding. The third group of studies is concerned with the dimensions of risk judgements for events that are not directly within the personal experience of people, and where there is very little frequency information upon which to base one's judgements of risk, such as is the case for new technologies, e.g., nuclear power or liquefied gas plants.

I will concentrate on the second and the third group of studies, which are presumably most relevant to the purposes of the present symposium but a few words about gambles are needed.

Gambles

Gambles are very attractive research tools for at least three reasons. Firstly, they are well understood: there is a normative theory which tells you how to maximize your earnings from gambling. Such a theory prescribes the rational approach to gambling, and research on gambling, therefore, was seen as a possibility of investigating whether or not people are rational. Secondly, a gamble consists of a limited number of well-defined components which can be varied experimentally in the way psychologists are accustomed to doing in their empirical work. Thus, gambles made it possible for psychologists to do research in this area with the methods they already know (Lopes, 1983). Thirdly, the normative theory for gambling (statistical decision theory) offered a general formal analysis of all decision problems—or at least that was what many psychologists thought. Thus, research on gambles was research on decision-making, and the results from these studies could presumably be generalized to all kinds of decision-making by virtue of the formal similarities among all decision situations as conceptualized by statistical decision theory. Whether or not people would consider, say, buying a car as the same kind of thing as buying a lottery ticket seemed to worry psychologists very little at the start. Research on gambling, then, followed the typical psychological research strategy of concentrating on the formal aspects with the hope of achieving generality by virtue of understanding such formal aspects.

While research on gambles has produced a large body of results, it has not led to any broader generalizations about decision-making or risk, except that people are not rational in the sense of statistical decision theory. That is, they do not follow the expected value principle when evaluating gambles. That had, of course, been known since Bernouilli formulated the St Petersburg paradox. (This work is reviewed in, e.g., Lee, 1971. See also Lopes, 1983, for an interesting discussion.)

The problem with the approach is that although formally speaking, all decision problems can be reduced to gambles, people do not seem to take such a formal approach to decision problems.

There is increasing evidence from research in cognitive psychology that content, rather than form, is the important psychological aspect and that we therefore have to study actual problems in context. A purely formal analysis will not provide a good basis for generalizations (Johnson-Laird, 1983). We will therefore not consider this line of research further in this paper.

Judgements based on personal experience

In this section, I will review three studies which involve judgements of risk of low probability events under circumstances which allow people to base these judgements on their own experience. The main question of interest is that of whether these kinds of judgements are made in the same way for these three domains.

Recently there has been a considerable amount of research on how people judge probabilities. Much of this work has been inspired by the pioneering efforts of Tversky and Kahneman (e.g., 1974) on the heuristics people use when making such judgements. These heuristics may be seen best as the operating principles of the mind when engaged in probabilistic judgement and they serve mainly to reduce the complex task of making probabilistic judgements to something the individual can manage. In this connection one of the heuristics, that of *availability*, is of special interest.

According to Tversky and Kahneman (1973), people base their judgements of probability upon the ease with which something comes to mind. Things that come to mind easily are judged to have a high probability and vice versa. Thus when asked about the safety of airline travel, we will give this a high rating if we do not remember any accidents and a low rating if we remember many accidents or if we happen to think of an accident very quickly. This is a useful way of making judgements because one of the reasons why things come easily to mind is that they have had a high frequency in our past experience. However, recall is also influenced by other factors, such as recency and vividness. Thus, accidents that happened yesterday are easier to remember than those that happened a year ago and a graphic description of an accident makes it easier to recall than a short pallid notice in the paper. Consequently, the availability heuristic, although generally useful, may introduce bias; the judgement of accident probability will be higher if there has been an accident recently and higher if the accident was given a vivid description or if the person making the judgement actually saw the accident. Indeed, more discussion of risks is likely to raise the subjective risk simply because it makes it easier to think of the risks.

The results on availability suggest that we can expect judgements of probability to be correlated with objective probabilities but that the correlation will not be perfect. However, availability is a slippery concept in that it is not always so easy to see what causes events to be available. This is very well illustrated in a study by Lichtenstein, *et al.* (1978). This study was concerned with how people estimate the probability of dying from different causes, such as being struck by lightning or from pneumonia. The results indicated that there was a correlation between objective and subjective risk but that the correlation was far from perfect. Specifically, the results indicated that low risks were overestimated and high risks were underestimated. This did not seem to be a general regression effect for closer inspection of the data showed that the low risks that were overestimated were risks that were violent and dramatic, such as poisoning from botulinus or homicide, while the high risks that were underestimated were nondramatic, such as dying from pneumonia. This seems to agree with the general prediction from availability that vivid events will be easier to recall and that they will be given an inflated subjective probability. However, this is probably only part of the explanation.

Combs and Slovic (1979) hypothesized that the estimates of causes of death are based on news-media reports and that these reports would be biased in the same way as the subjective risk estimates. They therefore recorded how deaths were reported in newspapers and found that there was indeed a bias in the newspaper reports; the newspapers tended to favour exactly those violent and dramatic deaths that the subjects overestimated.

These results are interesting in that they show that people are able to assimilate frequency information quite well, but that it is important to know what kind of information they actually have. Although there is bias in the subjective judgements of causes of death the bias is not only in the subjects but also and perhaps primarily in the data which are available to the persons.

Judgements without personal experience

In a series of studies in our department, we have investigated the relation between subjective and objective accident risk in car driving (TFD, 1982). In these experiments, subjects make judgements about the risk of an accident in different places in the town of Uppsala and their judgements are then related to actual accident probabilities. The accident data showed considerable stability, the correlation between accident rates for two four-year periods over the 100 places judged was about 0.80, and the reliability of the judgements showed similar values.

The correlation between subjective and objective accident risk was 0.40, not a bad value considering that the maximum correlation, taking reliability into account, was about 0.6. The question is what the basis of this correlation might be. To investigate this problem we studied four groups of subjects. They differed with respect to total driving experience and with respect to experience of driving in the town of Uppsala. The hypothesis was, of course, that the correlation between subjective and objective accident risk should be highest for the group of drivers who had most experience of driving in Uppsala. The results did not bear this prediction out: there were no differences among the four groups of subjects, and we have found that there is no difference between a group of driving instructors and a group of 13-year-olds with no driving experience. In this case, then, we found reasonably good risk estimates which are clearly not based upon experienced frequency, nor upon vicarious experience from reading newspapers; traffic accidents are not given much space in the newspapers, and the subjects who had little or no driving experience in Uppsala did not of course read the Uppsala newspaper either. Instead, we have to assume that those risk judgements are based upon some rather general intuitive theory about what constitutes dangers in the traffic environment and that the theory is not based upon actual driving experience but upon some more general form of experience involving what happens to moving objects.

We do not know very much about the nature of this intuitive theory, but closer analysis of the relations between judgements and objective accident rates showed that the correlations did not give an entirely correct picture of the relation between judgements and objective risk. Specifically, the results showed that practically all the judgements in the plot of subjective risk against objective risk fell *above* the 45-degree line. That is, risks were generally overestimated and almost never underestimated. This makes it impossible to understand how accidents could occur, until we remember that the judgements are not perfectly reliable and that, due to lack of reliability, errors of judgement are going to occur.

As part of a large project on the effects of police enforcement upon traffic safety, we have asked drivers to estimate the risk of getting caught by the police while committing various offences such as speeding and driving while drunk. The drivers have been stopped on the road and interviewed about the risk of getting caught by the police while speeding on a specified stretch of road. These results (not yet published) have shown that there is a close relationship between actual probability of getting caught and subjective risk of getting caught. The question is whether these judgements are based upon an intuitive theory about how the police operate of the kind employed by the subjects in the accident risk project or whether they are based upon actual experience. The results indicate that experienced frequency is the important factor in these circumstances. This conclusion is supported by three kinds of results. Firstly, we found in the original interviews that the drivers often refused to give an estimate of the probability of getting caught for stretches of road that they had not driven on or had driven on only very infrequently. Secondly, we found in a laboratory study, where subjects made judgements from video tapes of stretches of road, that the reliability of their estimates of probability of getting caught was very low for stretches that they had not driven on while it was high for stretches that they had driven on. Thirdly, we found in a study where we asked about the probability of getting caught while driving under intoxication that the subjective risk of getting caught was directly related to the number of times the driver had actually been subjected to a breathalyser test.

I have dwelled upon these results to emphasize the general conclusion that the subjective risk estimates are context dependent. We find that such risk estimates can be made in a variety of ways. They can be based upon vicarious experience through the media as in the case of causes of death, by means of an intuitive theory as in the case of accident risk or on the basis of direct personal experience as in the case of the breathalyser tests.

Presumably, there are even more ways of making these risks estimates; we have just not found them yet. This means that it is impossible to draw any general conclusions about people's ability to make judgements of risk, about how these risk judgements are made and how they may be influenced without taking the context of these judgements into account.

THE STRUCTURE OF JUDGEMENTS ABOUT RISK AND ACCEPTABILITY

Making risk judgements in situations where we have frequency information is a rather simple problem. The really difficult problems in the area of risk are, of course, those which concern events for which we have no frequency information or little such information or for which we choose to disregard whatever frequency information we have (as in the case of nuclear power plants). Such events, especially in relation to new technologies, are nevertheless often judged to be risky or safe, even though we have very little frequency information upon which to base the judgements.

In the last twenty years, a considerable amount of research has been directed towards the problem of finding which aspects of new technologies or events generally make them seem risky. This research has led to some interesting results. In this section, I will first review some results concerning the structure of judgements about risk. I will then discuss some results that relate to the acceptability of risky decision alternatives to provide some context for the results pertaining to risk.

Judgements about risk

Slovic et al. (1984), found that there was only a moderate correlation between people's risk estimates for a number of activities and actual fatality rates for these activities. On the other hand, there was very good agreement between different groups of people with respect to their subjective risk estimates. To explore these differences, Slovic and his associates had their subjects estimate a number of risks on a variety of scales such as annual fatality rates, catastrophic potential, the extent to which the events can be controlled, the extent to which the risks are known and so on. The intercorrelations among these estimates were then analysed by means of factor analysis. Figure 2.1, which is taken from Slovic et al. (1984) shows some typical results from such an analysis.

As can be seen from the figure, perceived risk seems to have two basic dimensions. The first of these, called 'dread', has to do with the extent to which the consequences of the event are catastrophic and uncontrollable. The second factor has to do with the extent to which the risk is known. The first factor is the most important one and the score on this factor predicts the extent to which the subjects want to see the risk reduced.

These results explain why the correlation between actual fatality rates and subjective risk is imperfect. It is because people incorporate aspects of risk that are not incorporated in the annual fatality rates. This is not irrational, it is simply another way of judging risk.

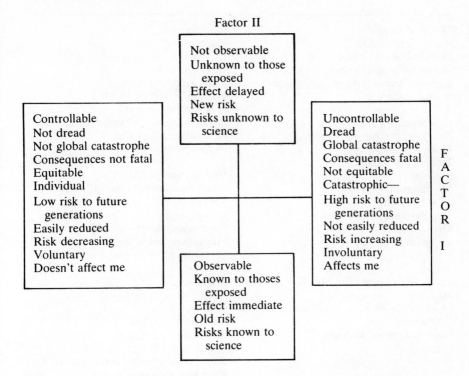

Factor II

Not observable
Unknown to those
  exposed
Effect delayed
New risk
Risks unknown to
  science

Controllable
Not dread
Not global catastrophe
Consequences not fatal
Equitable
Individual
Low risk to future
  generations
Easily reduced
Risk decreasing
Voluntary
Doesn't affect me

Uncontrollable
Dread
Global catastrophe
Consequences fatal
Not equitable
Catastrophic—
High risk to future
  generations
Not easily reduced
Risk increasing
Involuntary
Affects me

Observable
Known to thoses
  exposed
Effect immediate
Old risk
Risks known to
  science

F A C T O R I

Fig. 2.1. Factors I and II derived from the interrelationships among 16 risk characteristics. Each factor is made up of a combination of characteristics, as indicated by the diagram. (Source: Slovic *et al.*, 1984.)

While these results seem reliable, and have been obtained in a number of studies they are, nevertheless, method specific. Studies using other methods have given somewhat different results. Johnson and Tversky (1984), using cluster analysis to analyse judged similarities among different kinds of risks, found five different clusters of risks which differed with respect to the nature of the risky event: hazards (such as lightning and fire), accidents (such as traffic and airplane), violent acts (such as homicide and war), technological disasters (such as nuclear disasters) and diseases (such as cancer).

Perusse (1980), using the repertory grid technique for eliciting the concepts people use in thinking about risky events, found a highly differentiated picture with five major groups of concepts: origin of danger, threat, consequences, human intervention, and reactions, with a variety of subconcepts under each major concept, see Fig. 2.2.

Still other results have been obtained in studies where subjects have been asked to characterize risks choosing their own terms in a free response mode (Earle and Lindell, 1984).

Origin of danger
Natural/man-made
Human cause/no human cause
Blame assignable/no blame assignable
Self responsible/self not responsible
Internal/external

Characteristics of hazard
Necessary/unnecessary activity
Occupational/not occupational
Potential/present
Near/far
Moving/stationary
Slow/fast event
Specific/nonspecific location
Open/closed
Large/small concentration of people

Threat
Frequent/infrequent occurrence
High/low risk of accident
Most dangerous/least dangerous
Safe/unsafe
Sudden/continuous threat

Consequences
Major/minor
Large/small consequence
Fatal/survivable
Many killed/few killed
Many affected/few affected
Personal/impersonal
Instantaneous/long-term consequence
Reversible/irreversible
Painful/painless

Human intervention
Own control/out of control
Rely on others/rely on self
Avoidable/unavoidable
Preventable/unpreventable
Precautions/unforeseeable
Easy/difficult to escape

Reactions
Aware/unaware of danger
Sleeping/awake
Familiar/unfamiliar
Ugly-hideous/not ugly
Scaring/not scaring
Worry-concern/nonworry, unconcern
Acceptance/nonacceptance
Panic-chaos/orderly-calm
Public reaction/no public reaction

Fig. 2.2. Constructs elicited by means of the repertory grid technique (Data from Perusse, 1980).

Such a diversity of results need not lead to despair nor need they be interpreted to mean that there are no reliable results but only 'method variance'. Instead, I believe that these results indicate that people have no single and unitary mental representation of risks and that the representation they construct depends very much upon what questions are asked. Such an interpretation would agree with results from other domains of cognitive psychology (see for example, Johnson-Laird, 1983).

Such an interpretation raises an important issue. If it is true that different ways of formulating problems about risk lead to different representations there is an obvious possibility that discussions of actual risk problems may lead people to ignore important aspects of these problems because of the way in which the problems have been formulated (Slovic, Fischhoff and Lichtenstein,

1980). To avoid this we need more systematic information about how the formulation of a risk problem affects the cognitive representation of that problem. Our current understanding of this issue is only fragmentary. This should be one of the most important problems for future psychological research in this area.

Acceptability of risk

Risk as such is, of course, not of much interest except as an aspect of a decision alternative. In evaluating a decision alternative, the risk must be weighed against the benefits of that alternative. An important aspect of the psychology of risk is how perceived risks are combined with perceived benefits into an overall evaluation of decision alternative. This problem has received considerably less attention than the problem of risk as such. Two recent studies shed some interesting light upon the problem.

Vlek and Stallen (1981) analysed risk perception and acceptability of various activities, They interviewed 700 persons living in or near Rotterdam, a large industrial centre in the Netherlands. They were asked about risks, benefits, and acceptability of a variety of activities, ranging from personal activities (such as swimming at a remote beach in summertime), to labour and industrial activities (such as operating a nuclear power station close to a residential area) and societal organizations (such as storing personal data on all Dutch citizens in a central data bank). They report a number of detailed results but here it is sufficient to discuss some of the main findings. For risk judgements, Vlek and Stallen found two dimensions, similar to those reported by Slovic et al. The first dimension had to do with the size of the potential accident (related to 'dread') and the second with the degree of organized safety (related to the extent to which a risk is known). Judgements of beneficiality could also be described in terms of two dimensions. The first was described as personal necessity with narcosis and immunization scoring high and smoking in bed scoring low. The second factor had to do with the scale of production and/or distribution of benefits. On this factor, nuclear power scored high and swimming at a remote beach scored low. Judgements of acceptability could also be described in terms of two factors. These two factors were basically the same as those for beneficiality suggesting that the judgements of acceptability were based upon perceived benefits and that perceived risk was relatively unimportant. Further support for this conclusion came from the fact that there was a high (0.90) correlation between acceptability scores and beneficiality scores. Vlek and Stallen also found a number of interesting differences among subgroups of respondents. These differences were related mainly to the second, less important factor of the acceptability judgements. Thus, they found that people living close to the actual production centres of Rotterdam had a more favourable attitude towards activities involving large-scale production and benefits and that managers, administrators and industrial workers had a more favourable attitude to large-scale activities than respondents in the scientific, medical and artistic professions. It is not clear how these results should be interpreted. On the one hand, one might say that those who had the most personal experience with large-scale activities and knew most about those activities had a more positive attitude. On the other hand, one could note that those who have the most positive attitudes to large-scale activities are those who have a personal interest in such activities.

Similar differences among groups were subsequently reported by Kuyper and Vlek (1984) in a study involving attitudes to liquefied petroleum gas.

These results give some perspective on psychological risk. Clearly, the extent to which risk will be emphasized is dependent upon the benefits that people perceive. This calls for considerable caution in how the results from studies of risk perception are interpreted, for what is an important risk to one person may not be important to another person.

Sjøberg and Winroth

Sjøberg and Winroth (1985) point out that research on psychological risk and acceptability has focused too much upon the consequences and their associated probabilities and ignored the activities that produce these consequences. In actual decisions, these activities are an important aspect of the decision problem. One important attribute of activities is their moral value. They had four groups of subjects: prison inmates, deaconesses, ministers and pregnant women. They found that moral value of an activity was a more important determinant of acceptability than probability or value of consequences. The extent to which these results generalize is unknown but they point to an added complexity in determining the role of perceived risk in the evaluation of decision alternatives.

CONCLUSION

The results reviewed in this paper suggest that there is no one psychology of risk. How risk is judged depends upon the context in which the judgements take place. Risk is an aspect of a decision alternative and the weight it receives in the final decision depends on the benefits from that alternative as well as on how the activity as such is evaluated.

It is clear, however, that perceived risk has a structure that differs from the structure of expert judgements about risk. Expert judgements often focus upon fatality rates but this is only one of the aspects that affects perceived risk and therefore perceived risk does not always agree with the risk computed by engineers. Such differences do not mean that lay people are irrational in their risk assessment or that experts are wrong, it is simply that they often do different things.

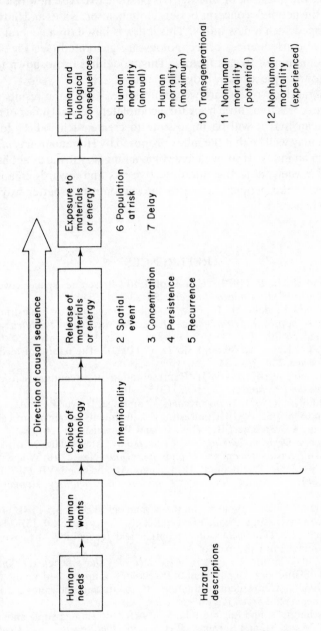

Fig. 2.3.

This raises the question of whether it is possible to devise new risk measures that reflect the people's concerns better. Hohenemser, Kates and Slovic (1983) have developed such a new index. This index is based on a general model of how negative consequences of technology are generated (see Fig. 2.3), and requires estimation of twelve factors. This model has been shown to predict quite well how people actually judge hazards.

How general these results are we do not know. Given the results reviewed above, there seems to be little hope for a completely general index of risk. This does not mean that it will be impossible to create such indices for special purposes. It may well be that the index proposed by Hohenemser *et al.* is a step towards such an index. If so, we have come a long way towards abolishing the distinction between subjective and objective risk and towards creating a risk index that will take people's concerns into account in a better way than do indices now in use.

REFERENCES

Combs, B. and Slovic, P. (1979). 'Causes of death: Biased newspaper coverage and biased judgments', *Journalism Quarterly*, **56**, 837–843, 849.
Earle, T. C. and Lindell, M. K. (1984). 'Public perception of industrial risks: a free-response approach', *Proceedings of the 1982 meeting of the Society for Risk Analysis*, **113**, 55–70.
Hohenemser, C., Kates, R. W. and Slovic, P. (1983). 'The nature of technological hazard', *Science*, **220**, 378–384.
Johnson, E. J. and Tversky, A. (1984). 'Representations of perceptions of risk', *Journal of Experimental Psychology: General*, **113**, 55–70.
Johnson-Laird, P. N. (1983). *Mental Models*. Cambridge: University Press.
Kuyper, H. and Vlek, C. (1984). 'Contrasting risk judgments among interest groups', *in* Borcherding, K., Brehmer, B., Vlek, C. and Wagenaar, W. A. (Eds), *Research Perspectives on Decision-Making Under Uncertainty*. Amsterdam: North-Holland.
Lee, W. (1971). *Decision Theory and Human Behaviour*. New York: Wiley.
Lichtenstein, S., Slovic, P., Fischhoff, B., Layman, M. and Combs, B. (1978). 'Judged frequency of lethal events', *Journal of Experimental Psychology: Human Learning and Memory*, **4**, 551–578.
Lopes, L. L. (1983). 'Some thoughts on the psychological concept of risk', *Journal of Experimental Psychology: Human Perception and Performance*, **9**, 137–144.
Perusse, M. (1980). 'Dimensions of perception and recognition of danger,' Ph.D. Thesis. Birmingham: University of Aston.
Sjøberg, L. and Winroth, E. (1985). *Risk, Moral Value of Actions, and Mood*. University of Goteborg: Department of Psychology. Unpublished manuscript.
Slovic, P. (1962). 'Convergent validation of risk-taking measures', *Journal of Abnormal and Social Psychology* **65**, 68–71.
Slovic, P., Fischhoff, B. and Lichtenstein, S. (1980). 'Informing people about risk', *in* Morris, L., Mazis, M. and Barofsky, I. (Eds), *Product Labelling and Health Risks*. Banbury Report 6. Cold Spring Harbor, New York: Cold Spring Laboratory.
Slovic, P., Fischhoff, B. and Lichtenstein, S. (1984). 'Behavioural decision theory perspectives on risk and safety', *in* Borcherding, K., Brehmer, B., Vlek, C. and

Wagenaar, W. A. (Eds), *Research perspectives on decision-making under uncertainty*. Amsterdam: North-Holland.

TFD (1982). *Form och styrka hos sambandet mellan upplevd och verklig olycksrisk*. Report 1982: 9. Stockholm: Transportforskningsdelegationen.

Tversky, A. and Kahneman, D. (1973). 'Availability: A heuristic for judging frequency and probability', *Cognitive Psychology*, 10, 34–52.

Tversky, A. and Kahneman, D. (1974). 'Judgement under uncertainty: Heuristics and Biases', *Science*, 85, 1124–1131.

Vlek, C. & J. and Stallen, J. P. (1981). 'Judging risks and benefits in the small and in the large', *Organizational Behaviour and Human Performance*, 28, 235–271.

Chapter 3

Risk from a Safety Executive Viewpoint

E. N. BJORDAL
Norsk Hydro a.s, Oslo

DEFINITIONS

It is important to describe what is meant by the words safety and risk from a safety point of view.

The word safety expresses:

— a feeling (to the individual),
— a mode (absence of accidents over a rather long period),
— a goal (both for individuals, organizations and the society).

Safety is important to all of us but we react as individuals. A rock climber has perhaps different feelings towards safety from most of us but the challenge for him also is to avoid accidents and safety remains his ultimate goal.

The word risk has another and more restricted meaning. In traditional safety work in industry it is not predominant and is used to qualify and elaborate what safety is. In this chapter however, risk is used in the modern way: risk is a function of probability and consequences for unwanted events, especially events which result in hurting people, or damaging the environment or materials.

Safety as such cannot be measured directly. Risk is introduced in technological safety work because it can be quantified under certain conditions. In recent years thinking about safety has concentrated on various ways of specifying risks.

41

MANAGEMENT AND RISK

The basic goals for senior management in industry are:

— profit for the company,
— market shares,
— new products/increased sales,
— influence.

Tools to reach these goals are:

— investments,
— organization changes,
— research,
— contacts, reports, analyses,
— decisions including all sorts of risks, of which some can be minimized through insurance.

Risk-taking for an executive is, in the broad sense of the word, a positive and necessary means to reach his goals. It is not only an integrated part of the executive's daily work, it is a condition for a senior manager's success; for him to cope with/to control risks is fundamental. Every decision involves uncertainty and the possibility of failing—a risk, or rather several risks. He uses several conscious and unconscious criteria for evaluating the risks and profits of a decision. Of these, the risk of accident is just one. His task is to make decisions where the probability of success is much greater than that of failure. He wishes to minimize the risks, but he must also be able to cope with the consequences of various failures and accidents. This is the justification for specialist safety officers. All organizations now have to meet strong safety regulations and to document how they are met. These requirements are the basis of risk-analysis.

It is important that the results of risk-analyses are suitable as input to the decision-maker and to the public. This question is more important than statistical methods and data bases.

RISKS AND SAFETY

Risks have several dimensions of which at least three are important for our discussion:

After effects

— accidents which hurt people,
— long-term severe health effects on people,
— disturbance of the environment,

— material damage,
— lack of availability/reliability,
— conscious sabotage and terror.

Seriousness (foreseen/unknown, probable/rare):

— numerous daily life incidents and accidents including, for instance, unsafe treatment of chemicals, which are known to be dangerous,
— serious accidents, but local in their effects,
— major accidents and disturbances.

Causes:

— man-made accidents,
— accidents caused by nature.

The management of a company or of a society feel responsibility:

— to consider and to have an evaluation system for all types of risk,
— to take 'reasonable' precautions against them,
— to have contingency plans and emergency organizations.

From a safety point of view it is crucial to understand that the different types of risks must be treated and analysed in different ways. For example, we cannot analyse the problem of numerous small accidents with the same tools appropriate for eventual long-term health effects. This is often overlooked in the risk literature.

From another point of view the safety tasks in our companies and in society can be divided into three main categories:

— *knowledge:* mathematical, biological, physical, behaviouristic, social, medical, and last but not least overall knowledge,
— *organization:* instructions, initiative, control and motivation,
— *acceptance:* political, sociological, economical and insurance.

The need for:

— more knowledge,
— better organization,
— clearer acceptance criteria,

has to be evaluated for all the three dimensions of risk mentioned above. The current situation is that our concrete knowledge is probably better developed than the other two categories.

RISK PHILOSOPHY

What are the limitations of 'the risk philosophy' today? How does it promote safety? Are there areas, important to safety, which the risk philosophy does not treat in an adequate way?

Normally in risk literature untreated areas are specified as 'the acceptance of risk', an area dealt with by the politicians. This is not acceptable from a safety point of view. There is a gap between the results of risk-analyses on one side and the managers' and the politicians' need for information on the other side. More research is needed to widen the field of risk-analysis, not accepting the current situation concerning 'the acceptance of risk'.

Another limitation of risk-analysts is that they take for granted a certain (but not defined) organization dealing with the risk. The management style, the maintenance systems, the qualifications of the staff, the systems of modifications are areas not dealt with in the risk-analyses. From a safety point of view, more research is needed to include such areas in the risk analyses.

The areas mentioned above are so dominant in the safety picture of technical activities that one can argue that risk analyses reveal so little about the safety level that they should not be used in important decisions. Procedures must be improved.

Another area of research relates to the kind of thinking and kind of analyses we need from a safety point of view. It is not enough to study risk, the study of risk is just a practical tool, a way to analyse and improve the real goal which is safety.

KNOWLEDGE OF RISKS

Knowledge of various aspects of safety is not independent of other disciplines and sciences. The more we know, the more we know we don't know and the situation undergoes rapid changes. We have to live with this, and it is important that our organizations and society as a whole have to make and accept analytical tools and systems which have significant shortcomings.

A pragmatic, but not cynical view, is that mankind can accept isolated accidents. The lack of knowledge is really important if today we are destroying irreversible ecological systems such as forests, deserts, water and the atmosphere. Genetic and sociological aspects are also important.

ORGANIZATION AND RISKS

For the last five years the organizational thinking in Norway concerning industry has been concentrated on what the authorities have introduced as the companies' 'Internal control'. Normally this is incorporated in the quality assurance system in the company. The system is an organizational one which takes care of safety principally in the same way as instrumentation, structure,

Table 3.1.

Type of recommendations	Three Mile Island, U.S.A.	'Bravo' blowout in the North Sea	'Alexander Kielland' accident in the North Sea
	%	%	%
Organization control, competence	90	80	70
Technical	10	20	30
	100	100	100

personnel qualifications and so on. It is intended to include aspects such as competence, education and behaviour, and is a big step forward. It is in its origin a technocratic system and is introduced as such. We still have to see if it can be a dynamic instrument in all parts of organizations. For instance, it is not clear how the unions will be able to use it.

On the human side we have big tasks in the future. This is obvious for the routine incidents but the study of official reports after major accidents such as Three Mile Island, 'Alexander Kielland' and 'Bravo' platforms in the North Sea reveals the same pattern. (Table 3.1)

ACCEPTANCE OF RISKS

The last of the three important problems mentioned above concerns acceptance. This has sociological, political, ethical and psychological aspects. The risk specialists have not yet been able to present a comprehensive and extensive theory of risk acceptance, neither at the company level nor at the society level. Does the phrase 'acceptance of risk' express a useful concept?

This can lead to a new question; perhaps we shouldn't care so much about the philosophical content of this concept but concentrate on specific projects. For instance, is quantification of risk as probability for fatalities per year the right way to go to improve safety in our societies?

The risk specialists for every project must learn to give answers which match the decision criteria of the management.

Risk and Decisions
Edited by W. T. Singleton and J. Hovden
© 1987 John Wiley & Sons Ltd.

Chapter 4

Risk: Culture and Concepts

JAN HOVDEN
SINTEF, Division of Safety and Reliability, Trondheim
and
TORE J. LARSSON
Institute for Human Safety and Accident Research, Stockholm

INTRODUCTION

The aim of this chapter is to contribute to an understanding of risk issues for policy-makers and managers in industry, authorities and elsewhere in their relationship to and coping with public opinions, parties, disagreements and decision dilemmas. A risk, though it has some roots in nature, is bound to appear in a social context and is subject to social processes and cultural patterns.

Cultural considerations of the risk concept refers mainly to those religious, magical or 'prescientific' aspects of risk that are part and parcel of every human group and society in history and today. In risk research we will find models and theories in both universalistic and relativistic/particularistic traditions. The pragmatic or practical utility of such knowledge for decision-making and risk-handling has been rather small. Introducing cultural considerations of risk-phenomena should avoid being so particularistic that every individual has to be seen as a special case without, at the same time, being so universalistic that everyone ends up the same (Thompson and Wildavsky, 1982). They also consider that: 'Culture, we begin to feel, confirms to neither of these contradictory extremes of total fluidity and rigid concreteness. Culture is plastic.'

Studies of cultural aspects of risk-handling can be based on two main empirical approaches:

— longitudinal: a historical, dynamic approach looking for trends and patterns of risk conditions, attitudes, behaviour and risk-handling, comparing past and present,
— lateral: comparative studies of today's differences and similarities between industrialized and developing countries, cultures, subcultures, and groups in society.

RISK EXPOSURE AND RISK HANDLING AT DIFFERENT LEVELS OF DECISION-MAKING

The individual's structure of decision-making during crisis handling is fundamentally different from the impersonal risk handling of safety executives. Under acute risk conditions the individual does not think in terms of probabilities in evaluating the risk. Most of the time we act as though life and health are immutable and harm and death nonexistent. Only occasionally are 'warning lights' of danger and threat perceived (Hovden and Larsson, 1984).

A starting point for the discussion of risk-perception is that the criteria, variables and relations encompassing the cognitive, emotional, and moral aspects of accidents and risk conception on different levels from the individual to the society represent different perspectives on reality and should therefore be treated separately (Hovden, 1980; Hovden and Larsson, 1984). It can be regarded as some sort of a continuum from concrete, specific and personally experienced risk in daily life to an abstract, general risk perceived through second-hand information, e.g., major hazards and general risk problems for anonymous groups or populations. Results from empirical research on risk-perception give support to this approach (Otway, 1977; Kahneman, Slovic and Tversky, 1982).

The distinction between different levels of decision-makers and groups may look rather obvious and simple, but nevertheless it is often forgotten in risk debates, communication on risk issues and in arguing about the rationality of different view-points. The interaction between the many groups of actors on different levels related to the risk source is crucial for all safety work and its effects on risk conditions in society (Hovden and Larsson, 1984).

Figure 4.1 is an attempt to illustrate the main points of the distinction between safety executives and exposed individuals which have a bearing on the meaning of the risk-concept. It is impossible to understand and to explain risk-exposure without knowledge about the different ways of risk-handling by individuals, groups and social systems. In the dualism between risk-exposure and handling risks issue from the dominant manners of reshaping nature—production and administration. The technical-economical structure and the market's offer of activities shape the pattern of high or low risk level arenas within which individuals and groups have to or choose to participate and act.

So far the differences in risk-conception have been focused. It is, however,

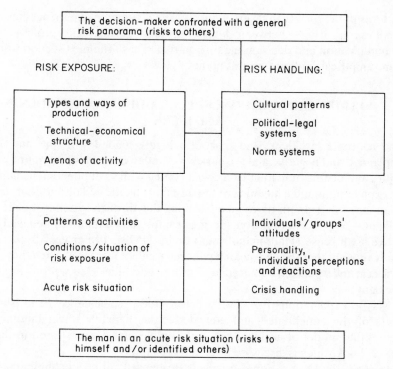

Fig. 4.1. Conceptual model illustrating the dualism between risk exposure and risk handling at different levels of decision-making from specific to abstract risks. (Hovden & Larsson, 1984, p. 5.)

some common aspects of risk-conception which are promising with respect to the possibility of communication and common understanding or risk matters between groups, parties and professions.

All of us, independently of position in society, have some common and similar experiences of risks and accidents. In some roles and activities we have all acted as safety executives and we have also been in acute risk situations and crisis handling. Most of us have also experienced minor accidents, as children we tested our limits of performance, skills and coping in using muscles, climbing and running, using tools like knives and so on. In that process we have fallen and hurt our knees, cut our fingers, been burnt and learnt how to cope with tools and the environment. We have experienced dangerous situations at work, in traffic, in sport or leisure time. We have in some circumstances been responsible for the risk exposure of others: our children, friends and colleagues. These common experiences highlight the knowledge that we share in today's society—how we were scared, how we reacted, how the peer-group interaction before and after risk exposure or accident taught us to think and behave, and how we grew up and were integrated into the subtle cultural patterns of the society that surrounds us. These common experiences may also serve as a bridge between levels, groups, parties and professions in communication and decision-making on risk issues. The next section will give some empirical evidence for this point of view.

ATTRIBUTION AND CONCEPTUAL MODELS OF ACCIDENTS AND RISKS

The concepts 'accident' and 'risk' are highly loaded with the unwanted, unplanned and negative and are closely related to outcomes in terms of losses, injury and death. Individual and social coping with such phenomena depends on explanations and a meaning to the threat of chaotic and disharmonic events (Larsson, 1985). In all times man has done this through systems of belief and religion—64 per cent of a large German sample stated that they believed in an active sixth sense (Hadjimanolis and Seiler, 1973), 10 per cent in the same study thought that the chance of having an accident increased when they saw a black cat and 9 per cent admitted to wearing a good-luck charm protecting from accident risks.

Maybe explanations like 'fate', 'act-of-God', 'coincidence', and 'sin' are parts of the enlightened and educated modern man's understanding and conceptual model of accident risk—not unlike that demonstrated in the old prayer book which is discussed later in this chapter.

In 1982, the Occupational Accident Research Unit in Stockholm commissioned the Swedish Institute for Opinion Research to put a number of attribution items before a nationally representative sample of the Swedish population between 18 and 70 years of age. Table 4.1 gives a summary of the results from nine items. The same questions were also put to high-risk groups such as air-force pilots, ambulance drivers and workers in explosives industry (Larsson, 1985). The same set of attribution items was also given to 130 participants at a seminar on risk analysis in November 1983. These respondents were mostly safety executives in industries and authorities.

The overall distribution of responses of the Swedish sample and the different high-risk groups were surprisingly similar, taking into consideration the differences in attitudes towards risks between occupational groups and subgroups (Larsson, 1985). Even the group of safety executives presented in Table 4.1 does not differ very much from the Swedish sample.

However, the percentages of safety executives which agreed on

— accident unimportance,
— accident proneness,
— fatalism,
— human factors,

as causes/reasons for accidents were significantly smaller than for the Swedish

Table 4.1. Distribution of nine items on occupational accident attribution for a representative sample of the Swedish population and of a group of safety executives.*

Statement on accident attribution	Sample of Swedes Agree %	Safety executives Agree %
Risk-taking	90	89
Human factors	89	60
Lack of planning and cooperation	88	96
Companies won't invest in safety	68	62
Technology makes accident unavoidable	60	60
Fatalism	52	27
Accident, small problem	46	25
Accident, big problem	37	37
Accident proneness	28	13
Sample size (n)	(982)	(130)

* The items are developed by Tore J. Larsson. For the full text of the items and the detailed distributions, see Hovden and Larsson (1984); Larsson (1985). The items were measured on a five-point scale: Agree—yes, fully/yes, partially/no, hardly/no, absolutely not. The table gives the percentages in the two 'yes' categories.

sample. Nevertheless, and maybe more important, quite a lot, even of the experts, believed in these statements.

Generally, in the risk research literature, there is a lack of empirical evidence on the extent of common interpretations of accidents and risks among all people, or the extent of stable differences connected with personality characteristics. The results from this study indicate that the pattern of accident attribution is related to general and stable cultural properties universal in time and space, differences related to roles and group properties, and properties specific to each person.

Attribution research and general cognitive psychology can give us some ideas about the relevant properties specific to each person. For example, in explaining the outcome of accident processes there seems to be a dimension that could be termed the person-situation dimension. This is related to the personal definition of responsibility (Larsson, 1985). Attribution researchers have interpreted this rather stable tendency as a personality trait (Shaver, 1970; Mischel, 1979).

The term 'locus of control' (Rotter, 1966) expresses a related distinction concerning the way risks are experienced with the added distinction of internal and external control. With a somewhat transferred significance it can describe a very important aspect of risk. The individual can see himself/herself as an object/victim or as a subject/actor in a risk situation. For example, this can explain traditional and stable differences between the sexes on attitudes and behaviour related to risks.

Table 4.2. The responses of a group of Swedish safety executives on items about the meaning of acceptable risk and items on attitudes towards risks.*

A: Statement on the meaning of acceptable risk	Agree %
A quantified safety level	74
No alternative way of solving the risk problem	61
Benefits outweigh the risk	50
No obvious benefits on risk reduction made	37
The risk is voluntary	35
The risk is eliminated, zero risk	19
The risk is equal for everyone	7

B: Attitude statement	Agree %
Prosecute those effecting accidents and harm	90
The society should protect the citizens against risks, even voluntary risk exposure	63
Money and costs don't matter when saving lives	58
Priority to the safety of myself/those nearest/dearest	50
The participants in sport accidents should pay the costs	29
Risk-taking—the individual's right to choose	16
Balloon-effects—fatalistic attitude	11

Sample size (*n*)	(130)

* The items are developed by Jan Hovden. For the full text of the items and detailed distributions of responses, see Hovden and Larsson (1984). See also the note of Table 4.1.

Table 4.2 presents results from the group of safety executives on statements about the meaning of acceptable risk and some attitude statements about risk issues. As for Table 4.1, the results can be interpreted from theories on:

— individual differences, unique individuals, a clinical perspective,
— group specific properties, roles and cultural patterns,
— general theories on cognition, motivation, emotion and ethics.

Table 4.2A shows that a majority of the safety executives agreed on interpreting the meaning of acceptable risk as:

— a quantified safety level,
— no alternative way of solving the risk problem,
— benefits outweigh the risks.

The most popular answer may be due merely to the fact that the respondents were attending a seminar on risk-analysis when they answered the questions.

The attitude statements in Table 4.2B reveal almost full consensus on law and prosecution in risk-handling. The respondents had a strong belief in society's obligation to protect people, even against themselves or so called 'voluntary' risks. This may reflect the general ideological framework of a welfare state.

Moving from basic meanings attributed to 'accidents' to a more intellectual decision-making construct like 'acceptable risk', and to attitude statements changes the approach from distinct, stable and rather latent psychological categories to more manifest and fluctuating expressions related to anthropological, sociological, and political theories. A great challenge for interdisciplinary behavioural research is to find ways of integrating these theoretical approaches on how to investigate and analyse the interaction between man's individual and collective representations of accidents and risk phenomena.

As a modest contribution, Hovden and Larsson (1984) combined the sets of items in Table 4.1 and Table 4.2 in multivariate analyses in order to get grouping across the three sets of items. It is a pilot study, the sample is small and the items need more elaboration and so the validity of the results can be questioned. Combining the three sets of items in different types of factor analysis and cluster analysis revealed some stable patterns of dimensions in the concept of risk phenomena (Hovden and Larsson, 1984):

Individualistic interpretation of risk:

— the individual's right to risk-taking,
— the benefits outweigh the risk,
— voluntariness.

System critique interpretation or risk:

— lack of planning and cooperation,
— society's duty of protecting people,
— the importance of the problem,
— companies won't invest in safety.

Legal interpretation of risk:

— risk-taking as accident cause,
— prosecute those responsible.

Ideal interpretation of risk:

— risk eliminated, zero risk,
— equal risk for everyone.

Fatalistic interpretation of risk:

— 'accidents happen now and then, there's not much we can do about it',
— immediate benefits in risk reduction,
— 'balloon effects', risk compensation.

Economic–moral interpretation of risk:
— the safety of myself/those nearest and dearest,
— cost of sports accidents should be paid for by the participants and not by society.

Technological-rationalistic interpretation of risk:

— a quantified safety level,
— risk criteria defined by science.

A more simple analysis of the correlation matrix of all items, bearing in mind the small sample and possible errors in scaling and measurement, gives three levels of clusters ranked according to their importance in explaining the group's overall interpretation of risk issues:

Level 1

— the individual's freedom *vs.* society's guardian role,
— risk benefit evaluations.

Level 2

— fatalism (four different aspects),
— person-oriented attitudes and attributions,
— ideal and moral attitudes.

Level 3

— the importance of the problem,
— system critical attributions and attitudes.

GROUPS AND SUBCULTURAL NORMS

It is established from research on attitudes towards risk and risk handling that:
— Women are more risk aversive than men (Brun-Gulbrandsen and As, 1973).
— Workers in traditional high-risk industries trust their individual coping with accident risks and accept high-risk levels. Typical examples from Norway are the coastal fisheries, mining, and forestry. A great deal of these occupational activities will be found in isolated communities with few, if any, alternative sources of income. Typical of these occupations are self-recruitment, strong traditions and socially established norms of risk acceptance and risk behaviour. A negative aspect of these norms is an attitude of fatalism. On the other hand, the traditions of risk taking in these occupations have developed skill and experience in risk coping and preparedness in crisis situations. Systematic studies in Swedish industries show the same picture (a review and analysis of these studies are presented in Hovden and Larsson, 1984).

— Subcultures among youngsters can develop rather odd attitude patterns towards risk. In traffic, for example, we have special risk problems of young drivers (Marek, 1975).

Some of these differences can be explained in terms of general sociological and social psychological theories of roles and norms. However, some aspects of differences between groups on risk attitudes and risk conceptions are perhaps better understood using an anthropological approach.

The combination of world view and strategy for handling what is appropriate to each social context results in an individual in that context perceiving his external world in a distinctive way. Psychology can tell us how we perceive and anthropology can tell us about the patternings that are socially imposed in order to support certain attitudes and moral commitments (Thompson and Wildavsky, 1982).

RISKS AND RISK PERCEPTION IN THE 'GOOD OLD DAYS'

The best Scandinavian original documents about risk conditions centuries ago are clerical handbooks for praying in church (Oden, 1977). An old book of prayers gives the following list of main risk sources:

— epidemic diseases,
— war and rebellion,
— bad weather,
— bad harvest and starvation,
— fires.

Prayers for specific high-risk groups were also said for fishermen, sailors, travellers, pregnant women and soldiers.

Dominant patterns of concepts and attributions of accidents, risks, and accident causation can be interpreted from such documents. Accidents were attributed to:

— 'acts of God',
— punishment for sins and immorality,
— destiny or fate.

In less complex societies in historical times, surrounding dangers were well known and risks of death easily attributed to nature, animals, illness or tribal warfare. The risk spectrum with time has widened and become more difficult to perceive and control for the local group or family. Today's risk coping is based more on decisions and actions taken by the single individual and by large organizations and national authorities.

Up to the end of World War II people in Europe primarily feared epidemics. No known catastrophes have had the magnitude of the Black Death. The

Spanish Influenza at the end of World War I killed more people than the war's shooting and bombing.

Thanks to better living conditions in general, scientific progress, better health services etc., we gradually got rid of the great infectious diseases in the first half of our century and life expectancy in Norway increased from less than 40 years in 1875 to more than 73 years in 1975. However, there is no evidence that it is the accident risk that has diminished, it is the great reduction in infant deaths that contributes most to the increase in life expectancy.

As shown in Table 4.3 we have had some dramatic changes in the pattern of fatal accident frequencies over the last hundred years.

Historical statistics show that except for the period of World War II, the relative number of fatal accidents in Norway has been approximately constant during the last century. There have been roughly 400 accident fatalities per

Table 4.3. Fatal accidents distributed by cause and/or type in the last hundred years. The figures are annual averages per 1 million population. (The table is compiled from data from the Norwegian Central Bureau of Statistics).

Causes/Types of accidents	Period			
	1876–85	1921–25	1951–55	1977
Motor vehicle transport	0	17	59	117
Fisheries and shipping	158	73	40	20
Other transport (railroads, land transport, air transport)	11	25	24	19
Drowning*	246	131	80	39
Falls, falling objects†	50	49	171	200
Fires, burns, strangulation	34	29	23	25
Poisoning	3	14	18	18
Firearms and explosives	12	17	11	3
Machinery and electricity	7	7	8	5
Nature, wind and weather	21	9	8	2
All other accidents	18	16	17	30
Annual average per 1 million population altogether	482	386	470	470
Total number of accident fatalities per year	915	1041	1515	1880

* Drowning while working in fisheries and shipping are included in the category 'fisheries and shipping'. On the other hand, passengers who drown when travelling by boat are included in the category 'drowning'.
† Registration practices were changed in 1939 with regard to injuries resulting from falls from the same level. In 1977, 537 out of a total 761 registered falls in or near the home that resulted in death involved persons over the age of 69.

million inhabitants per year. Figures from other countries reflect an analogous situation (Hovden, 1980). For a discussion of the relationship between accidents and the progress of technology, see Singleton (1982).

These facts have inspired some people engaged in safety matters to ask if there is a generally accepted risk level, a universal 'magic' number for risk acceptance, some sort of 'mysterious' societal adjustment to risk, theories of risk compensation and 'balloon' effects.

However, the stable trend in the historical statistics of fatal accidents can mostly be accounted for by changes in registration practices and the quality of registration. Controlling for such error sources gives at least 25 per cent reduction in the fatal accident rate in Norway over the last hundred years. The change in total figures is not dramatic, but great enough to reject the universalistic 'theories' of risk acceptance mentioned above, and stable enough to indicate that there may be some stable patterns in the way individuals and society handle risk problems regardless of changes in the pattern of accident risks (see Table 4.3.)

TODAY'S RISK PANORAMA—ATTITUDE CHANGES

There are a number of new hazards in connection with energy production, modern passenger transport, the transport and storage of large amounts of explosive and poisonous goods, new chemical substances which may be injurious to health, growing pollution and, not least, a greater chance of global destruction (NTNF's Risk Research Committee, 1983).

This has prompted us to concentrate on risks closely linked with the use of modern technology such as industrial accidents. However, risks to which we voluntarily expose ourselves in our leisure time and risks which have no connection at all with large scale technology are, according to official statistics, a more significant part of the overall risk picture.

In the last few years, attention has been focused increasingly on risks to life and health. This may be in the main traced back to three factors:

— People receive more information about risk conditions through mass media. On television, the entire world is our accident risk arena. Therefore, our fear of potential accidents has grown and become more pronounced. The criteria of 'good copy' in newspapers and TV sometimes give biased viewpoint effects on the receiver's perception of risks. The individual's concepts of risks are today relatively less dependent on personal experience and first-hand perception.

— Greater knowledge of and more critical attitudes towards risks in the rich part of the world due to education, higher standards of living and welfare. There are more stringent standards of safety than before for human life and health, emergency preparedness and health services. These are parts of general improvements in social welfare.

— The actual risk to which we are exposed, or expose ourselves, has changed. Among other things, it has changed because the historically great sources of hazard have been reduced. New accident areas have arisen in connection with the use of technology. Individuals seem to have a collective sound conservative reaction on new and unknown risks. For example, risk acceptance based on comparisons with traditional activities like mining and fishing will be rejected as irrelevant or even nonsense.

A brief historical overview like this one may also give some perspective on the risk scene in the developing countries, e.g.:

— major hazards due to natural disasters, starvation and epidemics,
— problems in handling modern technology.

Unsatisfied basic needs for food, clean water and housing as the main problem for many countries give a context where questions of traditional accident risks and environmental risks appear luxurious compared to more urgent problems of health and survival.

A typical example is the change of attitude that has taken place in the trade unions of Norway. In the past, the emphasis tended to be on the struggle for extra pay for hazardous and dirty work. Nowadays, the principle of providing compensation in the form of danger money has largely been done away with and, instead, the emphasis has shifted to increased safety and wellbeing inherent in technological and organizational improvements (Hovden *et al.*, 1979).

CONCLUSION

There is no reason to believe that risk carries fewer cultural aspects today compared to centuries ago. We tend to believe that we think and act more rationally today and therefore the investigation of the collective representations surrounding today's risks does not attract risk research. The success of risk-handling and safety work of all kinds is dependent on the cultural context of the risk scene.

REFERENCES

Brun-Gulbrandsen, S. and As, B. (1973). 'Kjonnsroller og ulykker', *in* Hem, L. and Holter, H. (Eds), *Sosialpsykologi*. Oslo: Universitetsforlaget.
Hadjimanolis, E. and Seiler, G. (1973). *Unfalle in Hausbereich*. Dortmund.
Hovden, J. *et al.* (1979). *Vurdering av ulykkesrisiko*. Trondheim: Tapir.
Hovden, J. (1980). Accident Risks in Norway. How Do We Perceive and Handle Risks. Oslo: NTNF's Risk Research Committee.
Hovden, J. and Larsson, T. J. (1984). *Olycka? Hantering av risker i svenskt arbetsliv*. Occupational Accident Research Unit. Stockholm: KTH.
Kahneman, D., Slovic, P. and Tversky, A. (Eds) (1982). *Judgement Under Uncertainty: Heuristics and biases*. Cambridge: University Press.

Larsson, T. J. (1985). 'The meaning of accidents', *in Fjarde Nordiska Olycksfallsforskningsseminaret, Rovaniemi, 1984,* Espoo: VTT Symposium 55.

Marek, J. (1975). 'Unge bilforere og deres ulykker', *Samferdsel*, **9**, 39–44. Oslo.

Mischel, W. (1979). 'On the interface of cognition and personality, beyond the person-situation debate', *American Psychologist*, **34**, 9, 740–754.

NTNF's Risk Research Committee (1983). *Perspektiv pa sikkerhetsforskining i Norge,* NTNF, Oslo. Draft in English (1985). *Perspectives on Safety Research in Norway.*

Oden, B. (1977). *Historiskt perspektiv pa riskpanoramaet i et foranderligt perspektiv,* Rapport 13–77, Projeket Riskbedomning och riskgenerering i ett samhalligt perspektiv. Gothenburg: University of Gothenburg.

Otway, H. J. (1977). *A Review of research on the Identification of Factors Influencing the Social Response to Technological Risks, International Atomic Energy Agency.* Salzburg.

Rotter, J. B. (1966). Generalized expectancies for internal versus external control of reinforcement', *Psychological Monographs*, **80**(1), 609.

Shaver, K. G. (1970). 'Defensive attribution: effects on servity and relevance on the responsibility assigned for an accident', *Journal of Personality and Social Psychology*, **14**, 101–113.

Singleton, W. T. (1982). 'Accidents and the progress of technology', *Journal of Occupational Accidents*, **4**, 91–102. Amsterdam: Elsevier.

Thompson, M. and Wildavsky, A. (1982). 'A proposal to create a cultural theory of risk', *in* Kunreuther, H. C. and Ley, E. V. (Eds), *The Risk Analysis Controversy.* Berlin: Springer-Verlag.

Discussion: Concepts and Measures

The calculus of probability is well established as a rigorous foundation from which to consider the description of risk and decision.

Suppose that a situation has a number of possible outcomes:

$$1 \ldots i \ldots n$$

with probabilities:

$$p_1 \cdots p_i \cdots p_n$$

where:

$$\Sigma_i^n \, p_i = 1.$$

Consider an individual who has to risk making a choice between these outcomes. Some are not desirable otherwise there would be no risk and some are desirable otherwise there would be no need to make a choice.

Suppose

— the outcomes up to and including j are desirable and those beyond j are undesirable

— collectively the desirable outcomes are labelled A and the undesirable ones are labelled B.

Then

$$\Sigma_i^j P_i = P_A \quad \text{and} \quad \Sigma_{j+1}^n P_i = P_B, \qquad P_A + P_B = 1 \tag{1}$$

The risk attached to this choice is P_B.

There are a number of features of this straightforward statement which are overlooked or confused in verbal discussions about risk and decision.

1. Possibilities are different from probabilities and both are significant in risk discussions.
2. Possibilities refers to the range of outcomes measured by a positive integer greater than one. If there is only one possibility no decision is required.
3. Probabilities, measured by numbers in the range 0–1, describe likelihoods of particular specific outcomes.
4. Risk is the sum of the probabilities of the undesirable outcomes—again a number in the range 0–1.
5. Risk-analysis is the search for data that can be fitted into equation (1).
6. In applying this calculus to decision-making we are implicitly assuming that a decision can be defined as a choice between alternative outcomes.

7. There is no implication that decisions are made entirely on the basis of risks. It is only when decisions are assumed to be direct functions of risks that it is necessary to incorporate other features such as consequences in the risk equation, i.e., risk $= f$ (probabilities, consequences). This is a retrograde step because consequences are often unmeasurable and are rarely directly comparable. This is how values creep in.

Inevitably real situations have other complications which make the formal definitions of risk a reference point rather than a comprehensively valid statement:

— it may not be feasible to enumerate all the possibilities n,
— it may not be feasible to decide that a particular outcome is unambiguously A or B in that it may have some desirable and some undesirable features,
— an outcome which is desirable at one level may be undesirable at another, e.g., in a military system the objectives of the system may be furthered although the subsystem involved may be lost which can hardly be regarded as desirable by the operators in the subsystem.

These pragmatic considerations should be supplemented by a corresponding contribution from the recondite literature on the classical philosophy of probability (Russell, 1948; Ayer, 1973). Unfortunately, this does not appear to contribute clarity to thinking about risk beyond an emphasis on the distinction between the calculus of probability and probability in decision-making. Popper (1976), as Doderlein has already reminded us, postulates a 'propensity interpretation' of probability which relates to his flexible methodological rules (in physics) that theories are only temporary and progress is by refutation. Accepting a refutation is also risky but not quite as risky as the formulation of the hypothesis refuted. Eddington (1928) pointed out a long time ago that there can be no unique probability attached to any event or behaviour, the probability changes with the extent of information. Similarly, Eddington graphically emphasizes the fact that probabilistic evidence is about populations and still leaves indeterminacy in relation to a specific case: 'we have admitted an uncertainty which may take or spare human lives: but we have yet to find an uncertainty which may upset the expectations of a life insurance company'.

More pragmatically, a decision-maker does not behave in relation to the probabilities as they are but to what he thinks they are. The subjective probabilities may be quite different from objective probabilities and may not conform to the above calculus. An individual may assign probabilities which add up to more or less than unity, e.g., in calculating the odds for the horses in a particular race a bookmaker makes no attempt to estimate odds such that when translated into probabilities they add up to unity. The decision-maker may not think in probabilities at all, his view of the problem may be entirely in terms of consequences or he may consider various consequences and be able to rank them in likelihood of success. He may, as Spjotvoll describes, begin with subjective estimates and proceed to refine these by examining further evidence thereby converging towards the objective probabilities.

Brehmer points out, from his studies of dangerous situations, that an individual may think of a risk as a degree of hazard and may estimate this hazard from a very broad knowledge of how the physical world works. Not surprisingly, his idea of risk as a psychologist is very different from that which fits neatly into probability theory, he sees judgements as 'a diffuse negative evaluation of a decision alternative, a general feeling this is something one does not want' (p. 26). The differences between objective and subjective risks in studies of risk assessment are not as clear as the terms suggest since 'objective' risks are also estimates. Lay assessments are often different from expert assessments; lay assessments are made in a wider context and include moral judgements but this does not justify regarding them as irrational.

The chapter by Bjordal presents yet another point of view. For the safety officer, the objective is reduced risks and accidents for the benefit of the individual, the organization and society generally. Procedures working towards this goal involve research and analyses and more particularly quantification. Evidence is needed to guide management decisions and also to demonstrate that the organization is functioning within the limits expressed by society in the form of regulations. The recent trend in Norway is to place the responsibility for procedures within each organization. The problem is now essentially an organizational one rather than a technical one.

Hovden and Larsson point out that risks and attitudes to risk cannot be separated from their social and cultural context. Attitudes to risk depend on the level of the assessor, from the individual considering his own situation to the senior administrator concerned with the overall situation, although the whole spectrum still has to be seen in the particular cultural context. This context is influenced by features such as communication through the mass media, the general wealth and social welfare situation and the changing position of risks. Communication between experts and decision-makers requires much wider evidence than risks expressed as probabilities, it requires a clarification of value judgements. Politicians in particular tend to reject any probing into their values. Values are not affected directly by scientific evidence but experts also are people and it is sometimes difficult to distinguish their values from their presented data.

Risk-analysis should be a procedure supporting decision-making but it appears to make a clearer contribution to management decisions within an organization than it does to politicians involved in larger and vaguer issues. For example, the broad criterion of 10^{-4} which is widely used as a risk limit for particular events in the Norwegian oil industry and 10^{-6} which is commonly used for acceptable catastrophe levels in aviation and nuclear power seem to have emerged by experience and debate over long periods rather than by any logically defensible process. Thus the size of consequences obviously reflects acceptable probabilities and consequences themselves are affected by the possibility of remedial action. These complications have resulted in some experts concluding that quantitative assessment of risks have meaning only within formal risk analyses.

Another approach is to suggest that probabilities express just one belief system, there are many others and a more individualized or organizationally agreed integration is needed in the context of policy decisions. The engineering concept of risk is a limited one, probabilities are not a suitable tool for describing major hazards and may even be misleading in presenting a false level of certainty. It remains the responsibility of the expert to describe the situation comprehensively and he cannot do this if he restricts his presentation to probabilities. There is no standard methodology which can be applied to every issue involving risk, even within formal risk-analysis different situations require different combinations of techniques. Values and choices already made should be visible within any presentation of evidence. In highly uncertain situations managers and politicians rely on experts, and their confidence will be undermined if the above principles are not followed. Complex decisions are influenced more by trust than by probabilities.

Typically a Yes/No decision has to emerge from an essentially probabilistic array of evidence, e.g., in law courts, and there is always a fine balance in the expression of doubt. Too much and there is indecision which in many circumstances is worse than a wrong decision. The flow of decision-making must continue and a wrong decision can be retrieved or adapted in the context of later decisions.

Risk to populations are qualitatively different from risks to individuals (indeed the latter may have no meaning) but precision and decision-making are greatly aided by the sensitive choice of the appropriate population. As in all other scientific problems, the identification and selection of appropriate categories must precede attempts to quantify.

REFERENCES

Ayer, A. J. (1973). *The Central Questions of Philosophy*. Harmondsworth: Penguin.
Eddington, A. (1928). *The Nature of the Physical World*. London: Dent.
Popper, K. (1976). *Unended Quest*. Glasgow: Collins.
Russell, B. (1948). *Human Knowledge*. London: George Allen and Unwin.

Section B

Risk and Behaviour

Risk and Decisions
Edited by W. T. Singleton and J. Hovden
© 1987 John Wiley & Sons Ltd.

Chapter 5

Subjective Risk

A. R. HALE
Delft University of Technology, Netherlands

INTRODUCTION

The point of view from which this chapter is written is a concern with the explanation, prediction and modification of behaviour in the face of danger. Danger here is preliminarily defined as a potential for harm to the individual, other people or to significant material elements of the system being considered. Typical operational questions in this area are:

— Why did an individual act in a particular way which contributed to events leading to an accident?
— How can behaviour which could materially contribute to an accident be predicted?
— Why do individuals in some circumstances take considerable precautions against accidents, whilst in others they ignore or even flout established safety measures?
— Why is the level of protest against the dangers of certain processes and technologies much greater than that against others?
— What training, motivation and changes in design of the environment (work or other) can modify behaviour so as to reduce the toll of accidents?

Some of the behaviours implied by the above questions would be labelled as 'risk-taking' in common parlance and in a considerable body of the safety and accident research literature.

67

68

DEFINITIONS AND SYSTEMS APPROACH

My analysis starts from the use of the systems approach to safety research (see e.g., Singleton, 1984; Leplat, 1984; Bernhardt *et al.*, 1984). This considers an individual person as one of the elements, both human and material, which interact within a defined system boundary to produce a dynamic, adaptive response to that system's environment and to move towards system goals. The human elements of the system differ from the material ones in being (at least potentially) aware of the existence of the system and its goals and being able to plan and carry out their behaviour in the light of their predictions about its outcome.

At any given point in time it is conceptually possible to take a snapshot of the current system state and then to predict potential future states by projecting different actions of the system elements or different influences from outside the system boundary. Some of those future states will involve harm to system elements, where 'harm' remains to be defined. As the time over which the prediction is made becomes longer the theoretical range of potential system states becomes larger, as does the number of those states which involve harm.

It is impossible to define any situation in which no potential for harm exists, provided that a long enough time scale is considered. It is only possible to conceive of a situation in which, at least over long periods, none of that potential is actually realized because the system is steered away from it. There is thus a distinction between the large range of theoretically possible future states and the much narrower range of ones which are credible; where credible implies certain assumptions about the 'control dynamics' of the system, and particularly of the likely actions of the people in it. Eventually 'harm' of a sort is inevitable for all system elements, since human elements die and material ones wear out.

On both of the above grounds, the concept of danger described in the previous section is useless as it stands, since there would be no situation excluded from consideration. The Gordian knot can be cut in two ways:

— either the definition of potential harm can be made reflexive so that it becomes the study of situations which the person(s) being studied consider 'dangerous';
— or an arbitrary definition can be imposed by an 'expert' as to how much harm and of what form is to be considered necessary to constitute 'danger'.

The former approach has been called the 'subjective risk', and the latter the 'objective risk' approach; but both of these solutions are, in fact, imposing a subjective, normative approach. All that differs is who is imposing the definition. In either case, it is relevant to ask what factors are taken into account and in what way and to ask whether the qualifications and authority of the person whose definition is used are suitable for the purpose to which the study will be put. Disagreements over this issue are clearly at the root of much acrimonious debate. This chapter largely reviews studies and questions rooted in the first of the two approaches, but comments will be made in passing about the contrasts between this approach and the other.

This section has already suggested two dimensions which must be considered in pursuing the definition of danger:

— the definition of 'harm' which people use,
— the completeness of the range of potential future states that people consider when making that assessment.

Relevant research

A number of reviews of work in the area of 'subjective risk', individual attitudes and response to danger, and their measurement have appeared in recent years (e.g., Fischhoff *et al.*, 1981; Lathrop, 1981; Vlek and Stallen, 1981; Covello, 1983; Royal Society, 1983; Brown and Green, 1980; Hale and Perusse, 1978; Hale, 1984). This research has sprung largely from what has come to be known as the 'Expressed Preference' approach which studies the way in which people think about, classify, or rate situations which contain danger. Three stages in this approach should be distinguished, since they may involve different decisions of an individual, and so be influenced by different factors.

(1) *Hazard elicitation*

To be truly a study of subjective risk the subjects should themselves define, as part of the research, the situations which they consider to be dangerous, e.g., by recording them on 'hazard and accident cards' (Perusse, 1980), pointing them out to another person during a site inspection (Abeytunga, 1978) or by using projective picture techniques in the laboratory (Perusse, 1980). In much of the published work, however, it is the researchers who define the range of situations which they present to the subjects as dangerous. In either case, I label these situations 'hazards'.

(2) *Scale elicitation*

The subjects should themselves then generate scales on which they differentiate between the hazards. This can be done using techniques such as Kelly's Repertory Grid (Green and Brown, 1976; Perusse, 1980). In most cases, however, the scales on which the hazards are to be rated are also given to the subjects (e.g., Fischhoff *et al.*, 1978c; Vlek and Stallen, 1981; Golant and Burton, 1969). This is frequently done to save time.

Even by this stage in the description of methodology, there are three different approaches which vary on one dimension already mentioned, namely who defines what range of 'harm' should be included.

(3) *Scale analysis*

The subjects then rate the hazards on the scales and the results are subjected to either factor or cluster analysis to produce a range of super ordinate dimensions which the subjects are using to make sense of the defined field of 'danger' or 'hazard'. These dimensions then have to be labelled by the researchers. Use of psychometric scaling techniques can also provide ratio scales which can be subjected to regression analysis to see which combination of scales best predicts the rating of the hazards on some 'objective' scale of seriousness (Green and Brown, 1980a).

It is clear from the above that, from a methodological viewpoint, the research in this field is based upon techniques which are not consistent. This may explain differences found between studies, and certainly adds an extra dimension of subjective interpretation to the work of any reviewer.

Additional insights come from the parallel approach of 'Revealed Preference' whereby the *behaviour* towards different hazards is considered. In the sense in which this term has been most used it refers to the approach pioneered by Starr (1969). He calculated the probability of death during a range of activities and then made the assumption that these current levels of risk were a good measure of 'acceptable' risks because they must have resulted from an accumulated process of decision-making and action which had levelled off when a point of indifference to the risk had been reached. He has been strongly criticized (e.g., Green, 1974; Fischhoff *et al.*, 1978b,c) for making that assumption. While accepting this criticism as valid, it attacks only Starr's use of the approach to assess acceptability. The use of observation of behaviour as a way of showing differences in the ways in which people respond to different types of danger is quite different (e.g., Hale, 1984). Indeed, as the *Royal Society Report (1983)* points out, studies of real behaviour are needed in this field in order to lessen the potential bias from subjects' uncorroborated reports of beliefs.

From those two sources of evidence I have drawn the following dimensions which appear to influence the assessment of danger and behaviour towards it, in addition to the two noted in the last section. As will become clear from the later discussion the distinctions and relations between the dimensions is far from clear cut. There are also semantic problems introduced where different authors have used the same word to refer to different things and vice versa. My list differs somewhat from others proposed (e.g., Risk Research Committee, 1980; Royal Society, 1983; Guttinger, 1984) and reflects my own attempts to integrate the dimensions into some coherent picture.

DIMENSIONS OF RISK

(1) Victims of the harm; whether these are the people making the danger assessment, or others, and if the latter whether they are a special group, e.g., children, future generations, perceived as skilled or expert etc. It is also relevant whether the potential victims are also those who reap the concomitant benefits from the exposure to danger.

(2) Whether the potential for harm in the situation is considered to be under the control of the victim or of another person or group who/which is either trusted or mistrusted.

(3) Whether the victim has a real choice to enter the danger or not, or to leave it once exposed.

(4) The time scale over which harm will occur; acute injury or death versus chronic or life shortening disease.

(5) The degree of uncertainty about possible future states of the system which might result in danger; the uncertainty or lack of knowledge may be in the person making the assessment alone, or may be perceived to exist also among those who are considered to be in control of the system.

(6) The complexity and plausibility of the combination of circumstances which would need to occur for the potential for harm to be realized.

(7) The vividness, dreadfulness and severity of the imagined consequences.

The following sections consider each of the seven dimensions or concepts and the two named in the first section of the chapter and summarize the evidence pointing to its importance.

Types of harm

In any work or living situation there are almost always several different types of threat or hazard which have potential. These may be to property (integrity, quality, etc.) or to persons. If to the latter, the hazards may be to:

— physical wellbeing (acute or chronic),
— mental wellbeing (stress, frustration, etc.),
— social wellbeing (embarrassment, loss of face, etc.).

From a systems perspective, hazards might be seen more globally as threats to system goals, which would add to the above list a greater range of errors and losses due to failures of communication or clashes between system components, e.g., strikes, missed deadlines, property theft, etc. Different disciplines and groups advocate differing clustering of such 'hazards' for different purposes. For example, Loss Control (e.g., Bird and Lofthus, 1976) starts from an organizational viewpoint and clusters all loss resulting from nonspeculative (and insurable) causes, thus grouping property damage and theft with physical injury. Psychologists (e.g., Reason, 1982) often group situations using the causal factor of human error, and hence would cluster selected situations from almost all of the categories above. One influential tradition in safety (Heinrich, 1931–80) places emphasis on the 'near miss' or 'quasi-accident' as a member of the same family as the accident, having the same causes and lacking only the physical damage. More restrictively, much discussion of the dangerousness of different industries confines its metric to deaths (Fatal Accident Frequency Rate, e.g., Kletz, 1977), and much analysis in the nuclear power debate considers only loss of core containment in the definition of safety-related plant (see e.g., CEGB, 1982; Ergonomics Society, 1983).

Where the term 'risk', tout court, is used in a discussion, there may be a failure to specify which cluster of outcomes is being considered and so a clash of perceptions may occur. A number of studies provide insights into the way in which people cluster the various hazards. Steiner (1967) showed marked differences between individual's responses to 'risks' in the differing spheres of physical injury, social embarrassment, and financial loss. Many others have also criticized the attempt to draw analogies between behaviour towards physical damage and towards financial or social loss (e.g., Slovic, 1962; Ross, 1974; Council for Science and Society, 1977), and no further inclusion of nonphysical damage will be made here. However, even this restriction does not solve the problem. As Singleton (1983) has pointed out, the making, detection and correction of error is the fundamental mechanism on which human skill works; hence, it should never be the goal of anyone involved in accident prevention to eliminate all error, but only that subset which goes undetected and uncorrected. The reverse of this coin is that changes which aim to reduce the potential for physical harm in a situation may not always result in the expected reduction in accident rates because people may adjust their behaviour to compensate, and so reap a reward in other payoffs than increased safety (see Cownie and Calderwood, 1966; Saari, 1984).

Leplat (1984) quotes work comparing damage accidents and near misses ('traffic conflicts') which shows that these have significantly different characteristics. Similar results were found by Bamber (1975) in the occupational sphere, while Laitinen (1984) showed that incidents in a steel works reported as near misses had a greater potential seriousness of outcome than the accidents which actually happened in that works. All of these findings can be interpreted as evidence that some types of incident which can be labelled by certain criteria as potential threats are much less likely to result in actual harm than others, presumably because they are more likely to be picked up by the error detection mechanism discussed by Singleton (1983).

Green and Brown (1980b) showed consistent differences from their regression analyses in the factors which people use to consider acute, immediate hazards as compared to chronic (delayed in effect) hazards. They therefore argue that straight comparisons of the two types of hazard (which usually use only the probability of death from each) are invalid when assessing priorities for action; yet this comparison is frequently made when tables compare the risk of death from, e.g., nuclear loss of containment, cigarette smoking and road accidents (e.g., Kletz, 1977). They also (1977, 1978) found that people consistently differentiate between situations with a potential only for minor injury and those with a potential for 'nearly as bad as death, death, and supralethal injuries' (quadriplegia and brain damage).

Two conclusions can be drawn from this evidence. Firstly, human behaviour towards danger, whether to protest about it or to take action against it, cannot be explained or predicted using an undifferentiated concept of harm. Behaviour is likely to be qualitatively different dependent upon the type of harm inherently (and subjectively) possible. Much more research is needed to specify what clusters relate to what sort of behaviour and so what hazards can be meaningfully grouped together for what decision-making purposes. Secondly, if we want to predict the likelihood of harm occurring in a situation, we must take into account the different probabilities of the humans in the system detecting and so avoiding the danger. The system has an important feedback loop mediating between potential and actual output.

Range of causal links considered

Perusse (Hale and Perusse, 1978) studied how people assess a situation to see what hazards exist in it. He found that the process was one of hypothesis generation and testing. In effect, the subjects projected onto the situation a number of potential events or actions. (What if a child were to come into this room? What if that machine were left switched on without someone knowing? etc.) They then assessed these scenarios for their potential consequences. The range and type of hypotheses generated varied considerably. One factor in this is likely to be experience (Hale, 1980). However, that is not the only factor. Fischhoff et al. (1978a) gave to their subjects fault trees showing with different degrees of completeness the possible causes of engine failure and asked them to rate the probability of the car failing to start. They found that experience as a mechanic was only one factor which played a part in the degree to which the subjects overcame the incompleteness of the trees and extended the range of possibilities they considered.

The peer review of the NUREG human factors reliability document (Brune et al., 1983) revealed the marked differences in the estimates of failure probability on the sample calculation that the 'peers' were asked to carry out. The differences would appear to be mainly the result of significant differences in the range of potential causative factors considered and again experience (this time of the nuclear industry) was clearly not the only factor at work.

The models which people possess to explain the harm process seem also important here. Thus Burton et al. (1978) showed how false beliefs about the regularity of natural disasters, and supernatural explanations for them determined behaviour towards them. Mason (1982) and Hale and Perusse (1978) also contain examples of misconceptions in causal beliefs which lead to unsafe behaviour, and of fatalistic attitudes to accidents which inhibit rational exploration of causal structure. It is likely that other factors relevant here may include creativity (cf. the creativity test used by Guilford (1967) requiring lists of potential uses for common objects) and cognitive style (what could be called constructive mistrust, cf. Hale, 1984).

Victims of the harm

Green (1979) and Lathrop (1981) point out the importance of the concept of 'equity' in the assessments which people make of hazards. Different assessments are arrived at if the person at risk of being hurt is also the one who benefits from the dangerous activity, as opposed to situations where the potential victim must accept the danger as a part of an activity from which someone else is the main winner. The dichotomy may partly explain the differing reactions to dangers in voluntary activities such as rock climbing and those in work situations which the individual must accept as part of the price of obtaining the job. Within the second category of dangers we also need to differentiate between the ordinary work situation and that of the firemen or mine rescue personnel who put their own person at risk as part of their job in order to save others from injury. Quite different assessments apply because of the different distributions of benefits in the situation and because of different beliefs about the awareness of danger and the skill of the protagonists. The important conclusion is that the negative aspects of risky decisions are not treated in isolation from the benefits (Vlek and Stallen, 1981); this is in contrast with the treatment in papers on 'objective risk assessments' where attempts are made to fix criterion levels for acceptable probabilities of death with no consideration for the benefits 'bought' by that death.

The greater importance attached to a 'named' life or known individual compared to a statistical or anonymous one has also been noted (Royal Society, 1983).

Abeytunga (1978) studied the attitudes of construction site supervisors' to hazards on their sites and the responsibility for their removal. He showed the importance of the supervisors beliefs about the level of skill possessed by those exposed to the danger in determining the level of concern about such dangers. Those considered capable of choosing or controlling their own safety were less a matter for concern. At the other end of the spectrum, more concern is generated for those who are considered particularly unable to exercise this control on their own behalf, e.g., children, the unborn, etc. This view is also reflected in the way in which the law on health and safety has developed. In the U.K., intervention of the state in working conditions was justified in 1833 on the basis of the belief that those protected (children and later, in 1844, women) could not choose for themselves (GB 1833/4, Mess, 1926), while it is only with the 1974 law that self-employed persons in the U.K. were required by law to protect themselves.

The literature on attribution theory, risky shift and locus of control (see Hale (1980) for a brief review) suggests that threats and actions against them are perceived very differently if the person themself or someone else is threatened. There is a tendency for people to recommend less 'risky' actions to others than they accept for themselves. This may be because an observer attributes less personal control to other people over their actions than to himself over his own (e.g., Jones and Nisbet, 1971). Accidents to other people are more likely to be attributed to failures in their personal care or skill, while the individual's own accidents are attributed to misfortune or external circumstances. Hence, others are seen as intrinsically less skilful than oneself when it comes to avoiding accidents. Leplat (1984) quotes evidence that assessments on this dimension are affected by satisfaction with and integration into work, and also with hierarchical position in the organization. These general findings coincide with a major outcome of Green and Brown's research (Green, 1979) that people see differently threats to personal safety and to the safety of society.

Control

The research cited in the last section already introduces the concept of the degree of control which the potential victim can exert over the occurrence of danger. This is the primary dimension which emerges from Perusse's analysis (1980) and which he calls 'Scope for Human Intervention'. It also emerges in much other work, e.g., Guttinger (1984) (personal responsibility), Vlek and Stallen (1981) (organized safety). The dimension of 'familiarity' which emerged from Champion's study (1977) may also be similar. It is a recognition by people of Singleton's concept of the intimate interaction of error and skill. Those who believe themselves knowledgeable about and in control of a dangerous situation, even where the magnitude of the consequences is great, show little concern about it (Wilson, 1975; Williams, 1976; Melinek et al., 1973; Ross, 1974). This can be a serious source of overconfidence in skilled personnel such as research chemists or toolroom personnel. Green and Brown (1980b) showed that people asked to allocate money for fire prevention between different types of fire did so not on the basis of fire frequency but on the basis of their beliefs about control, allocating most to fires which they thought were beyond the control of the victim.

Personal control is not the only factor. Trust may be placed in others to keep the situation safe. Hale and Perusse (1978) quote an example of workers who showed little concern about a dangerous situation because of a misplaced trust that medical monitoring was keeping them safe from it. The work of Vlek and Stallen (1981) can be interpreted to suggest that one element of the cluster of beliefs characterizing those who oppose large nuclear and chemical plant developments is insecurity and lack of trust in those controlling the technology.

A related concept is the distinction between situations which are essentially governed by chance (e.g., roulette or dice throwing) and those which are, in principle, controllable by human skill. The literature on gambling shows that erroneous beliefs about the susceptibility of chance events to human intervention are rife in that field (Cohen, 1970; Cohen and Christensen, 1970). Cohen suggests that this may arise from a confusion in the mind of gamblers between predictability and controllability. Different assessments of the susceptibility of danger situations to chance or control is therefore likely to be a factor in responding to them. It may produce changes in the external versus internal attribution of locus of control and so may result in differing actions towards danger ranging from fatalism to strenuous action (Hale and Perusse, 1978). The field of health education has produced the concepts of self-efficacy (Maddux and Rodgers, 1983) and of psychological action thresholds within the health belief model (Becker and Rosenstock, 1974). These appear to have in common the importance of a person's belief that an action taken by them can succeed in removing the danger or its consequences.

Choice to enter danger

A frequently suggested dichotomy in attitudes to danger is that between involuntary and compulsory activities (Starr, 1969). The difference lies in the freedom to choose whether or not to expose oneself to the dangers which lie in the activity. This dimension emerges also from Green and Brown's studies (1977), as a predictor of perceived safety, from Fischhoff et al. (1978c) and is a subconcept of scope for human intervention in Perusse (1980).

Time remoteness of harm

The differences in assessments reported by Green and Brown (1980a) between immediate and delayed-in-effect hazards show the importance of the time dimension. Conventionally 'risk' estimates are quoted on an annual timebase (e.g., accidents per man year), or over a convenient 'life span' (e.g., an average human working life of 40 years, or the life of a plant or machine). I can find no specific research which indicates the time base(s) which people actually use in their assessments of danger. Findings are, however, reported in the decision-making and probability literature on the distorting effects of time remoteness (e.g., Kahneman and Tversky, 1973; Kahneman et al., 1982). In that literature also the lack of symmetry between assessments of past and future probabilities is clearly demonstrated (Fischhoff, 1975). Events which have occurred always appear with hindsight to have been more probable than they actually appeared with foresight before the event.

The interpretation of this time dimension is difficult because the work of Slovic *et al.* (1980a) suggests that 'delayed-in-effect' hazards also tend to be seen as unfamiliar and uncertain (see below).

Uncertainty versus obviousness

Fischhoff *et al.* (1978c) in their study of the attitudes towards a range of hazards found that the most important dimension was one which they called 'technological risk' and which loaded heavily in their factor analysis on dimensions such as 'known to science', 'known to the exposed', 'newness', 'controllability' and 'voluntariness'. There would appear to be a strong element here of how commonplace as opposed to unknown the risk was. This result was replicated by Slovic *et al.* (1980b). Perusse (1980) also found a dimension relating to obviousness and prominence of the hazards.

The Royal Society (1983) suggested that there were three elements to 'familiarity':

— adaptation (habituation) to proximity to the hazard,
— more information about the benefits, costs and control techniques relevant to the hazard,
— the availability of reminders that the hazard is present.

The first element is likely to reduce worry, the last to increase it, while the second could act either way. The elements appear rather to overlap with each other and with other concepts already set out here.

A common feature of these reported dimensions appears to be the degree to which the respondents feel that they or anyone else fully understands the potential effects that the hazard could have in the future. Respondents would appear to be making a judgement about the degree to which the map of future states of the system contains significant areas of 'Unknown Territory' which might need to be labelled, in the manner of old charts; 'Here be Dragons'. The issue of trust and confidence may also enter at this point, since lack of certainty might not be a problem if respondents felt that some trusted person in control of the area was guaranteeing to guide them through the uncertainty. The comments made in the section on 'Control' could therefore apply here also.

Complexity and credibility

A concept already central to the Probabilistic Risk Assessment approach is the 'credible accident'. Only those events which are considered by experts to be credible are included in the quantitative analyses (e.g., U.S. NUREG, 1982). A similar cutoff seems to be applied by people in other circumstances. Perusse

(1980) asked subjects to verbalize their hazard searching process in looking at pictures of hazardous situations. He found that they would sometimes state a hypothesized sequence of events leading to harm and then reject it with statements such as: 'That's too far-fetched'. This is an example of 'bounded rational choice' (Burton et al., 1978), where certain simplifying assumptions are being made before any detailed assessment is made. Low probability is only one dimension on which such cutoffs are made. Other hypotheses in Perusse's study seemed to be rejected for reasons which looked far more like an unwillingness to believe that someone could possibly act in a particular (usually stigmatized) way.

Vividness, dreadfulness and severity

The dimension of the severity of the consequence of an incident emerges from both Fischhoff et al.'s (1978c) and Perusse's (1980) study as the second most important dimension. Vlek and Stallen (1981) and Green and Brown (1978) also demonstrate its importance. The latter also developed a ratio scale on which to measure the dreadfulness of different outcomes and found that respondents could generate assessments on it consistently and found it meaningful to do so (Green and Brown, 1976). From this scale they showed that there were some injuries (quadriplegia and brain damage) which were consistently rated as worse than death. Similar scales have been developed for diseases (Wyler et al., 1968). Burton et al. (1978) have postulated a series of action thresholds (of awareness, action and intolerance) on a similar scale for natural disasters, as have Becker and Rosenstock (1974) for health threats.

In their study of decision-making and probability assessment Tversky and Kahneman (1974) describe the bias of availability, (which includes the recency and memorableness of events) which tends to make people believe that the events will be more likely to occur again. Fischhoff et al. (1978b), Slovic et al. (1979) and Green and Brown (1978) ascribe some of the results they note in assessments of the probability of hazards to these biases. They also point to the importance of 'kill-size', both actual and potential as an important factor in 'availability'. Combs and Slovic (1979) investigated the issue directly by showing that subjective assessments of frequency of a range of hazards correlated well with the amount and intensity of newspaper reporting, but not with objective frequencies.

At the other end of the scale of severity, there is evidence that a finite level of danger is positively valued, or at least willingly accepted (Drasdo, 1969). This indicates that the zero point of the subjective utility scale for danger is not fixed at the zero of the 'objective' scale, but floats somewhere around it, varying with individual differences.

The experience of having an accident or disaster and having survived it also seems to affect this dimension. Survivors often seem to rate the magnitude of that hazard less than those who have never experienced the accident (Kates,

1967; Green and Brown, 1976). Reality seems to be less frightening than imagination.

Individual differences

The previous sections have considered evidence related to dimensions which have an influence on widely different groups of people in their assessment of danger. Within many of the studies there is also evidence of significant individual differences in the absolute or relative importance of the various dimensions, and the way in which particular hazards are classified on those dimensions (e.g., Vlek and Stallen, 1981). Some of the factors explaining these individual differences have been mentioned in the relevant sections. Much more research will be needed to see how far such individual differences can account for, or be useful in predicting, individual differences in behaviour towards those dangers. However it is already clear that assessments cluster within an individual in ways which suggest cognitive styles. Thus Otway and Fishbein (1976), Green (1980), Eiser and v.d. Pfligt (1979) have found different attitude clusters or ratings on dimensions which characterize opponents and supporters of the development of 'hazardous technologies' such as nuclear and chemical plant. These findings also raise questions about the direction of cause and effect in this area; to what extent are ratings on the individual dimensions derived from, rather than combined to form an overall rating of the dangerousness of the situation. (Do I believe that this situation is dangerous because it is out of my control, or that it is out of my control because it is dangerous?)

GENERAL COMMENT ON DIMENSIONS

The choice of titles under which I have reviewed the evidence from studies on subjective risk is to an extent a personal one. It is often not possible to say with certainty that a dimension described in one study is the same as one given the same (or a different) name in a different study. It is clear also that there are strong interrelationships between some of the dimensions. Those studies which have attempted to put some order into the dimension through factor or cluster analyses (Fischhoff *et al.*, 1978c, Slovic *et al.*, 1980, Perusse 1980, Vlek and Stallen, 1981) show a remarkably similar overall structure, with two main dimensions, one having the flavour of controllability/intervention and the other of seriousness.

Within those dimensions the picture is far less clear. It is clear that the factors which individuals consider relevant to their behaviour depend upon what decisions they are being asked to make: to accept a dangerous job; to have a dangerous plant built next door to them; to stop using a dangerous work method, etc. This suggests that, before plunging into a discussion of the factors affecting each 'risk taking' situation we must always be sure we know what decision we want to take (or have others take) based upon that discussion. We must also consider not only the potential harm that can flow from any course of action, but, as Rowe describes it, 'the whole gamble', including the potential benefits and their distribution.

The tentative interpretation I would like to propose of the factor structure which emerges from the research is of two clusters of questions which the individual asks himself when assessing dangerous situations. The first revolves around his own relationship with the system: Can I influence it? Do I understand how? Do I trust the people in control? Who is getting the benefit out of the situation? Am I just a cog in the system? The second cluster revolves around the consequences of things going wrong: How bad would it be? Who suffers? How reversible are the consequences? It seems likely that questions under the second heading only get asked if the individual has given an unsatisfactory answer to the first group; i.e., has decided that things are out of control, so the harm could happen and what matters now is how serious it could be.

More painstaking work is needed to clarify and firm up this structure. It is, however, clear that a quite complex structure of distinguishable dimensions does exist which takes into account more aspects of both the causal structure of the harm process and the type of outcome of that harm than appear in the classic formulation of utility theory, which uses only functions of probability and consequences in its equation.

What is far more important is that, though both utility theory and subjective risk studies come up with two main dimensions, they are not the same two. It may be noted that no section in the above discussion had the label of 'probability' or 'likelihood'. This does not appear to emerge clearly in any factor structures. Thus Perusse (1980): 'A great deal of attention has been devoted in the literature on hazards to the assessments of likelihood. There were, however, indications that perceived likelihood may be only a minor aspect of hazard assessments.' His own study found it subsumed under 'dreadfulness' as a concept.

IMPLICATIONS FOR THE CONCEPT 'RISK'

It would be possible to force the dimensions which I have discussed into the straightjacket of a conceptualization according to two elements of probability and consequences of dangerous situations. This might go as follows: (see also Vlek and Stallen, 1981):

Consequences

— types of harm included,

— dreadfulness/vividness of consequence,
— range of potential future states considered.

Probability

— remoteness in time,
— lack of knowledge/predictability,
— choice and controllability,
— number of rare events needing to occur together (combinatorial remoteness).

Such an assessment is attractive to those who wish to bring these subjective studies into line with classical utility theory and with the Probablistic Risk Assessment approach derived from plant reliability studies. The term 'risk' could then be used for the probability part of the equation, as it is in those approaches. Even if this were done, as the Royal Society Report (1983) suggests, the assimilation of the objective and subjective approaches would still pose formidable problems in combining the subjectively important subscales into the two major scales. However, I am sceptical of the psychological validity of such a logical scheme. The growing evidence which I have quoted seems to indicate that the factors do not group themselves psychologically in this way. For example, there would appear to be more subjective kinship between the dreadfulness of an outcome and its assessed likelihood than there is between either the assessments of the controllability of risk exposure or risk occurrence.

Such a conclusion produces a communication problem, since the dimensions used in calculations by one group of people do not exist in the same form in the other's theory. Subjective studies seem to call for more concepts than just probability and consequence of hazards. Moreover, they assign a low importance to the former.

I have not made much use of the word 'risk' in this paper, and where it has appeared it has usually been in quotation marks or in a reference to how others have used it. This is some indication of my mistrust of the word. Its use in common parlance in talking of 'risk-taking' is frequently only a post-hoc judgement that harm has occurred, that a person was involved in the accident, and hence that risks 'must have been taken'. Its use by others is more precise; 'By risk-taking, is understood an intentional choice of behaviour which is known— from accident statistics—to increase the probability of having an accident. The risk-taking behaviour is chosen although there is time and opportunity to choose a safer way.' (Sundstrom-Fisk, 1984.) However, there are still great problems in operationalizing what is meant by 'intentional' and 'known'.

The word 'risk' is sometimes used as a synonym for what I have here called 'danger' (i.e., the overall descriptor for the field). This is confusing given its equally common use to describe only the probability element. I have no objection to this more restricted use, except that I would strongly advocate, for reasons explained above, that it should always be qualified by the consequences to which it is being attached and never be used on its own. However, as my analysis shows, this particular definition is not particularly useful for the field I have been reviewing. It is at the wrong level of abstraction. This leaves it rather in the position of an ageing prostitute, with an unfortunate past and little current function.

REFERENCES

Abeytunga, P. K. (1978). 'Construction safety: the role and training needs of the supervisor'. Ph.D. Thesis. Birmingham: University of Aston.

Bamber, L. (1975). 'Loss control and accident costing.' Department of Safety and Hygiene. Unpublished report. Birmingham: University of Aston.

Becker, M. H. and Rosenstock, I. M. (1974). 'Social-psychological research of determinants of preventive health behaviour', *Behavioural Sciences and Preventive Medicine* 4, 25–35.

Bernhardt, U., Graf Hoyos, C. and Hauke, G. (1984). 'Psychology safety diagnosis', *Journal of Occupational Accidents*, 6, 61–70.

Bird, F. E. and Lofthus, R. G. (1976). *Loss Control Management*. Loganville Georgia: Institute Press.

Brown, R. A. and Green, C. H. (1980). 'Precepts of safety assessments', Journal of Operational Research Society 31, 563–571.

Brune, R. L., Weinstein, M. and Fitzwater, M. E. (1983). 'Peer review study of the draft handbook for human reliability analysis with emphasis on nuclear power plant applications', NUREG/CR 1278. Sandia Laboratories Report SAND82-7056.

Burton, I., Kates, R. W. and White, G. F. (1978). *The Environment as Hazard*. Oxford: University Press.

CEGB (Central Electricity Generating Board) (1982). Statement of case for the public inquiry into the siting of a pressurized water reactor at Sizewell B. Barnwood: C.E.G.B.

Champion, A. (1977). 'Perception of danger'. MSc. Dissertation, Department of Safety and Hygiene. Birmingham: University of Aston.

Cohen, J. (1970). 'The nature of gambling', *Scientia* 105, 699–700 1–25.

Cohen, J. and Christensen, I. (1970). *Information and Choice*. Edinburgh: Oliver & Boyd.

Combs, B. and Slovic, P. (1979). 'Causes of death: biased newspaper coverage and biased judgements', *Journalism Quarterly* 56, 837–843.

Council for Science and Society (1977). 'The acceptability of risks.' Report of a working party. London.

Covello, V. T. (1983). 'The perception of technological risks: a literature review, *Technological Forecasting and Social Change*, 23, 285–297.

Cownie, C. and Calderwood, J. (1966). 'Feedback in accident control', *Operational Research Quarterly* 17, 253–262.

Drasdo, H. (1969). 'Margins of safety', *Mountaineering Journal*, 159–168.

Eiser, J. R. and v.d. Pfligt, J. (1979). 'Beliefs and values in the nuclear debate', *Journal of Applied Social Psychology*, 9, 524–536.

Ergonomics Society. (1983). 'Proofs of evidence for the public inquiry into the siting of a pressurized water reactor at Sizewell B.' ES/P/1–4.

Fischhoff, B. (1975). 'Hindsight does not equal foresight: the effect of outcome knowledge on judgement under uncertainty', *Journal of Experimental Psychology: Human Perception and Performance* **1**, 288–299.

Fischhoff, B., Lichtenstein, S., Slovic, P., Derby, S. L. and Keeney, R. L. (1981). *Acceptable Risk*. Cambridge: University Press.

Fischhoff, B., Slovic, P. and Lichtenstein, S. (1978a). 'Fault trees: sensitivity of estimated failure probabilities to problem representation', *Journal of Experimental Psychology: Human Perception and Performance* **4**, 330–344.

Fischhoff, B., Slovic, P., Lichtenstein, S., Layman, M. and Combs, B. (1978b). 'Judged frequency of lethal events', *Journal of Experimental Psychology: Human Learning & Memory*, **4**, 551–578.

Fischhoff, B., Slovic, P., Lichtenstein, S., Read, S. and Combs, B. (1978c). 'How safe is safe enough? A psychometric study of attitudes towards technological risks and benefits', *Policy Sciences* **9**, 127–152.

G.B. (1833/4). Reports from the Commissioners appointed to collect information in the manufacturing districts relative to the employment of children in factories. Parliamentary Papers **XX**, 450; **XXI**, 519; **XIX**, **XX**, 167.

Golant, S. and Burton, I. (1969). 'The meaning of a hazard: application of the semantic differential.' Natural Hazard Research Working Paper No. 7. University of Chicago: Department of Geography.

Green, C. H. (1974). *Measures of Safety*. Centre for Advanced Studies. Urbana: University of Illinois.

Green, C. H. (1979). 'Public perception of risk.' Symposium on the acceptability of risks.' Pollution Research Unit, UMIST/Manchester University.

Green, C. H. (1980). *Not Quite Dr Strangelove*. Conference on Energy and Planning. Ayr: Craigie College.

Green, C. H. and Brown, R. A. (1976). *The Perception of and Attitudes towards Risk, E2 Measures of Safety*. Dundee: School of Architecture University of Dundee.

Green, C. H. and Brown, R. A. (1977). 'The perception of, and attitudes towards risk.' Final Report. Dundee: School of Architecture, University of Dundee.

Green, C. H. and Brown, R. A. (1978). 'Counting lives', *Journal of Occupational Accidents* **2**, 55–70.

Green, C. H. and Brown, R. A. (1980a). 'Revealed preference theory: assumptions and presumptions', *in* Conrad, J. (Ed.), *Society, Technology and Risk Assessment*. London: Academic Press.

Green, C. H. and Brown, R. A. (1980b). 'Risk: beliefs and attitudes', *in* Canter, D. V. (Ed.), *Fires and Human Behaviour*. Chichester: Wiley.

Guilford, J. P. (1967). *The Nature of Human Intelligence*. New York: McGraw-Hill.

Guttinger, V. A. (1984). 'Risicoperceptie en riskant dedrag in de arbeidssituatie: een onderzoek bij lassers.' Leiden: T.N.O.

Hale, A. R. (1980). 'Attributing cause', *Occupational Health 32* **10**, 519–521.

Hale, A. R. (1984). 'Is safety training worthwhile?', *Journal of Occupational Accidents* **6**(1), 17–34.

Hale, A. R. and Perusse, P. (1978). 'Perception of danger: a prerequisite to safe decisions.' Institute of Chemical Engineers. Symposium Series No. 35.

Heinrich, H. W. (1931). *Industrial Accident Prevention*, (4th Ed. with Petersen, D. and Roos, N. 1980). New York: McGraw-Hill.

Jones, E. E. and Nisbet, R. E. (1971). 'The actor and the observer: divergent perceptions of the causes of behaviour', *in* Jones, E. E., Kelley, H. H., Nisbett, R. E., Valins, S. and Weiner, B. (eds), *Attribution: Perceiving the Courses of Behaviour*. General Learning Press.

Kahneman, D., Slovic, P. and Tversky, A. (Eds) (1982). *Judgements Under Uncertainty: Heuristics and Biases*. Cambridge: University Press.

Kahneman, D. and Tversky, A. (1973). 'On the psychology of prediction', *Psychological Review* **80**(4), 237–251.

Kates, R. W. (1967). 'The perception of storm hazard on the shore of megalopolis.' Research Paper No. 109. Department of Geography. Chicago: University of Chicago.

Kletz, T. A. (1977). 'What risks should we run?', *New Scientist*, May **12**, 320–322.

Laitinen, H. (1984). 'Estimation of potential seriousness of accidents and near accidents', *Journal of Occupational Accidents* **6**(3), 167–174.

Lathrop, J. W. (1981). 'Evaluating technological risk: prescriptive and descriptive perspectives.' Laxenburg: International Institute for Applied Systems Analysis. (WP 81-78.)

Leplat, J. (1984). 'Occupational research and systems approach', *Journal of Occupational Accidents* **6**(2), 77–90.

Maddux, J. E. and Rodgers, R. W. (1983). 'Protection motivation and self-efficacy: a revised theory of fear appeals and attitude change', *Journal of Experimental Social Psychology* **19**, 469–479.

Mason, I. D. (1982). 'An evaluation of kinetic handling methods and training.' PhD. Thesis. Birmingham: University of Aston.

Melinek, S. J., Woolley, S. K. D. and Baldwin, R. (1973). 'Analysis of a questionnaire on attitudes.' Fire Research Note No. 962. Borehamwood Fire Research Station, U.K.

Mess, H. A. (1926). *Factory Legislation and its Administration*. London: King & Sons.

Otway, H. J. and Fishbein, M. (1976). 'The determinants of attitude formation in application to nuclear power.' International Institute for Applied Systems Analysis. Laxenburg. AM 76-67.

Perusse, P. (1980). 'Dimensions of perception and recognition of danger', PhD. Thesis. Birmingham: University of Aston.

Reason, J. (1982). 'Slips, lapses, biases and blunders', *Proceedings of the British Association*. Liverpool.

Risk Research Committee, (1980). Accident Risks in Norway: How do we Perceive and Handle risks. Oslo: Royal Norwegian Council for Scientific and Industrial Research.

Ross, H. E. (1974). *Behaviour and Perception in Strange Environments*. London: Royal Society.

Royal Society Study Group (1983). Risk Assessment. A Study Group Report. Royal Society, London.

Saari, J. (1984). 'Accidents and disturbances in the flow of information', *Journal of Occupational Accidents* **6**(2), 91–106.

Singleton, W. T. (ed.) (1983). 'The study of real skills', Vol. 4, *Social Skills*. Lancaster: MTP Press.

Singleton, W. T. (1984). 'Application of human error analysis to occupational accident research', *Journal of Occupational Accidents* **6**(2), 107–116.

Slovic, P. (1962). 'Convergent validation of risk taking measures', *Journal of Abnormal and Social Psychology* **65**(1), 68–71.

Slovic, P., Fischhoff, B. and Lichtenstein, S. (1980a). 'Perceived risk: psychological factors and social implications', *Proceedings of the Royal Society* **A376**, 17–34.

Slovic, P. Fischoff, B. and Lichtenstein, S. (1980b). 'Perceived risk', *in* Schwing, R. C. and Albers, W. A. (Eds), *Societal Risk Assessment: How Safe is Safe Enough?* New York: Plenum Press.

Slovic, P., Lichtenstein, S. and Fischhoff, B. (1979). 'Images of Disaster: perception and acceptance of risks from nuclear power', *in* Goodman, G. T. and Rowe, W. E. (Eds), *Energy Risk Management*. London: Academic Press.

Starr, C. (1969). 'Social benefit versus technological risk', *Science* **165**, 1232, 1238.

Steiner, H. (1967). 'An experimental study of risk taking', Dissertation. London: D.P.M. University of London.

Sundstrom-Fisk, C. (1984). 'Behavioural control through piece-rate wages', *Journal of Occupational Accidents* **6**(1), 49–60.

Tversky, A. and Kahneman, D. (1974). 'Judgement under uncertainty: heuristics and biases', *Science* 185, 1124–1131.

US Nuclear Regulatory Commission (1982). 'PRA procedures guide.' NUREG/CR 2300.

Vlek, C. A. J. and Stallen, P. J. M. (1980). 'Rational and personal aspects of risk', *Acta Psychologica* **45**, 273–300.

Vlek, C. A. J. and Stallen, P. J. M. (1981). 'Judging risks and benefits in the small and in the large', *Organizational Behaviour and Human Performance* **28**, 235–271.

Wilson, A. (1975). 'Attitudes of workers to hazardous substances: understanding and evaluation of hazards due to trichloroethylene, asbestos and ionizing radiations.' MSc. Dissertation. Department of Safety and Hygiene. Birmingham: University of Aston.

Williams, J. B. (1976). 'Knowledge and attitudes in relation to toxic substances: benzene and cyanide.' M.Sc. Dissertation. Department of Safety and Hygiene. Birmingham: University of Aston.

Wyler, A. R., Masuda, M. and Holmes, T. H. (1968) 'Seriousness of illness rating scale', *Journal of Psychomatic Research* **11**, 363–374.

Risk and Decisions
Edited by W. T. Singleton and J. Hovden
© 1987 John Wiley & Sons Ltd.

Chapter 6

Risk Cognition

A. I. GLENDON
Department of Applied Psychology, Aston University, U.K.

INTRODUCTION

'When I use a word' Humpty Dumpty said in a rather scornful tone, 'it means just what I choose it to mean—neither more nor less.'

If Humpty Dumpty's categorical semantics are applied to the term 'risk', then we have the beginnings of an answer to Singleton's first question in the introduction to this book, for it does appear that different disciplines do use the word to mean different things. One way to conceptualize approaches to risk is by way of a multidisciplinary context comprising three nested domains as shown in Fig. 6.1. In Fig. 6.1, the innermost domain is risk-appraisal in its various forms such as calculating probabilities, cost/benefit analysis and risk analysis. Disciplines involved include mathematics, economics and engineering. The second domain is concerned with perceptions, cognitions and behaviour and is part of the subject matter of psychology and to a lesser extent of philosophy. The outermost domain is the social and political environment which provides the broader context and is the concern of disciplines such as sociology, geography and politics. Very broadly, the three main sections of this book correspond to these three domains.

In this chapter some attempt is made to provide a link between the second and third domains. In this task only some of the ways in which links between risk and behaviour may be explored are considered and the approach is selective. While 'risk' has a number of types of meaning, use of the term in this chapter is restricted to physical risks, outcomes from which could harm potential victims, mainly in the short term.

The title of this chapter reflects the notion that 'risk' as such cannot be perceived but that, for an individual, risks are appraised in a cognitive context which involves decision-making as well as perception. Physical hazards may be perceived—directly or indirectly, but the risk cognition process implies an evaluation of a range of possibly relevant stimuli in the light of experience. Thus, in seeking to measure elements of risk cognition processes, a model is required which takes account not only of dynamic properties of risks in the external environment but also of individual differences and if possible of interactions between these elements. These desired properties for an adequate

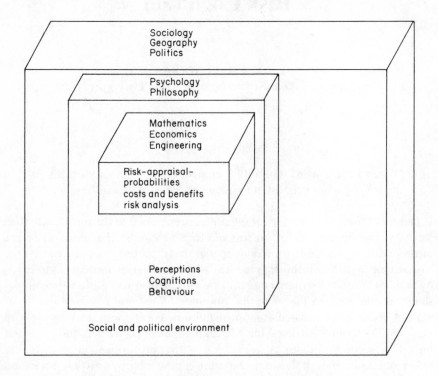

Fig. 6.1. A multidisciplinary context for the study of risk.

model of risk cognition will guide the course of this chapter. However, it must still be recognized that a cognitive approach to risk, while providing a framework for data collection, may be theoretically inadequate to account for observations in the social and political domain and therefore also of behaviour.

The chapter first considers environmental factors in hazard perception before going on to examine some empirical work on perceived responsibility and individual differences. This leads to an outline embryonic theory of risk cognition. Limitations of both survey and cognitive approaches are considered within the framework of an argument which highlights the problematic nature of risk and which by implication also questions its usefulness as an analytic tool.

THE IMPORTANCE OF THE ENVIRONMENT

A simple illustration of people's perceptual differences between environments comes from a small community survey on attitudes to safety. Among other questions asked was 'Who do you consider to be responsible for your safety: in your own home? in the street? at work?' Although the sample size was small, the results were nevertheless interesting and indicative of differences in this responsibility dimension. Table 6.1 shows the findings.

Table 6.1. Perceived responsibility for safety in three environments.

		Environment		
		Home	Street	Work
Agent of responsibility	N	74	74	35
		%	%	%
Self		55	67	23
Self and others		15	13	40
Others		31	20	37

The results suggest that:

— This sample of individuals considered that they personally were most responsible for their own safety in the street, then in their own homes and least of all at work (where the sample size was even smaller as less than half these respondents were in paid employment).
— Others were much more likely to be perceived as responsible for safety at work—either alone, or in conjunction with self than in the other two environments.
— As well as an overall pattern there were complex patterns of differences between individuals.

The results from this small study suggested a need for further research in at least three directions. First, do perceived likelihoods of accident injury in different environments show significant differences? Second, are there differences between 'amateur' and 'professional' perceptions of responsibility for safety and related phenomena? Third, how important are individual differences? Among other topics for research are the degree of heterogeneity of various environments, the ways in which attributions are made and the development of perceptions in this area.

A larger-scale survey provided some evidence on the first of these questions and also pointed to the importance of considering other variables, such as injury severity. There were large differences in perceived likelihood of injury depending upon whether this was identified as either serious or minor. Thus, serious injury was perceived to be more likely in the street with the home and work environments a similar distance behind. Minor injury was perceived to be most likely at home, followed by work and street environments respectively. There were also significant differences in responses associated with age.

It might be tempting to try and assign causal connections between these findings. For example, to postulate that because people perceive a greater likelihood of serious personal injury in the street than in other environments, they attribute greatest personal responsibility here. This might be predicted from a defensive attribution approach. However, the difficulty of interpreting responses to such questions alone should be sufficient caveat in drawing any such conclusions. As will be seen, 'safety' and 'injury likelihood' are distinct concepts.

In an attempt to answer the second of these questions, various groups of 'professionals' were questioned about workplace hazards. Findings from these *ad hoc* studies appeared in McKenna (1975) and in Glendon (1979, 1980, 1981). The main findings were:

(1) Manual workers had consistent and logical beliefs about prevention of injury to themselves based upon physical proximity to workplace hazards, i.e., they considered themselves to have primary responsibility followed by other workers, supervision, management and other parties.

(2) Both management and supervisors had broadly similar views about accident/injury prevention to the views of the sample of workers, that is, seeing workers themselves having primary responsibility for accident/injury prevention.

(3) Views on responsibility for safety were quite different from those on accident prevention. Management and supervision were considered by all parties to have primary responsibility for safety. Views of professionals such as safety personnel and occupational health nurses on responsibility for safety and accident prevention were similar to those of workers and managers.

(4) Relevant professionals from outside the workplace, in this case factory inspectors and risk control managers, tended to see less of a distinction between safety and accident prevention than did all parties within the workplace.

(5) There were considerable differences in views of responsibility for safety and accident prevention among different professionals. It is a matter of definition who are the professionals in this case:

  — those who work with the risks,

— those who have managerial responsibility,

— those who are specially trained—safety advisers or safety representatives,

— those who advise, enforce or undertake research.

(6) Views of responsibility for occupational health and the prevention of occupational disease were much more in alignment for all those sampled than was the case for safety and accident prevention. Management, followed by occupational health professionals were seen to have greatest responsibility in both cases.

Clearly, responsibility is a concept which has different meanings for different professions and in different contexts. For those outside the workplace, it may be viewed in legalistic terms—who would be responsible if an accident injury occurred. For those who are closest to the hazards, it is interpreted more in terms of immediate scope for prevention. For managers, it may be related to notions of accountability.

These *ad hoc* studies suggest:

— that the issue of who is a professional and who is an amateur in hazard perception is problematic,

— there is unlikely to be any single model applicable to the process of hazard perception because of the different ways in which risks are defined by an individual (e.g., short-term/safety *vs.* long-term/health, disease),

— it seems certain that social and cultural factors affect hazard perception. For example, Lancianese (1980) found that financiers in the U.S.A. and the general American public were often willing for employees to bear financial responsibility not only for injuries incurred on the job but also for occupational disease incurred on a job years before. Congress and Government regulators were more likely to attribute financial responsibility to employers in such circumstances.

INDIVIDUAL DIFFERENCES AND THE ENVIRONMENT

In his chapter, Hale reviews some of the studies which have considered dimensions used by individuals in the perception of danger and the general tendency for findings from such studies to converge to two main dimensions, typically labelled 'controllability' and 'seriousness'. Hale briefly considers individual differences and how these might relate to the 'objective' hazards presented by situations.

Among the problems encountered by most studies of hazard perception are:

— Hazard perception is taken out of an everyday context, for example, respondents may be asked to compare hazards or risks which are unusual or remarkable to them in some way.

— Individual differences in hazard perception are either ignored or are subsumed within a larger model or category.
— There is an implicit assumption that similar dimensions are used to perceive different hazards. This is at least partly a problem of measurement.
— There is a corresponding assumption that environmental changes are unimportant to perception of similar hazards in different environments.
— They tell us little or nothing about behaviour.

Hazard perception studies have generally used either experimentally derived stimuli (Perusse, 1980; Brown and Green, 1981) or else have been field studies initiated on the premise that it would be interesting to see how people view one specific risk (Eiser and Van Der Pfligt, 1979) or a number of risks (Prescott-Clarke, 1982). While it may be deemed desirable to hold experimental stimuli constant, there is no evidence that hazard perception is a static phenomenon and this approach is therefore not without methodological problems. In the case of the cross-sectional survey approach, extreme caution must be exercised to ensure that methodological sophistication, for example, in respect of sampling framework or statistical analysis, is not accepted by way of compensation for conceptual inadequacy. In a complex and dynamic area such as risk cognition it is inappropriate to rely upon any single methodology as a benchmark for theoretical advances. A further danger is the use of data from a single nonvalidated source in the political or policy-making field.

Both experimental and survey approaches largely ignore the potentially great variety which exists in the less glamorous and nonlaboratory world which people inhabit for most of their lives. It is in this everyday world that most human risk-taking behaviour occurs and in which most of those who die 'prematurely' do so as a result of injuries or disease incurred in what may be described as risk-related behaviour and its associated cognitions. Even to speak in terms of 'premature' death implies a value judgement that the only 'acceptable' form of death is that which is not associated with risk-taking activity.

However, considerable methodological problems would beset any research team seeking to study the many facets of risk and behaviour even after a rational conceptual framework had been devised. The triangulation likely to be required for rigorous investigation could well include:

— systematic observation of up to half a dozen, or more in some cases, environments for each individual.
— measures of perceptual changes occurring as individuals move between environments; validation of these measures.
— longitudinal assessments of broader-scale changes over time.
— behavioural measures to assess the validity or appropriateness of self-report data on behaviour.
— experimental manipulation of key issues to relate behaviour to hazard perception.

— measures of permanent or temporary change resulting from exposure to hazard outcomes, e.g., accident or disease experience.

Such large-scale research is never likely to be undertaken for reasons both of cost and of feasibility. Therefore, risk researchers are likely to continue the traditional process of scholarship involving interplay between small-scale empirical studies to consider different aspects of the subject, reviews of research in an area, and armchair theorizing—all of which are important.

As a small contribution to this continuing effort, some findings from an as yet unpublished study are reviewed in outline for any indications for promising future research in this area. The study used 31 subjects who might be described as professionals of the future. They were students of occupational health and safety. Two main techniques were employed—a diary hazard-spotting exercise followed by a repertory grid study. The hazard-spotting exercise was used to elicit everyday hazards encountered by subjects. The term 'risk' was not used on the grounds outlined in the introduction to this chapter, namely that it is hazards which are actually perceived, while the term 'risk' should be used in the context of cognitive appraisal, which includes decision-making processes. Figure 6.2 shows the relationships between the concepts.

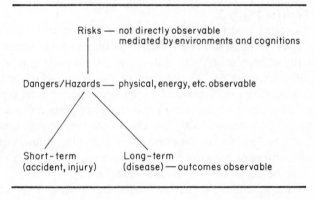

Fig. 6.2. Simplified relationship between risks, hazards
and outcomes.

Almost all hazards reported in this study could be categorized as occurring in one of three environments: the home, the road or street and 'public places'. Virtually no health hazards were reported spontaneously (one subject reported 'air pollution'). This finding should serve to reinforce caution in interpreting findings from any study which asks respondents to evaluate long-term (delayed action) hazards such as cigarette smoking, air pollution, nuclear power or contaminated work environments, as dimensions used for conceptualizing these are different from those used to assess short-term physical hazards (Green, 1979).

Forty-nine hazards recorded by the subjects were pooled and used as elements in the repertory grid. Subjects then elicited 26 common constructs which were used to rate the elements on a five-point scale. Problems associated with this approach are discussed by Perusse (1980). All subjects completed the 49 × 26 grid—a total of 39, 494 responses. For the purpose of this chapter, the answers to two questions might reasonably be sought from a consideration of this study:

— Is there any evidence that different risk dimensions are used as a framework for perceiving hazards in the three types of environment?
— If there are such differences between environments, is there evidence of marked differences between individuals in the risk dimensions used by them to perceive hazards within each environment?

The answer to the first question is that different dimensions are used in the three environments, although there are similarities between them. Although the methodology of deriving consensus grids may be suspect, it provides a general guide to the way in which different environments may shape perceptions of hazards and thereby provide insights into cognition. Analysis of consensus responses for each environment was undertaken separately and the results are shown in Fig. 6.3.

Figure 6.3a shows that three of the principal components which emerged from the analysis of the home environment consensus grids accounted for 76 per cent of the variance in these data. The first component is a 'control dimension' and accounts for 37 per cent of the variance while the second component accounting for 26 per cent of the variance, is 'fixed aspects of the environment' incorporating the notion that there are certain given features in the home which present hazards. The third component was similar to the second and is labelled 'the commonplace in a specific home environment' suggestive of features or hazards which are peculiar to a person's own home and therefore to be expected from local knowledge.

Dimensions for the other two environments are shown in Figs 6.3b and 6.3c respectively. For road hazards, the first component—accounting for 38 per cent of the variance is labelled 'hazards not under the control of the road user'—suggesting that unlike the home environment it is a lack of control which is considered to be most important. In the case of public place hazards there is a very similar, and identically labelled, first component accounting for 30 per cent of the variance in this grid. The second component for the road grid is 'design of the environment' offering little scope for individual intervention (26 per cent of the variance in this grid) and for the public places grid the second component (accounting for 21 per cent of the variance) is rather different, being labelled 'unnecessary hazards which can be avoided'. The third

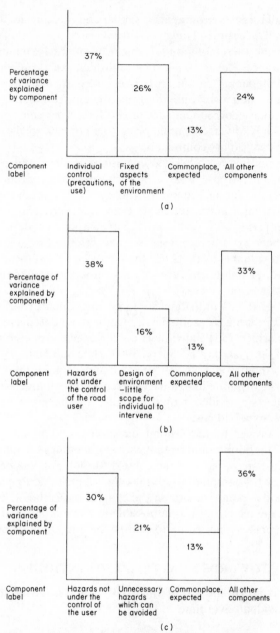

Fig. 6.3. (a) Principal components from a consensus grid for home hazards ($N = 31$). (b) Principal components from a consensus grid for road hazards ($N = 31$). (c) Principal components from a consensus grid for public place hazards ($N = 31$).

component in all three environments is similar and accounts for 13 per cent of the variance in all three grids. However, subsidiary components are also part of risk cognitions and these components might be of crucial importance under certain circumstances; for example, in establishing skills and expertise which distinguish a 'professional' from a lay person for a particular environment. It is interesting that in the most 'familiar' of the three environments considered— the home, subsidiary components accounted for 24 per cent of the variance whereas in the most diverse—public places, 36 per cent of the variance was accounted for by subsidiary components.

Figure 6.3 simplifies hypothesized cognitions in the three environments. However, its main purpose is as a heuristic to aid comprehension of the postulated principle that such changes do take place. Emphasis should be given to the difficulty of interpreting repertory grid data—particularly those derived from consensus grids. Only the principal components derived from the analyses have been considered here. Neither differences between groups of subjects nor individual constructs nor the degree to which these differentiate between hazard elements in each of the three environments have been considered.

Examination of the 31 individual subjects' components revealed consider-able individual differences despite the derivation of models deemed to account for the way in which (all) individuals perceive, make decisions and act in response to risk or hazard (e.g., Surry, 1969; Hale and Hale, 1970; Hale and Perusse, 1978; Andersson et al., 1978). Although some of these models may be adaptable to incorporate individual differences this relatively homogeneous sample of subjects provided ample evidence of the great variety in risk cognition between individuals.

A tentative answer to the second question posed by Singleton in the introduction to this book would be that we can sometimes say something about individuals or instances, but that the context for doing so will be bounded by the methodology (idiographic) used, making it impossible to generalize with accuracy. A similar point is made in the chapter by Brehmer. Furthermore, random variation means that it is impossible to make other than probabilistic predictions and makes it necessary to confine these to populations.

TOWARDS AN ATTEMPTED SYNTHESIS

A further issue concerns the way in which risk cognition and hazard perception develops in individuals over time.

The development of risk cognition

On the basis of the findings described it might be hypothesized that there are three dimensions in regular use by individuals in their assessment of risk. For the cognitively complex—the 'professionals' in any particular environment, it is likely that further dimensions could be incorporated—either a fourth or fifth or even more in certain circumstances. In chapter 8, Marek and his colleagues suggest that this is the case. For the cognitively simple—or amateurs, it is possible that a single dimension or perhaps two might well suffice in the appraisal of a wide variety of risks. It may be that complexity is related to need and that cognitive appraisal of risks develops to the point at which particular needs for any environment are met.

A basic model to be postulated is of individuals moving through a series of environments with a number of orthogonal cognitive dimensions which are used to assess risks and which interact with behaviour. Environmental feedback is important—particularly when learning about new hazards, for the development and labelling of new dimensions. In developmental terms, the first environment that has to be learned about is the home and so dimensions are developed and labelled according to early experiences there. Typically, the next move is to the street and road environments where existing dimensions may be largely inappropriate for the range of hazards encountered there—witness the disproportionately large numbers of children killed and injured in road accidents (W.H.O., 1976). This is likely to be a critical phase in the development of risk cognition, for essentially two processes are involved: the individual is required to relabel say up to three dimensions when moving from home to road environments, and crucially for future learning about risk, the individual must learn to adjust in time at environmental transitions—for example, in the time it takes to get from home to the street. In learning terms, this ability to access the relevant dimensions which define how risk is understood may be crucial to an individual's future survival. Inevitably, many do not make the adjustment every time and often those that do survive do so as a result of good fortune.

In this learning process, one or more near-miss experiences may be highly functional. A number of authors have pointed to the importance of errors in the learning process (e.g., Singleton, 1983 and Rasmussen in chapter 7). As each new environment is encountered, the transition phase may be marked by an increase in accident injury outcomes for the population (teenagers riding motorcycles or young people at their first factory job are other examples). At these major transitions as well as cognitive changes there are also likely to be changes in the affective dimension, as costs and benefits of risk-taking are assessed by each individual as well as in skilled behaviour. In the broader context, risk cognition is liable to be influenced by reports of the types of accidents and disasters described in chapter 9 by Hedge as well as from accounts or predictions of those outlined in Rowe's discussion. These may be incorporated into the cognitive labelling process by vicarious experience.

Environments next likely to be directly encountered are school and a variety of public places. In terms of hazard perception, each individual must be able to switch risk dimensions when moving between environments. As the appropriate dimensions (for that individual) for each new environment are acquired, there will be again a cost in terms of accidents and injuries. However, as mastery of the dimension-switching process improves it is likely that the speed of learning increases and that accidents and injuries which may be attributed to elements of the learning process are never as high as when the first switch was required—that between home and street environments.

Thus, by the time a person starts work, he or she will have acquired; first, a variety of cognitive labels which define the dimensions used to perceive hazards in different environments; second, an ability to label new dimensions as a substantially new environment is encountered and third, an ability to switch dimensions as environments change. For many people, work may be the last substantially new environment encountered. For this reason and because such a large proportion of people's lives is spent at work, the development of appropriate cognitive dimensions for the work environment is likely to be crucial. Acquisition of initially inappropriate cognitive risk dimensions may not result in immediate misfortune but in some cases it will do so. Accidents might also result from individuals applying incorrect labels or to environmental changes which are too subtle to merit new labels—for example, working on a different machine or driving a different car. Subsequent changes might be associated with further job moves, transfer to a different country or culture and retirement.

Some points in relation to the hypothesized process outlined above are pertinent:

(1) Evidence for it is scanty and in some places, nonexistent. For example, there are few studies on developmental aspects of risk cognition (Sheehy, 1982 is an exception) and therefore the approach is largely speculative.

(2) Evidence has been selected which is suggestive of a developmental framework for risk cognition; for example, the large numbers of under five-year-olds killed and injured in road/street accidents, the role of inexperience in work accidents, (Powell *et al.*, 1971; Richer, 1973) or unusual or novel activities being associated with a greater proportion of more serious (major and fatal) accident injuries to young people starting work activity (Glendon and Hale, 1985).

(3) Both developmental and dynamic cognitive elements are required before substantial improvements in our understanding of processes involved in hazard perception and risk behaviour can be made. An explanatory model needs to be developed to indicate how to proceed in order to collect evidence which can support, refine or disprove this notion.

(4) In hazard perception, it is highly improbable that any two individuals use the same combination of dimensions for the different environments they encounter. Human beings cannot be treated as a homogeneous factor in any environment. One possible cause of viewing individuals as cognitively

simple is that we are bound by the limitations of our measuring techniques. Thus, if we only measure in one dimension—for example, an attitude survey, or in two dimensions such as probability and outcomes, then we should not be surprised if we are only able to explain our findings in terms of this number of dimensions.

For a population, it may be legitimate to consider risk exposure in terms of two dimensions—length of time of exposure and degree of risk. However, for an individual or small group this is inappropriate because it ignores dimensions used to evaluate a particular environment. Nevertheless, from the consideration given to the cognitive approach in this chapter as well as the more detailed reviews in the chapters by Brehmer and Hale, it is clear that by itself it cannot provide a comprehensive framework for the analysis of risk. It is therefore necessary to look further afield for such a framework.

ONE-, TWO- AND THREE-DIMENSIONAL APPROACHES TO RISK

If many professionals do not treat 'risk' as a multidimensional concept should we be searching for more adequate ways of expressing the complexity of the concepts that are our concern?

In proposing a theoretical framework for alternative conceptions of risk dimensionality, the insight provided by Lukes (1974) into dimensions of political power is acknowledged. However, in applying an analogous approach to risk there are at least two serious difficulties. The first is that it is problematic that risk is a multidimensional concept in its most common usages and that therefore higher level concepts such as a feedback systems model may be required to explain it adequately. A second difficulty is that the term 'dimension' also has different meanings. For a sociologist like Lukes it refers to the depth of explanation for a concept, while for a psychologist it may be used to define cognitive space.

A one-dimensional view

An example of a one-dimensional view of risk is provided by a survey commissioned by the U.K. Health and Safety Executive and carried out by Social and Community Planning Research (Prescott-Clarke, 1982). This survey could be considered to have high respectability in terms of its sponsorship, the agency conducting it and the survey's internal methodological integrity. The survey also produces the type of data which might be used to support certain types of policy decision-making so that its findings could have wider political implications which make it an example of the expressed preference approach to risk acceptability (Brown and Green, 1981).

This survey sought to compare six different types of 'risk':

— home-based hazards,
— cigarette smoking,
— work-related hazards,
— air pollution,
— nuclear plant hazards,
— chemical and other major industrial plant hazards.

The survey made no attempt to determine the existence of qualitative differences in the ways that these 'risks' were 'perceived'—a series of common scales were used for respondents to rate the various hazards. The interview defined 'risk' in one-dimensional terms as being the 'likelihood of such an event happening' although it is known that people are poor judges of absolute likelihood (Tversky and Kahneman, 1974) and the survey itself demonstrated this.

One aim of the survey was 'to examine the extent to which public assessment of risk probability compares with expert assessments'. However, restricting a survey of public knowledge to likelihood estimates permits only one point of comparison with expert judgements. One series of questions asked respondents to estimate the number of people who die each year from a particular cause. While this has not been shown to be a prominent feature of individuals' risk cognitions, studies have shown that for immediate effect hazards people do use 'assessed number of deaths that might occur in any single accident' as one criterion for judging relative detriment (Green, 1979; Green, 1980; Vlek and Stallen, 1981). However, in asking respondents to compare different types of risk the important distinction between threat to society and threat to individual is ignored. Therefore, it may be asked whether it matters if respondents do not know offhand the 'correct' answers when many lay people could as well as any professional find the answers to such questions. It is unrealistic for professionals to expect lay people to perceive things which are outside their normal range of experience and so asking them to estimate very small probabilities (say over four orders of magnitude) is a pointless exercise. To use one dimension only and one that was known from the pilot study and from previous research to be one that individuals cannot handle ignores a number of features about risk judgements which are known to be important. These include: the confidence that individuals have in their judgements and the relevance of the risks to themselves (Green, 1984b), whether they have direct knowledge or experience of the hazards (Green and Brown, 1980) and whether they personally are able to do anything about the risks (Green, Brown and Goodsman, 1985). Green et al. (1985) point out that if risk is defined as the risk of death per year then respondents will answer in those terms, even if the definition does not correspond to their own ideas.

A two-dimensional view

An example of a two-dimensional approach to risk is Fischhoff et al. (1981)—a text which is scholarly, plausible, tightly argued and written by a highly respected team of professionals. The book exemplifies a two-dimensional approach to risk in the sociological sense of being in essence a critique of an empiricist one-dimensional approach. The book effectively demolishes a simplistic approach to data gathering on facts, probabilities, values, costs and benefits relating to risk which it is pointed out are highly subject to context.

However, the analysis considers neither individual differences—human responses to hazards are treated as being unpredictable, nor the wider political issue of the power of one party effectively to dictate another's risk exposure. On the one hand, individual differences are taken as being subsumed within collectivities or interest groups, while on the other, it is implicitly assumed that in any decision-making process the existing order is acceptable and all interest groups will be equitably represented. While making token genuflection to notions such as political acceptability and power imbalances, the analysis is prescriptive and pluralist. For example, the political power dimension is reduced to a mere value judgement issue and values are implicitly treated as being synonymous with the values of the dominant group.

The focus of the book is upon three approaches to acceptable-risk problems and the criteria for judging them. The authors systematically consider: professional judgements, bootstrapping—an approach based upon historical precedent of which revealed preference is an example, and formal analysis—of which cost/benefit analysis is one example. Existing decision-making methods are appraised but not challenged. Who controls access to any of the three decision-making processes is not considered.

Acceptable risk problems are considered not as political issues but as decision-making problems where the two dimensions of risk and cost are used as a guide but in which risk measurement is assumed to be nonproblematic. While acknowledging the interrelationship of facts and values and cautioning use of any of the three types of decision-making approaches, this book is ambivalent about the role of values in judgements about risk.

The notion of acceptable risk problems as capable of being neatly categorized into approaches to decision-making, seduces those who adopt a two-dimensional approach to risk into believing that answers to such problems do exist—even if only in theory. However, an approach to decision-making on risk which considers consensus and agreement to be desirable objectives (as in Chapter 3 of Fischhoff *et al.*, 1981), which sees workers and consumers who are exposed to risks as requiring increased communication but only within existing democratic institutions (as on p. xiii of Fischhoff *et al.*, 1981) and which ultimately treats the 'public' as a single entity, cannot be based upon a complete analysis of the power structure within society. A pluralism which acknowledges the possibility of conflicts between experts and public in risk decisions serves the functions of the politically powerful by ignoring the point that both experts and public may be manipulated by politically powerful groups.

Towards a three-dimensional view

At this stage of our knowledge it may be easier to define a three-dimensional approach to risk in terms of what it is not than in terms of what it is. One reason for this is that researchers and professionals in the field of risk have not yet succeeded in generating a widely acceptable paradigm for risk (Kuhn, 1962). This partly reflects the disciplinary diversity of those with an interest in risk and it seems likely that there can be no single three-dimensional approach possible but rather a number of these based upon different types of models, for example; cognitive models, behaviour models or sociological models. A three-dimensional approach stresses the vital nature of an adequate analysis of risk at a conceptual-theoretical level. Two-dimensional approaches may be adequate conceptually and theoretically within a limited framework but may for example ignore a broader context. As Perrow (1984) notes, 'the issue is not risk but power'.

However, even before attempting a three-dimensional approach to risk, the problematic issue of whether 'risk' is an adequate concept for use beyond two dimensions must be addressed. We may be faced with the problem of an absence of satisfactory alternatives and therefore accord 'risk' a default status which creates difficulties for interdisciplinary debate. For example, if we are seeking a three-dimensional cognitive model for risk then this must take account of individual differences and also of temporal and environmental changes. If a behavioural model is sought then environmental, cultural, spatial and other differences and the way in which these relate to behaviour change are also important. Although aggregates may be useful for description, a three-dimensional psychological approach should not submerge individual and environmental differences within aggregates.

If risk is being considered beyond the individual behaviour level, then a three-dimensional approach must recognize that power differences and associated conflict are inherent in social decision-making processes. Thus, as well as making no *a priori* judgements regarding the desirability of consensus on risk decision-making, a three-dimensional view acknowledges an enduring imbalance between those who are obliged to accept risks and those who make the essential decisions which define the parameters for risk analysis and who ultimately determine what risks are taken in society.

Chapter 13 by Page is an excellent illustration of this view for it highlights the important point that for those who make the principal decisions the term 'risk' is not used. Issues are settled not by debate but by power politics—manoeuvring, strategy and tactics, for example, attempting to influence another party's view of your strength as in the deterrence philosophy. This is qualitatively no different from addressing risk (or power) in other contexts—it merely represents the extreme of a continuum. In this case, those making decisions are not obliged to and therefore do not consult those who are duty-bound to accept the risks. Risks relate to behaviour as well as to the decision-making process. This reflects a power relationship not so much between the senior decision-makers on each side as between those on each side who give and those who are required to transmit or to act upon orders. It is functional for those in power to deny the validity of the concept of risk as one means of confirming the nonlegitimacy of wider debate.

Perrow (1984) considers the importance of system failures resulting from multiple interactions of failures which by their complex nature are impossible to foresee. Nevertheless, their existence means that accidents are built in to complex systems ensuring that they will happen somewhere sooner or later. Thus, Perrow's view runs counter to the more conventional wisdom as exemplified by Cyert and March cited in the chapter by Rasmussen, that maintains a self-correcting tendency towards an equilibrium position. However, a tendency towards equilibrium and a tendency towards imbalance may exist simultaneously within an organization so that in nearly all observed cases the system is self-correcting. However, it always remains a possibility that there will be occasions when it is not so because organizational and human behaviour does not correspond to hard and fast laws but rather to probabilistic event trees.

The dimensions used by Perrow are; system complexity, degree of coupling (on a loose–tight continuum), and the value dimension (used as a basis for deciding whether any given risk is acceptable). Coupling refers to the degree to which there is flexibility or slack within the system to respond to situations. Perrow's analysis uses the value dimension to arrive at decisions as to which risks are acceptable and why, and thereby goes beyond a two-dimensional view of merely describing an idealized decision-making process. While a three-dimensional analysis cannot be expected to influence directly the political decision-making process, it may, nevertheless, provide a polemic for challenging the politically powerful.

The broadening of debate on risk is further exemplified by other considerations introduced by Perrow. One of these is the four categories of those affected by risks which includes not only the operators and system users but also 'bystanders' and the unborn—including future generations. The decision-making context is set within three rationalities. The first is termed absolute, being narrow, quantitative and with precise goals. The second is bounded rationality which characterizes the framework used by risk assessors and which prescribes limits on an individual's thinking capacity. The third emphasizes diversity of skills and characterizes lay judgements being referred to as social/cultural rationality. Organizations may be efficient in the third type of rationality even if they are not efficient in the first.

Perrow is critical of the role of risk assessors in supporting elites and of those cognitive psychologists who relate that the 'public' are poor at making 'risk judgements' (i.e., estimating probabilities) and by implication should not be given effective decision-making opportunities. The role of risk assessors or other 'experts' should neither be to assure the public nor to provide answers, but to provide the necessary data for the public to make decisions and to present as much of the complexity of decision-making as possible. While experts may solve problems faster and better than others, they also run a higher risk of posing the wrong problems. Thus, despite the undesirability of this, problems are likely to be defined to suit methods rather than the other way round. The issue of control—prominent in cognitive studies, also emerges here as a dichotomy: do the experts and their masters or the 'public' control the essential decision-making processes?

In Perrow's analysis, the highest risk systems are tightly coupled and complex. However, some of these may be judged 'acceptable' on the grounds that they do not possess catastrophic potential. This leads to a three-way partitioning of high-risk systems. The first category of high risks should, according to Perrow, be abandoned on the grounds that the inevitable risks outweigh reasonable benefits and includes nuclear power and nuclear weapons. A one-dimensional approach could not arrive at that conclusion even if it revealed that 99 per cent of the population considered the risks of these systems to be unacceptable, because the result would only be an aggregation of attitudes. A two-dimensional approach could only go so far as to reveal that there was conflict between a large majority and a small minority and that there should be mechanisms for listening to the view of the majority.

The second category includes those activities to which considerable effort should be devoted to making them less risky, including DNA work and marine transport. The third category of risks which should be further reduced with modest effort includes chemical plants, airlines and air traffic control.

A power-based approach to risk such as that of Perrow is useful firstly because it makes explicit the context within which decisions are made and therefore is a guide towards greater understanding of the complete range of issues involved, and secondly because the analysis can be used as a basis for making testable predictions.

CONCLUSION

Kluckholn and Murray's often restated dictum may be restated yet again: 'A person evaluates risk like all other people, like some other people and like no other people.' In terms of everyday experience every person is a professional risk-taker. Conversely, all professional risk-takers are amateurs in all but the specific context of their expertise. If a characterization of differences between professionals and amateurs were required then it seems likely that these would be focused first upon behaviour—skills acquired from learning and experience, and second upon cognitive dimensions.

Researchers into hazard perception or risk cognition have often concentrated upon spectacular or glamorous risks. This has served to narrow theories of hazard perception and risk-related behaviour as everyday phenomena, leaving our statements often at a common-sense level. Social scientists in their search for the counterintuitive and the statistically significant may ignore the mundane but nevertheless important accumulation of data which are relevant to much of human behaviour. In seeking to understand human behaviour in the face of 'high-technology' risks, baseline measures and understanding of how people learn from the risks they encounter throughout their lives are needed. To improve understanding of risk and behaviour, research effort needs to be concentrated in a number of so far underresearched areas.

(1) It is important to study relevant cognitions, meaning those which are act-oriented rather than object-oriented (Fishbein and Ajzen, 1975) if greater behavioural prediction from psychological studies is to be achieved.

(2) There is a need to discover ways of sampling from the universe of hazards which form the environment for risk cognition, distinguishing between those hazards which individuals can directly influence and those which they cannot (Perusse, 1980; Green, 1984b; Green et al., 1985). This is unlikely to be an easy task.

(3) Before it is possible to appreciate fully how 'new' hazards are perceived and new risks appraised, greater understanding is required of the developmental processes involved in acquiring relevant cognitions.

(4) The hypothesized environmental categorization outlined in this chapter needs to be rigorously tested to determine whether this is a valid and useful approach to the way in which people appraise risk or whether some metalevel categorization is more appropriate.

Links between hazard perception, risk cognition and behaviour therefore remain problematic. For an individual it is dysfunctional for other behaviour and therefore not cost-effective to consider risks all the time. Once established, appropriate cognitive dimensions are likely to be called on only when triggered by certain environmental stimuli. Models of risk behaviour need to take these points into account. Links between hazard perception and behaviour mediated by individual cognitions and by environments are therefore in need of study in the way that links between attitudes and behaviour (Ajzen and Fishbein, 1977; Deutscher, 1973) and between attributions and behaviour (Kelley, 1971) have been considered. If correlations between perceptions and behaviour are low, then the importance of perceptual/cognitive components in risk behaviour may need to become subordinate to environmental influences. These might include: power relationships, norms, customs, responsibilities, rules, laws, commands, policies and constraints within organizational frameworks.

It is probably neither possible nor desirable to attempt a 'grand theory' of risk from the individual/cognitive through the organizational to the social/political as this would be too broad to be useful in either a practical or a theoretical sense. However, it is important when conceptualizing risk to be aware that it may be considered as a topic for different domains of study and in more than one dimension. Thus, the individual cognitive approach may be contrasted with the sociological collective approach as a dynamic which helps us to work towards an interactive behavioural model. Psychologists have regularly and frequently been accused of being 'soft' on power and one reason why they are generally unable to deal with this dimension is that they possess neither the methodology nor the critique (outside the laboratory) to do so.

To return to the initial three-nested domains outlined at the beginning of this chapter, a model which could go some way towards incorporating the diverse positions expressed in this book might consider risk as the probability of failure, decision-making as a function of probability times perceived consequences and control or power as the context or environment within which decisions are made and in which risks exist.

REFERENCES

Ajzen, I. and Fishbein, M. (1977). 'Attitude-behaviour relations: a theoretical analysis and a review of empirical research', *Psychological Bulletin*, **84**, 888–918.

Andersson, R., Johansson, B., Linden, K., Svanstrom, J. and Svanstrom, L. (1978). 'Development of a model for research on occupational accidents', *Journal of Occupational Accidents*, **1**, 341–352.

Brown, R. A. and Green, C. H. (1981). 'Threats to health or safety: perceived risk and willingness to pay', *Social Science and Medicine* **15C**(2), 67–75.

Deutscher, I. (1973). *What We Say/What We Do: Sentiments and Acts*. Glenview, Ill.: Scott, Foresman.

Eiser, J. R. and Van Der Pfligt, J. (1979). 'Beliefs and values in the nuclear debate', *Journal of Applied Social Psychology*, **9**, 524–536.

Fischhoff, B., Lichtenstein, S., Slovic, P., Derby, S. L. and Keeney, R. L. (1981). *Acceptable Risk*, Cambridge: University Press.

Fishbein, M. and Ajzen, I. (1975). *Belief, Attitude, Intention and Behaviour*. Cambridge, Mass.: Addison-Wesley.

Glendon, A. I. (1979). 'Accident prevention and safety: whose responsibility?', *Occupational Health*, **31**(1), 31–37.

Glendon, A. I. (1980). 'Whose responsibility 2?', *Occupational Health*, **32**(8), 408–412.

Glendon, A. I. (1981). 'What does responsibility mean?', *Occupational Health*, **33**(5), 245–250.

Glendon, A. I. and Hale, A. R. (1985). *A Study of 1700 Accidents on the Youth Opportunities Programme*. Sheffield: Manpower Services Commission.

Green, C. H. (1979). *Risk: Beliefs and Attitudes in Regard to Major Hazards*. Regional Studies Association/School of Town and Regional Planning Conference on the Implications of Large-scale Petrochemical Development. Dundee. 5 December 1979.

Green, C. H. (1980). 'Revealed preference theory: assumptions and presumptions', *in* Conrad, J. (Ed.) *Society, Technology and Risk Assessment*. London: Academic Press.

Green, C. H. (1984a). *The Justification of the CEGB's Fundamental Reliability Criteria*. Proof of Evidence FOE/P/4, Sizewell B Inquiry Secretariat, Snape.

Green, C. H. (1984b). *Risk, Uncertainty and the Nuclear Energy Option*. London: Social Statistics Sections, Royal Statistical Society. 19 June 1984.

Green, C. H. and Brown, R. A. (1980). *Through a Glass Darkly: Perceiving Perceived Risk*. Eugene, Oregon: Invitational Workshop on Perceived Risk.

Green, C. H., Brown, R. A. and Goodsman, R. W. (1985). 'Injury or death by fire: how people rate their chances', *Fire*, March, 44–48.

Hale, A. R. and Hale, M. (1970). 'Accidents in perspective', *Occupational Psychology*, **44**, 115–121.

Hale, A. R. and Perusse, M. (1978). 'Perception of danger: a prerequisite to safe decisions', *Institute of Chemical Engineers Symposium*, Series No. 53.

Kahneman, P., Slovic, P. and Tversky, A. (Eds) (1982). *Judgement Under Uncertainty: Heuristics and Biases*, Cambridge: University Press.

Kelley, H. H. (1971). *Attribution in Social Interaction*. Morristown, N.J.: General Learning Press.

Kluckholn, C. M. and Murray, H. A. (1953) 'Personality formation: its determinants', *in* Kluckholn, C. M. and Murray, H. A. (eds.). *Personality in nature, society and culture*, 2nd edn. 53–67. New York: Knopf.

Kuhn, T. S. (1962). *The Structure of Scientific Revolutions*. Chicago: University of Chicago Press.

Lancianese, F. W. (1980). 'Survey probes risk in a complex society', *Occupational Hazards*, October, 109–113.

Lukes, S. (1974). *Power: a Radical View*, Harmondsworth: Penguin.

McKenna, S. P. (1975). 'Accident attitudes', *Occupational Health*, **27**(8), 330–332.

Perrow, C. (1984). *Normal Accidents: Living with High-risk Technologies*. New York: Basic Books.

Perusse, M. (1980). 'Dimensions of perception and recognition of danger', PhD. Thesis. Birmingham: Aston University.

Powell, P. I., Hale, M., Martin, J. and Simon, M. (1971). *2000 Accidents: a Shopfloor Study of Their Causes*. London: NIIP.

Prescott-Clarke, P. (1982). *Public Attitudes Towards Industrial Work-related and Other Risks*. London: Social and Community Planning Research.

Richer, M. (1973). 'Factors affecting the incidence of accidental injuries in manufacturing industry', Ph.D. Thesis. Birmingham: University of Birmingham.

Sheehy, N. P. (1982). 'The perception of hazard by children and adults in familiar environments', Ph.D. Thesis. Cardiff: University of Wales Institute of Science and Technology.

Singleton, W. T. (1983). 'The study of real skills', Vol. 4, *Social Skills*. Lancaster: MTP Press.

Surry, J. (1969). *Industrial Accident Research: a Human Engineering Appraisal*. Toronto: Labor Safety Council of Ontario.

Tversky, A. and Kahneman, D. (1974). 'Judgement under uncertainty: heuristics and biases', *Science*, **185**, 1124–1131.

Vlek, C. and Stallen, P. J. (1981). 'Judging risks and benefits in the small and in the large', *Organizational Behaviour and Human Performance*, **38**, 235–271.

World Health Organization. (1976). *The Epidemiology of Road Traffic Accidents*. Copenhagen: W.H.O.

Risk and Decisions
Edited by W. T. Singleton and J. Hovden
© 1987 John Wiley & Sons Ltd.

Chapter 7

Risk and Information Processing

JENS RASMUSSEN
Risø National Laboratory, Denmark

INTRODUCTION

Two trends in the industrial and technological development have had major impacts on the problems in coping with the risk involved in industrial operations. First of all, there has been a general trend towards large and centralized operations, not only in production plants but also in administrative systems, commercial companies and outlet chains, with the consequence that faults and errors can lead to drastic damage and economic loss. Examples from recent years are legion. This situation has immediately two consequences in the present design context. On one hand, during system design it is now becoming necessary to consider the consequences of events and conditions of very low probability. On the other, due to the short time span between conceptualization of new products or processes and full-scale operation, this cannot be done from direct empirical evidence or operation of prototype systems. During periods of rapid development and with changes of basic technologies, piecemeal adjustment of prior designs is no longer adequate. Instead, new analytical methods have to be found, and a 'top-down' design approach based on proper predictive models is necessary. Such a design approach has to include a consideration of the ultimate risk related to operation by means of systematic analytical risk assessment.

This industrial development has led to a widespread public concern with the safety of such installations, and the designers have made serious attempts to explain and document the safety targets underlying the design and the probabilistic considerations by which the design is validated. Such attempts have had limited success, with the consequence that the difference between the objective risk concepts of system designers and the subjective risk perception of the general public has been widely studied and discussed. Based on the assumption that quantitative risk figures are not understood by the general public, designers have made great, but largely unsuccessful attempts to compare their risk figures with other categories of natural and man-made risks, and many attempts have been made to explain the lack of acceptance in terms of differences in risk acceptance depending on the degree of voluntary exposure, in acceptance of individual or collective risk, etc. This approach in turn is based on the assumption that a kind of more or less conscious risk evaluation is underlying the different personal choices. This argument may be misleading in two respects. First of all, the lack of acceptance of the risk figures resulting from quantitative risk assessment may not only be related to acceptance of the risk level *per se*, but also to a lack of confidence in the underlying assumptions of the analysis. Secondly, the concept of risk cannot be separated from other aspects of personal value judgements underlying intuitive human choice.

In the following sections, it is argued that the present rapid development of information technology may increase the difficulty in formulating a credible basis for risk analysis and point to areas where basic research is needed in order to improve the model framework behind risk analysis.

TECHNOLOGICAL TRENDS

Analysis of major accidents has invariably shown that human activities have been involved in the causation and further development of the course of events. Reviews show that human errors have been significant in typically 70–80 per cent of accidents reported. Coping with the human role is clearly important, but the new technology is presenting special problems since analytical assessment requires predictive models of human performance, models which are not presently well developed.

Another important industrial trend is the introduction of modern information technology in the interface between humans and their actual work content. Information technology will now allow, both technically and economically, the design of very complex control systems. This means that all frequent and, therefore, well formulated tasks are likely to be automated. Left to the human supervisor are the more creative tasks related to problem solving. In consequence, system design cannot be based on the traditional analysis and description of tasks and functions. Instead, design should be in terms of an envelope within which an operator can adopt effective strategies during situations which have only been foreseen by the designer in kind, not in particular. Modern computers and information displays are effective means for system designers in their attempts to match the selection and presentation of information to the various human tasks and roles. This optimization cannot be based on traditional task analysis in terms of action on the system, but an analysis in terms of cognitive or mental activity is necessary. Misconception in this aspect of design may leave the human in a situation which is worse than it would be by less advanced technology. In consequence, methods for analytical risk assessment including the human activities in system operation and maintenance become necessary for design of large-scale industrial installations.

OBJECTIVE AND SUBJECTIVE RISK

The basic risk concept involved in the objective evaluations applied by designers and in the subjective judgements of the general public is in both cases related to an aggregated measure of probability and magnitude of actual negative effects. The actual decision processes are, however, basically different. The evaluation performed by designers is based on a conscious, analytical comparison of quantitative measures of separate aspects of costs and benefits, such as productive output and losses caused by disturbances.

Most human choice is not, however, based on such rational analysis which is mainly typical of formal professional activities, but on holistic, intuitive and mostly subconscious judgements. Risk will be only one feature of the value perception underlying intuitive choices, and will not be considered separately, except maybe for after-the-fact explanation. From research on social judgement, it is well known that judges use fewer, and frequently different cues than they can rationalize when asked. The context in which risk may influence judgement will vary widely with the particular setting. In general, public acceptance of new technologies, such as, for instance, nuclear energy or genetic engineering, depends on value judgements which involve features of a general political nature and emotional reactions to unknown technologies. In questioning whether to choose to live close to such installations, features of immediate quality of life aspects interfere. When entering activities like skiing, mountain climbing, or high-speed driving, risk perception probably has much less weight in judgements than the immediate feedback from perception of the limits of control which is necessary for improvement of skill, together with the joy experienced from such skill improvement. Considering choice of the individual acts of an activity, risk considerations may be involved during conscious preplanning, but when once absorbed in the performance of a skilled task, our analysis of accident reports and verbal protocols indicates activity to be controlled by immediate functional criteria like 'choosing the way of least effort' and control by higher level features like risk potential appears less likely.

The role of risk features in judgement, therefore, cannot be separated from the context by objective analysis, and rational arguments based on comparison of the perception of risk across activities and situations cannot be expected to change people's actual judgements.

An important reason for the lack of acceptance of risk in spite of the objectively acceptable quantitative figures may be the lack of confidence in the assumptions underlying risk analysis, a criticism which is difficult to formulate by the general public, and which may, therefore, be expressed in terms of risk level.

One major problem in analytical risk assessment is to obtain a clear and explicit formulation of the coverage of an analysis. The final result of a risk-analysis is a theoretical construct which relates empirical data describing functional and failure properties of equipment and processes to a quantitative or qualitative statement of the overall risk to be expected from the operation of the system. The analysis depends on a decision regarding the boundaries of the system to be considered; on a model describing the structure of the system and its functional properties in normal and in all relevant abnormal modes of operation, including the activities of the people present in the system; together with a number of simplifying assumptions which are necessary to facilitate a systematic analysis. These assumptions, the model, and the characteristics of the sources of the empirical data used, are just as important results of the assessment study as is the resulting risk figure, since they are the necessary precondition for the operation of the system in correspondence with this risk target.

Unfortunately, neither this basis of analysis nor the strategies used to identify the mechanisms and courses of events to include in the analysis are generally explicitly formulated in present analytical techniques. This makes it difficult to use the analyses for control of the actual conditions during operation. The conclusion is that a major problem in presentation of credible risk analysis is the formulation of the underlying models and assumptions in a way which makes possible an independent verification of the correspondence with the actual installation. The aim of the present paper is to point to several aspects in the technological development which aggravate this problem and, therefore, require more active research efforts, in particular with respect to models including human activities and the effects of modern information technology.

THE NATURE OF HUMAN ERROR

The trends discussed in the introduction invite a closer look at the nature of human errors. In the industrial or technical context, the definition of a human error has typically been made in analogy to component faults. For analytical risk assessment, a technical installation has been considered an aggregation of standard components for which failure characteristics and frequencies could be determined empirically from application in other systems. The overall risk involved in system operation can then be calculated or simulated by means of a model of the causal structure of the system. In analogy, human performance was considered an aggregation of standard acts or routines for which error characteristics and frequencies could be collected from similar activities in other task settings.

This approach has close links to Taylorism in industrial engineering and behaviourism in psychology, and has been fruitful in analysis of systems where human activity has been manual assembly tasks, repair, and calibration. Such tasks can often be decomposed into more or less separate, manual routines, and analysis can be based on the overt activity which to a large degree is controlled and sequenced by the system. Another important feature is that many tasks have been repetitive and that performers have reached a stable level in a skill in which errors can be considered stochastic variations going beyond the limits acceptable for proper system performance.

The application of modern information technology is rapidly changing the basis for these assumptions. Automation has removed many repetitive tasks and given humans the role of supervisors and troubleshooters. This means that their performance is more related to decision-making and problem-solving and, consequently, cannot be adequately decomposed into standard routines in terms of overt, observable elements. Analysis has necessarily to be performed in terms of cognitive information processing related to diagnosis, goal evaluation, prioritizing, and planning. Such mental functions are much less constrained by the external task conditions. They can be solved successfully by several different strategies and the individual choice will depend on very subjective criteria. Another important point is that performance in a task can no longer be assumed to be at a stable level of training. Learning and adaptation during performance will be significant features of many situations which are relevant for analysis of the ultimate risk. It follows that analysis of the human role in this risk can no longer be based on a model of the external characteristics of the task. Design has to be related to a model of human performance in psychological terms referring to cognitive capabilities and limitations.

Furthermore, when performance can no longer be judged with reference to a stable normal performance, the definition of 'human error' becomes dubious. Considering a highly-skilled performance of a task, there will generally be no difficulty in identification of errors and no dispute between the performer considering his actual goals and intentions and a posterior analysis. However, considering performance during complex abnormal situations which are part of an accident scenario there is no clear reference for identification of 'errors'. They are found during the search for causes of the accidental event, but the identification in terms of component fault, operator error, manufacturing error, or design error depends entirely upon the stop-rule applied for termination of the search. This stop-rule will be purely pragmatic and be something like: an event will be accepted as a cause and the search terminated if the causal path can be followed no longer, or a familiar, abnormal event is found which is therefore accepted as explanation, and a cure is known. Paradoxically, human errors seem to be allocated under two typical circumstances. On one hand, human errors are found when human variability brings an otherwise stable task outside acceptable limits. On the other, human errors are found when human variability or adaptability proved insufficient to cope with variations in task content; if, on hindsight, a 'reasonable' human ought to be able to cope with disturbances.

It appears to be a more fruitful approach not to look for errors as causes of accidents, but to consider the related events to be occasions of human-task mismatches and to look for factors which are sensitive to improvement, whether or not they are considered causes, i.e., irrespectively of their location on the causal path. Accidents can be avoided by breaking the path, as well as by removing causes, as everybody will know (Leplat and Rasmussen, 1984).

The nature of the tasks in modern systems, being related to problem-solving and decision-making in which adaptation to unfamiliar situations is crucial, makes it very doubtful whether a category of behaviour called errors can be meaningfully maintained. The term 'error' in a way implies that something could be done to the humans in order to improve the state of affairs. Recent work on the problem indicates that effective means can more readily be found when considering design of 'error-tolerant' systems—by means of modern information technology.

Basically, system designers have to accept human variability as an integral element in human learning and adaptation (Rasmussen, 1984). Fine-tuning of manual skills depends upon a continuous updating of the sensory-motor schemata to the time–space features of the task environment. If the optimization criteria are speed and smoothness, adaptation can only be constrained by the once-in-a-while experience gained when crossing the precision tolerance limits, i.e., by the experience of errors or near-errors. These, then, have a function in maintaining a skill, and they neither can nor should be removed. Also at the more consciously controlled rule-following level, development of know-how and rules-of-thumb is dependent on a basic variability and opportunity for experiments to find shortcuts and identify convenient and reliable signs which make it possible to recognize recurrent conditions without analytical diagnosis; in short, to develop quasirational heuristics. Involved in genuine problem-solving, test of hypothesis becomes an important need. It is typically expected that operators check their diagnostic hypotheses conceptually—by thought experiments—before operations on the plant. This, however, appears to be an unrealistic assumption, since it may be tempting to test a hypothesis on the system itself in order to avoid the strain from reasoning in a complex causal net. For this task, a designer is supplied with effective tools like experimental set-ups, simulation programmes and computational aids, whereas the operator has only his head and the plant itself. And—'The best simulation of a cat—is a cat.' In this way, acts which on afterthought are judged to be mistakes, may very well be reasonable acts intended to gain information about the actual state of affairs.

In other words, considering the human role in modern systems, human errors should rather be considered to be 'unsuccessful experiments in an unfriendly environment', and design efforts should be spent on friendly, i.e., error-tolerant, systems.

The view that 'errors' are integral parts of learning mechanisms has long roots. Already Ernest Mach (1905) notes: 'Knowledge and error flows from the same mental sources, only success can tell the one from the other', and Selz (1922) found that errors in problem-solving were not stochastic events but had to be seen as results of solution trials with regard to the task, which is somewhat misconceived. Hadamard, the mathematician, states (1945): '... in our domain, we do not have to ponder with errors. Good mathematicians, when they make them, which is not infrequent, soon perceive and correct them. As for me (and mine is the case of many mathematicians), I make many more of them than my students do; only I always correct them so that no trace of them remains in the final result. The reason for that is that whenever an error has been made, insight—that same scientific sensibility we have spoken of—warns me that my calculations do not look as they ought to.'

This means that human errors cannot be studied in isolation, only as a part of an analysis of the psychological mechanisms controlling cognitive activities in general. Only quite recently has research in cognitive psychology again taken up the interest in such studies (Reason, 1982; Norman, 1980). The findings match very well those found from analysis of industrial accidents (Rasmussen, 1980), and indicate that the great variety of errors can to a large degree be explained as the effect of a very limited number of psychological mechanisms when folded onto the variety of the work environment—as Simon (1969) argues:—'man is quite simple, complexity of his behaviour reflects largely the complexity of the environment'.

DESIGN OF ERROR-TOLERANT SYSTEMS

It follows that system designers have to accept that humans make errors all the time, and that this is just the other side of the generally successful adaptation of the user's behaviour to the peculiarities of the system. Or, as Reason has put it: 'Systematic error and correct performance are two sides of the same coin' (Reason, 1985). The task of the designer will be to aim for error-tolerant systems, in which errors are observable and can be reversed before unacceptable consequences develop.

This brings the use of advanced information technology in the work interface into focus. It is now possible to match the interface to the requirements of individual users and their immediate tasks. From a risk point of view this may lead to problems, considering the importance of certain categories of rare events for the safety of many kinds of systems. Optimizing an interface to the requirements of the more frequent members of the task repertoire for which performance can be evaluated empirically may create difficulties in more unfamiliar task situations. Furthermore, optimizing for support of task execution may violate requirements for error recovery.

Task execution is based on procedural information of the form: if (situation, cue), then do (action, task). For familiar tasks, this information is immediately available in terms of skilled users' know-how, and computer support of the less skilled can be developed in computerized procedure retrieval systems or, in more recent terms: expert systems. For monitoring the effect of the activity, and for recovery from disturbances, quite a different kind of information is needed. Error detection is not simply a question of monitoring the outcome in comparison with the goal. In many cases, this will lead to detection far too late—you cannot save the cake when tasting the final result. Monitoring depends on the equivalent of Hadamard's 'scientific sensibility' which is something like understanding of the functioning of the system behind the task and knowledge of the intended dynamic behaviour. It is important to understand and to monitor the process, not only the product. Of major concern from a risk point of view, when attempts are made to transfer the heuristic rules of 'know-how' of human experts to 'expert systems', should be the problems in transferring also the 'sensibility' to the limits of expertise. The applicability of 'expert systems' in centralized systems very much depends on the ability to appeal to analytical performance when the preconditions for heuristic rules break down (Barnett, 1982).

In other words, monitoring of routine activities probably depends on the same kind of information as diagnosis and intervention during infrequent tasks: ability to predict the behaviour of the system and to compare with the intended performance. This additional need should be carefully considered in the design of interface systems.

CAUSES AND REASONS

Decision-making is, in general, a kind of resource allocation in a problem space which can be organized in a means–end hierarchy reflecting the fact that the system involved can be described at several different levels of abstraction in the mapping of the purpose/function/equipment relationships. A decision task involves the identification of discrepancies between the actual state of affairs and the target states, which may be done at any of the levels in the means–end hierarchy. In this hierarchy, the effects of changes in the physical world propagate bottom-up, and the reasons for proper functions are derived top-down. In the design of information systems, emphasis is typically placed on representation of factual information from measurements and statistics, i.e., bottom-up data. This is due to an assumption that decision-making for supervisory plant control as well as executive management depends on rational analysis of the system involved and is performed in accordance with the formal, theoretical decision models. The information about purposes, reasons and policies is only implicitly formulated; it is assumed to be available from general training and instruction. This may be the case for undisturbed routine tasks, but for infrequent tasks and for error detection it is not necessarily true. When introducing information systems as an interface to the task content, the disturbance of informal top-down paths for communication of reasons should be carefully considered.

A decision-making task which has been in the focus of discussion during the recent decade has been that of industrial operators during system failures. In industrial process plant control rooms, a large amount of measured plant status data is presented to the operators and great effort is spent on development of proper presentation of this information and support of the operators in diagnosis, i.e., bottom-up identification of the actual physical state of the plant. In addition, support of the operators' memory of the functional structure of plant is given in terms of mimic diagrams, etc. Operators are generally supposed to assess the operation of the system from understanding of the functional structure and knowledge of physical variables. This is frequently not the case. Many systems, for instance control systems, are too complex and operators will rather try to judge correctness of function with reference to their perception of the designer's intentions, i.e. from information derived top-down in the hierarchy.

At present, data bases for industrial control rooms include only little information about the complex relationship between overall purposes and goals and the intentions behind the design at the lower levels of functions and equipment. This is so, partly because such information is difficult to formalize, but also because it is only implicitly present in the form of company policies, design practices and system designers' subjective preferences which do not find their way into drawings and technical manuals. Instead, reliance has been on *ad hoc* advice facilities, e.g., supervisors on call, communication with designers, etc. In the nuclear industry, great effort has been spent in formalizing such systems in terms of 'resident technical advisors', 'technical support centres', data links to design teams and authorities. There is, however, a movement towards exploitation of advanced information systems, 'expert systems', for such advice giving, and direct transmission of plant status data to outside advisors by data links is considered. At the same time, there is a tendency towards an integration of the process computer systems and the computer systems used for production and maintenance planning. This integration of plant control and executive decision-making may have implications for risk management, if based on a conception of decisions transferred from normative theories.

NORMATIVE MODELS AND EMPIRICAL EVIDENCE

In general, there is a discrepancy between the normative theories for management decision-making which are typically derived from economics, and the empirical evidence. It is generally assumed that the decisions of high-level executives are based on careful analysis of statistics and factual reports, the kind of information which is normally considered for computerized management data bases. Several studies indicate that this is an unreliable assumption. Dreyfus and Dreyfus (1980) find that the normative, theoretic models of decision-making are only representative of the behaviour of novices, and Minzberg (1973) concludes from a study that top level executives prefer face-to-face interaction and even hearsay and gossip to analysis of factual reports. A reasonable explanation may be that management executives are not faced with a causal system, the response of which can be predicted bottom-up by factual analysis. They are actors in a social game and predictions have to consider intentions and motives of other people rather than objective facts. Predictions have to be derived top-down from a reliable perception of other people's value structures, for which face expressions and gossip may be more reliable sources than statistical reports.

Communication of values and intention is not only required for strategical planning. It is a precondition for the error correction features which seem to be inherent in social organizations. Cyert and March (1963) call it 'bias discount'. When people are making frequent errors, one could fear that errors would propagate willingly in a social system and add up until a major mistake is at hand. However, this appears not to be the case. The individual agents are correcting faults in messages and data and will complete ambiguous orders and instructions from their implicit knowledge about policies and other people's intentions and goals.

Therefore, failure-tolerant management systems basically depend on the continuous and efficient communication of corporate and individual values and intentions. One of the major risk problems related to the introduction of information technology in centralized systems may therefore be the temptation of rational, scientifically minded experts to design large systems in which centralized data banks with factual information are the basis for communication between decision-makers, and, unwillingly, disturb the communication of values and intentions which is necessary for error recovery.

There may, however, be another dimension to the communication of value structures. Such communication is crucial for error recovery but may lead to a very tightly coupled system with short time constant, and, consequent stability problems. Losses and time delays are fundamental tools for maintaining stability in technical systems. Are similar measures now necessary in social systems? The consequences of effective communication of attitudes and values can be seen on a grand scale, as a consequence of the effective communication of values by the mass media. It took the French Revolution half a decade to initiate a change in Denmark, where a new constitution was the result of a meeting. The student revolt in Berkeley was, however, followed next morning in Copenhagen. Small-scale experiments and adjustment of approaches at a reversible level may be difficult in tightly coupled, fast systems. Is it now necessary to consider stability theory of social systems on a control theoretic basis? If so, approaches like Forrester's (1971) modelling should be supplemented with models of propagation of values.

ADVICE ACCEPTANCE

Closely connected to this reliability problem is the problem of advice acceptability. When several people cooperate in decision-making, they will be exchanging messages communicating factual information, results of analysis, and plans for action. The form of the messages may vary, depending upon the role of the participants and upon their authority. For data, the form ranges from statements of facts to hypotheses of varying likelihood, and plans for actions may be stated as proposals, advices, instructions, or orders. It is crucial for the reliability of cooperative decision-making that messages are received in the mode they were intended by the sender, e.g., the designer of a computer-based decision support system. For orders, this is no great problem, but the question of criteria for proper understanding and acceptance of advice and recommendations is crucial. What kind of information is needed to ensure that a client understands advice? The problem has been discussed in some detail for 'expert systems' for support of medical diagnosis like MYCIN (see for instance Shortliffe, 1983), but the solution proposed, which is a replay of the inference rules used by the advisor, does not appear to be convincing. Understanding a piece of advice depends not only on a step-by-step tracing of the way in which the result was found, but also on reasons why that path was chosen. It is important to consider that human decision-makers are quasi-rational; underlying analytical reasoning there is a background of intuitive judgement and expectations. The composition of intuition and analysis depends entirely on the familiarity of the problem context to the decision-maker and, consequently, so does the kind of information required to make advice understood.

The interaction between user, computer and designer changes in a very important way when the routine tasks are automated and only the *ad hoc*, on-line decision-making is left as an interactive task. For frequent tasks, a 'task allocation' can be made. From empirical evidence the human will have definite expectations about the automated functions and intuitively be able to 'understand' them. He will not need conscious, analytical evaluation of the automatic functions, he will be allowed to forget details, reasons, and necessary preconditions. This is not the case for interactive decision-making where the computer is supposed to take over the data collection, preprocessing, and transformation during various phases of the decision process. The human user is then supposed to accept the result from the computer and to take over information processing during particular—and frequently badly structured—parts of the decision process. This presupposes, however, that the human accepts the immediate results of the computer, and this in a situation when the human may have no intuition and no well-structured expectations of the message. The user will need to evaluate the reliability of the message in some way and will need an explanation which is not just a replay of the algorithm, but information matching the user's intuitive expectations. If this is not possible a mode of competitive rather than cooperative interaction may develop. In such systems, design is not a question of task allocation, rather a question of allocation of authority; the task is performed more or less in parallel by the user, the computer, and the programmer. What is shifting is the role as performer, monitor, and advisor, and, with that, the mode of processing applied.

ETHICAL QUESTIONS OF DESIGN

The difficulty in highly automated systems of establishing a clear reference in terms of 'normal behaviour' raises some problems for designers of large-scale systems in terms of compatibility between their expectations to user behaviour in cases of accidents. The allocation of guilt after the fact depends on a concept of a 'reasonable person' which may be very different for behaviour in very familiar situations and in case of problem solving during disturbed situations. This 'reasonable person' at times seems to be rather similar to the normative decision theorist's 'rational agent', and an interaction among professionals from systems design, psychology, sociology, and legal matters might be useful to probe the need for changes in the perception of human errors.

CONCLUSION

The conclusion of this discussion will be that the present rapid technological development, in particular within information technologies, makes it increasingly important to realize that conditions for systems design have changed. Up to now, systems design and planning of human work conditions have been considered two independent activities on each side of a man–machine interface which is taken care of by human factors specialists. It is symptomatic that the International Federations of Automatic Control (IFAC) and Information Processing (IFIP) have had two committees. One on 'Social Effects of

Automation' taking care of systems considered as the work environment of humans, and another on 'Modelling Man–Machine Interaction' considering humans as functional systems components. A consequence of the tight coupling of the activities of humans and computers at the intellectual level will be that this separation is no longer possible. Human values and attitudes will not only be a question of quality of working life, but directly influence functional effectiveness and reliability. It also means that proper design is no longer a question of having practitioners in Human Factors to use the available results from academic research; no acceptable design model of higher level intellectual processes and of affective states is as yet available, and a change in academic research is needed towards analysis of complex man–machine systems in cognitive psychology, linguistics, semiotics, etc. Furthermore, it will be mandatory that researchers within these fields have a solid basis in technological knowledge and understanding. As the sociologist Peter Winch (1958) notes: 'A sociologist of religion must himself have some religious feeling if he is to make sense of the religious movement he is studying and understand the considerations which govern the lives of its participants.' It will, in the same way, be impossible to study human interaction with technical systems without fundamental knowledge of the technology. This is particularly so for the design of high risk man–machine systems.

There are, fortunately, several signs of changes in the proper direction. University faculties are discussing the plans for technical-humanistic lines of education, and programmes for psychological experiments in complex decision-making situations are taking over interest from the classical experimental psychology paradigm. Also, committees like those of IFAC/IFIP are mutually trying to reach an integrated view of the criteria for systems design.

REFERENCES

Barnett, J. A. (1982). 'Some issues of control in expert systems', *Proceedings of the International Conference on Cybernetics and Society*. Seattle, October 28–30, 1982, pp. 1–5.

Cyert, R. M. and March, J. G. (1963). *A Behavioural Theory of the Firm*. London: Prentice-Hall.

Dreyfus, S. E. and Dreyfus, H. E. (1980). *A Five-Stage Model of the Mental Activities Involved in Direct Skill Acquisition*. ORC-80-2 Operations Research Center. Berkeley: University of California.

Forrester, J. W. (1971). *World Dynamics*. New York: Wright-Allen Press.

Hadamard, J. (1945). *The Psychology of Invention in the Mathematical Field*. Princeton: University Press.

Leplat, J. and Rasmussen, J. (1984). 'Analysis of human errors in industrial incidents and accidents for improvements of work safety', *Acc. Anal. and Prev.* **16**(2), 77–88.

Minzberg, H. (1973). *The Nature of Managerial Work*. London: Harper and Row.

Mach, E. (1905). *Knowledge and Error*. English Edition: Reidel, 1976.

Norman, D. A. (1980). *Errors in Human Performance*. Report No. 8004, Center for Human Information Processing. San Diego: University of California.

Rasmussen, J. (1980). 'What can be learned from human error reports?', *in* Duncan, Gruneberg, and Wallis (Eds), *Changes in Working Life*. New York: John Wiley.

Rasmussen, J. (1984). 'Human error data. Facts or fiction?', 4th Nordic Accident Seminar. Rovaniemi, Finland. Risø-M-2499.

Reason, J. (1982). *Absent-Minded?* London: Prentice-Hall.

Reason, J. (1985). 'General error modelling system (GEMS)', *in* Rasmussen, Duncan and Leplat (Eds), *New Technology and Human Error. Proceedings of 1st Workshop on New Technology and Work*. Bad Homburg, Chichester: John Wiley. (To be published.)

Selz, O. (1922). *Zur Psychologie des Productiven Denkens und des Irrtums*. Bonn: Friederick Cohen.

Shortliffe, E. H. (1983). 'Medical consultation systems: design for doctors', *in* Sime and Coombs (Eds), *Designing for Human Computer Communication*. New York: Academic Press.

Simon, H. A. (1969). *The Sciences of the Artificial*. Cambridge Mass.: MIT Press.

Winch, P. (1958). *The Idea of a Social Science*. New York: Routledge and Kegan Paul.

Risk and Decisions
Edited by W. T. Singleton and J. Hovden
© 1987 John Wiley & Sons Ltd

Chapter 8

Risk, Organization and Safety on an Oil Platform

J. Marek, E. Iversen and O. H. Hellesøy
University of Bergen, Norway

INTRODUCTION

Issues which arise in relation to social and organizational aspects of risk and safety are reviewed in the context of a particular study of operator personnel on an oil platform.

Measures oriented towards specific objectives, such as risk control and safety management, have to be fitted into the general organizational framework of the enterprise. The fit is usually general and not specified, i.e., of a 'more-or-less' type. The point of this study was to articulate the connection as follows:

(i) To show that the effect of organizational and social aspects of work on control of specific risk sources and on general safety is selective and that the extent of the effect varies. One would generally expect that the effects of organizational factors on risk control and safety would be on the whole weaker than the corresponding effects of specific safety measures. Organizational conditions act primarily as a general facilitating background for the introduction and implementation of safety measures.

(ii) Similarly, the effect of safety measures on control of specific risk sources is also selective. This is to be expected because safety measures are specific in their design, but the extent to which they satisfy the intentions of their design is rarely, if ever, assessed. Yet the size of these effects directly indicates the effectiveness of safety measures in controlling specified hazards. Again the question is: which safety measures contribute to the control of which sources of risk, and by how much?

123

These are then our working hypotheses, and their evaluation has to take into account both the size of the observed effects and their pattern.

The study reported here forms part of the Statfjord Project that covers working conditions, safety and hazard on Statfjord A, the first and at the time the only platform extracting oil and gas from the Statfjord field of the Norwegian Continental Shelf. Statfjord A was covered by an extensive survey in 1980, the results of which were published in a series of reports and articles, a book in Norwegian (Hellesøy, 1984) and an English edition of the book (Hellesøy, 1985). The part of the project which concerns risk and safety and which serves as the background for the present study is given in Part IV of the book—see especially chapters by Marek (1985a and b), and Marek, Tangenes and Hellesøy (1985a and 1985b).

WORKING MODEL AND METHOD

Registration of the effects stated in our working hypotheses is of considerable interest since they provide an evaluation of the safety climate of an enterprise in general (Zohar, 1980). From an operational point of view, however, it is important to decompose such a general effect into contributing factors. In doing this one has to take into account both those aspects of organization which promote given safety measures, and the safety measures which are important for control of specified risks and for general safety.

Consequently the model contains the following influences:

(a) Organization   → safety measures.
(b) Organization   → risk control and safety.
(c) Safety measures → risk control and safety.

The relationships are shown in Fig. 8.1.

The boxes represent domains which are evaluated by the employees themselves. Organizational and social conditions and social conditions and specific safety measures serve as two separate blocks of predictors (independent variables), while specific sources of risk and general safety serve as a block of criteria (dependent variables).

The type of evaluations provided by the employees is of central importance to the interpretation of our data and results.

In the case of criteria, a list of hazards, or potential sources of risk was presented with the question of how safe the respondents felt about them. The questions concern objectively existing conditions which are subject to various controls; their aim is to keep the potential risk at an acceptable minimum. An evaluation of the kind 'I feel safe' or '... very safe' means that the control of a given risk source is in the view of the respondent effective, and vice versa when

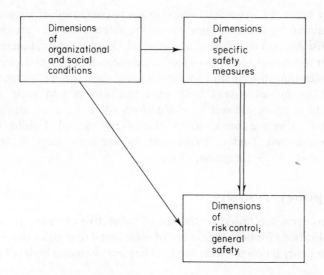

Fig. 8.1. Working model for present study. (Double line
indicates relative primacy of relationship.)

the evaluation is 'unsafe' or 'very unsafe'. We shall refer therefore to these
evaluations as concerning *risk control*. It should be kept in mind that the
operators consist of highly experienced employees.

The same question was posed concerning safety measures which include:
equipment, specialized training, education, routines and procedures oriented
towards prevention and handling of specified types of dangers such as fire or
explosion. Again, an evaluation of a safety measure in terms of 'I feel safe' or
'... very safe' means that the respondent views the measure as adequate for the
purpose. We shall refer to these evaluations as concerning *specific safety
measures*.

The evaluations of organizational and social aspects of the job were of a
different kind. They concern the personal consequences of organization of
work: the structure of the job, the relationships between superiors and
subordinates, autonomy of the employees on the job, variation of tasks
assigned to one person, use of abilities, job pressure, social interaction and
overall satisfaction with the job, (O'Brien *et al.*, 1977; Marek *et al.*, 1985b). As
such these are general background characteristics of any organized work and
are usually known as effects of the 'organizational climate' of the enterprise
(James and Jones, 1974; Drexler, 1977). We asked our respondents whether
they were satisfied with them or not. An evaluation of 'very satisfied' or
'satisfied' indicates that a given aspect is acceptable to the person in question.

Each domain in Fig. 8.1 is composed of a number of dimensions, and each
dimension is in turn composed of specific elements. Thus for the group

considered here, the organizational domain is composed of six dimensions, each containing from one to nine elements, safety measures are covered by four dimensions, and risk control and general safety by seven dimensions.

Whether the model refers to objective or subjective effects depends on the operationalization of domain components and their evaluative measures. In principle, the model covers both objective effects and their subjective parallels. In practice subjective evaluations often have to supplement or replace the objective ones, as is shown by use of Delphi technique (MacCrimmon and Taylor, 1976) and by methods used in ergonomics (Singleton et al., 1973; Chapanis, 1976).

Use of subjective evaluations

Several problems are raised by the use of subjective evaluations. They have direct implications for both the design of scales used to register the evaluations and for the general design of the study. They are discussed in detail elsewhere (Marek, 1985a).

Perceived risk, based on a person's subjective assessment, may be quite different from the real risk of an accident. Varied interpretations of risk and its operational and social consequences exist. Extensive discussions of the subject are given by Døderlein (1978), Hovden (1979), Kahneman and Tversky (1982), Lowrance (1976), Otway (1977), Rowe (1977), Schwing and Albers (1980), Singleton (1986) and Starr, Rudman and Whipple (1976). The Norwegian Directorate of Oil publishes cumulative statistics of accidents on the Continental Shelf. The point at issue in this study is not whether the risks considered here actually caused accidents on the oil platform. They are of interest as hazards, i.e., potential sources of danger which have to be secured by appropriate controls, and they are evaluated as such by the respondents. Although the evaluations and their consequences are assessed by quantitative methods, the main focus is on their qualitative aspects: on how the risks are interpreted, on how they are related to each other, what other factors influence them and what practical implications follow from the way the employees view and evaluate them.

Subjective evaluations have important operational implications for safety. Knowledge concerning potential risk, what one thinks and feels about the risk involved and about its causes, can be decisive for handling of a critical situation. Given the same external situation, the individual's experience, background, personality, etc., will together determine which aspects of the situation should be considered as especially important, whether action should be taken or not, and what kind of action—see for example Joyce, Slocum and von Glinow, 1982; Hale, 1984; Mowday, Stone and Porter, 1979; and Dunn, 1972.

It is significant that control system designers and other professionals, who at the outset are principally interested in the objective control of process failures and accidents, had to turn their attention to the operator error as an important source of information concerning the malfunctioning of the system—see for example Rasmussen (1982). Operator error in this context refers broadly to combined effects of knowledge, experience, vigilance and errors 'encouraged' by the objective system although they are ostensibly committed by the operator. Rasmussen (1983, p. 265) refers explicitly to the usefulness of qualitative evaluations for the assessment of system design; these concern especially the match between the predicted and actually used strategy of control. Knowledge about the employees' subjective experiences of risk and risk control on an oil platform is thus highly pertinent to the design and evaluation of safety measures and safety policies.

The operator personnel is responsible for all central functions on the platform such as control, maintenance and production, and some of the supporting functions, such as organization of all personnel and material transport, and radio and other communications. As a group they cover administrative functions and medical services and are responsible for the safety of the platform. Compared with other groups of platform employees they have the most extensive education and training in safety. For a detailed description of the group see Milcarek, Hellesøy, Marek and Tangenes (1985).

These operators are generally recognized as the most experienced and most knowledgeable group of employees on the platform. They are indeed 'experts in their situation' (Glendon, 1986). The contents of our previously published results and their consistency across different areas of concern fully support this view (Marek *et al.*, 1985a, and Tangenes *et al.*, 1985).

Generally, employees' evaluations prove to be a useful source of information concerning work conditions. When they concern hazards, whose probabilities of risk on the whole cannot be based on objective assessments but on estimates, employees' evaluations of the adequacy of hazard control measures are especially important and ought to be considered as relevant input.

When such evaluations come, as is the case here, from a knowledgeable group of employees, they ought to be accepted as considered reflections on the realities of the situation. This does not mean that evaluations coming from badly informed employees should be disregarded, as they may point to the source and possible consequences of misinformation.

Method

Using five-point scales ranging from 'very safe' to 'very unsafe', the respondents were asked to evaluate 20 potential sources of risk as to how safe they felt about them. At the end of the list they were in addition asked to give a summary evaluation of safety in their work, taking into consideration all the specified sources of risk together with any additional factors which in their view may have been relevant.

The scale for general evaluation was extended by subdividing each of the primary five categories into three subcategories yielding a 15-point scale. The 20 risk items accounted for 59 per cent of variance of the general evaluation of safety (Marek *et al.*, 1985a).

The list consists of items covering both direct sources of risk such as blow-out, explosion, wind and weather conditions, and indirect ones such as safety measures which represent danger only when they are inadequate to give the protection they were designed to give. For the purpose of this study, only the direct sources of risk are considered as the criterion measures of risk control. The list was prepared on the basis of discussions with the employees on the Statfjord platform and on the basis of findings from a pilot study (Hellesøy and Gogstad, 1979).

As in the case of risk assessment, the respondents were asked to evaluate, using a five-point scale, a list of 22 items pertaining to the organizational and social aspects of their jobs. At the end of the list they were similarly asked to assess their job as a whole by stating how satisfied they were with their job. They were to include in this general assessment all preceding 22 aspects of the job and any others not included in the list but considered to be relevant. Following our standard procedure a 15-point scale was used for the general evaluation.

It ought to be stressed that general evaluations of the kind 'I am satisfied with my job' are not necessarily an expression of direct satisfaction. They are, rather, a form of conditional acceptance of the job, having considered factors like nature of work, pay, shiftwork, recreational opportunities, family relationships, alternative opportunities in the labour market, etc. When, for example, 75 per cent say that they are satisfied with the job, it does not mean that they actually like it, but that they accept it in view of certain criteria.

RESULTS AND DISCUSSION

This study addresses the question of how important are the socio-organizational conditions and specific safety measures at work to control of specified sources of risk and to general safety—see Fig. 8.1 above.

The three blocks of variables were evaluated by experienced employees of an operator company of a large Norwegian oil platform. The evaluations were factor analysed, and indices were formed as follows.

The evaluations of the 22 specific items concerning organizational and social conditions at work were grouped into five dimensions:

— Job variation and use of abilities.
— Job management and reward systems.
— Job pressure.

— Social interaction,
— Housekeeping.
   Overall job satisfaction was in addition included as a separate dimension.

The composition of these dimensions (Table 8.1) varies considerably from those usually yielded by factor analysis of occupationally heterogeneous groups (O'Brien *et al.*, 1977 and Marek *et al.*, 1985b). For the understanding of a particular group of employees it is necessary to establish dimensions which are typical for them, and which reflect the existing routines and requirements of their jobs.
   Four dimensions were established on the basis of nine items of indirect risks, or specific safety measures. They are listed in Table 8.2.
   Eleven sources of risk together with the general evaluation of safety were reduced to the six dimensions shown in Table 8.3.
   After factor analyses and index-forming, multiple regression analyses were used to assess the contributions of the socio-organizational dimensions and dimensions of safety measures (predictors) to each of the risk dimensions (criteria).
   Effects of organizational and social conditions. The two most prominent contributors within this block of predictors are *job management and reward systems*, and *housekeeping*—see Table 8.4.
   Inspection of the constituent items of these dimensions point to the importance of clarity and orderliness on the job.
   Importance of reward systems in the form of good pay and promotion opportunities could be interpreted in two ways, either as a fair compensation for working offshore which helps to commit the employee to his work and therefore to the safety on job, or as a payoff for danger and for acceptance of inadequate safety. Our discussions with representatives of the employees following the presentation of our preliminary results pointed clearly to the first of the two interpretations in the sense that 'a well-paid worker is a safe worker, because he cares more'. There was an explicit rejection of danger payoff on the grounds that workers on an oil platform can ill afford the indifference towards safety which such payoff encourages.
   Worthy of note is the lack of contribution from *job variation and use of abilities*, since this dimension is considered usually as the most important for job satisfaction (O'Brien, 1980). Its relevance for risk control and general safety is, in the view of the operator crew, decidedly minor, except for a small contribution to the control of falling objects; general experience, which it conveys, is understandably of value here. Otherwise, however, it seems that specific experience and skills are required for adequate control of specific risks and for maintaining safety at work.
   Similarly surprising is the total absence of *job pressure* as a significant contributor. Despite a considerable variation in the evaluations of the two

Table 8.1. Operator personnel: General organizational and social factors.

	% Satisfied	Not satisfied	N
Job variation and use of abilities			
The amount of change and variety in my job	70	30	234
The chance to do different jobs	65	35	231
Opportunities to do challenging and interesting work	62	39	229
The chance to use my abilities, training and experience in my job	63	37	231
Opportunities to grow as a person	55	45	226
The chance to learn new things in my job	72	28	232
Chances of really achieving something worthwhile	57	43	232
Being able to change the things I don't like about my job	50	50	232
Having a say about the way I do things in my job	75	25	232
Job management and reward systems			
The sharing of responsibilities and leadership between foreigners and Norwegians	49	51	228
Clarity of job description	43	57	231
The use of Norwegian language in relation to the use of the English language in the job	43	57	229
Promotion opportunities	43	57	231
The amount of pay I get	54	46	233
Quality of supervision	43	57	233
Being able to do my job without a supervisor worrying me	84	16	230
Job pressure			
Having enough time to do my job properly	68	32	232
The amount of pressure and stress	56	44	320
Social interaction			
The people I talk to, and work with in my job	91	9	233
The chance I get to know other people in my job	86	14	232
Opportunities to be open and frank, and to be oneself	72	28	232
Housekeeping			
Physical conditions at work (cleanliness, noise levels)	59	41	232
Overall job satisfaction			
General satisfaction with the job	79	21	231

items which constitute the dimension it is likely that, in comparison with other jobs on the platform, the general level of strain among the operator personnel is not high (Marek *et al.*, 1985b).

Table 8.2. Operator personnel: Specific safety measures.

	Safe %	Not safe %	N
Emergency training and equipment			
Protective measures/equipment	68	32	229
Education/training in safety	50	50	230
Fire/smoke alarms	56	44	226
Alarms at your worksite	75	25	230
Escape possibilities			
Escape routes	46	54	229
Evacuation facilities from the platform	35	65	229
Surveillance of installation			
Surveillance and protection of the installation	55	45	225
Medical services			
Access to and sufficiency of medical services	72	28	225
Access to first aid	71	29	227

Table 8.3. Operator personnel: Risk-dimensions.

	Safe %	Not safe %	N
Major hazards			
Explosions	37	63	231
Blow-out	50	50	231
Fire	36	64	230
Transportation of people (helicopter)	55	45	230
Destruction of installation			
Sabotage	62	38	227
Presence of hydrocarbons on the platform	65	35	228
Effect of corrosion/rust on the installation	55	45	230
'Dangerous acts'	41	59	226
Weather conditions			
Weather conditions	78	22	229
Cargo-handling			
Transport and loading (cargo)	74	26	221
Falling objects			
Falling objects	52	48	230
General evaluation of safety			
General feeling of safety considering potential hazards and other relevant factors	65	35	223

That *overall job satisfaction* is not relevant with respect to safety is on the other hand not surprising at all. General experience otherwise shows clearly that a positive attitude towards an activity is in general not related to its danger or safety, even though some dangerous activities, like mountain climbing, seem to offer excitement. Work of the operator personnel does not belong in this category.

Social interaction is important only in connection with the harsh weather conditions of the North Sea, and with handling of cargo. In general, the emotional aspects of social sharing are likely to matter for the former, while operational aspects of cooperation are clearly relevant for the latter. Contribution of social interaction to cargo-handling is markedly stronger than in the case of weather conditions. Additional analyses showed that the element of friendship in social relations is most important, especially in the case of cargo-handling. Although in general, cooperation may not require friendship (Axelrod, 1984), handling of heavy loads under difficult conditions underscores the importance of trust and reliance on the reliability of a fellow worker.

Absence of any noticeable contribution of social relations to the evaluations concerning destruction of installation and major hazards is both unexpected and worrying. Does it mean that no help from fellow workers and friends is expected to be given and received in the event of a major catastrophe? Without going into further discussion of this finding we raise the point as meriting a serious examination of the existing contents of safety education and training, of their practicalities and general guidance.

Effects of specific safety measures. The two most pervasive and consistent contributors to the control of potential risks are, in the view of the operator personnel, *emergency training and equipment*, and *escape possibilities*—see Table 8.4. These two dimensions are primary contributors in the case of major hazards, weather conditions, cargo-handling, falling objects and general safety. In view of their pervasiveness it is significant that 50 per cent of the group do not consider safety education and training as adequate and 44 per cent do not feel safe concerning fire and smoke alarms. Similarly, 54 and 65 per cent do not think that escape routes and evacuation facilities are adequate.

Only for the assessment of destruction of installation is the contribution of emergency training and escape possibilities exceeded by that of another measure; as could be expected the effect of surveillance of installation is in this case considerably stronger. Surveillance of installation contributes also to the evaluation of general safety and major hazards, but on a considerably lower level.

Medical services are, according to the operator employees, important for major hazards and destruction of installation, and it is reasonable to expect that they should be both adequate and accessible under these extreme

Table 8.4. Significant contributions from safety measures and organizational/social dimensions to the evaluations of risk.

Dimensions of risk	Specific safety measures				Organizational and social dimensions					
	Medical services	Surveillance of installation	Escape possibilities	Emergency training and equipment	Housekeeping	Interaction	Job pressure	Job management and reward systems	Job variation and use of abilities	Overall job satisfaction
Major hazards	X	X	X	X	X			X		
Destruction of installation	X	X	X	X	X			X		
Weather conditions			X	X			X	X		
Cargo-handling			X	X	X	X				
Falling objects			X	X	X			X	X	
General evaluation of safety		X	X	X	X			X		

Stepwise multiple regression. Safety measures and org./social dimensions were run as separate blocks. $N = 234$.

conditions. It is worth noting that a high proportion of the group, over 70 per cent, judge them as being adequate, yet almost 30 per cent of employees do not feel safe concerning them—see Table 8.2.

General vs. specific effects. The question of how relevant are general organizational and social conditions for safety was raised by Zohar (1980) concerning the overall safety climate. This study makes it possible to articulate these general effects by decomposing them.

In addition, the evaluations of components of general organizational and social conditions are accompanied by those of specific safety measures. This combination makes it possible to assess their respective contributions in relation to each other, and their combined effect—see Fig. 8.2.

The working model adopted for this study (Fig. 8.1.) postulated that the general organizational and social conditions act as a facilitating background for specific safety measures. As such, their effects in terms of explained variance ought to be lower than those of the specific safety measures.

For three dimensions of risk this is certainly so—see Fig. 8.2. The effects in

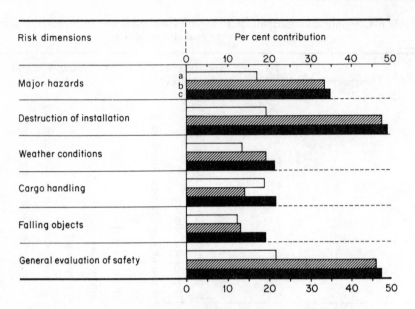

Fig. 8.2. Operator personnel: per cent contribution to evaluation of risk
from evaluations of (a) all significant organizational and social dimensions;
(b) all significant safety measures; (c) all significant organizational and social
dimensions and safety measures combined. (c is less than a + b because of
overlaps)

question concern major hazards, destruction of installation and general
evaluation of safety. For destruction of installation, which is the most
illustrative example here, the total variance explained by both blocks of
predictors amounts to almost 49 per cent. Specific safety measures alone cover
47.6 per cent, while only 19.4 per cent is explained by general organizational
and social conditions. The effects of the two blocks of predictors overlap to
some extent, but their respective values clearly show their potential, and
similar relative proportions are registered for the two remaining dimensions of
major hazards and general safety.

Although the same tendencies could be observed for weather conditions and
for falling objects, the effect of organizational and social conditions is relatively
stronger. The absolute levels of values are here considerably lower.

For cargo-handling on the other hand, the tendency is reversed and the
component contributions form a mirror image of those for weather conditions.
The organizational and social conditions are here the stronger predictors.

CONCLUSION AND SUMMARY

One could well conclude that our working hypotheses are supported by our inquiry. It is clear that both the size and the pattern of contributions is interesting and useful.

Firstly, existing safety measures are clearly oriented towards control of major hazards and protection of installation against its destruction (Table 8.2). General safety of the platform is strongly influenced by these two dimensions, (Marek *et al.*, 1985a).

Secondly, specific safety measures are considerably less oriented towards handling of cargo, control of falling objects and the consequences of weather conditions. The question of what could or should be done in these respects cannot be answered here, but the question itself should be of value to those concerned with safety.

Thirdly, it seems that contribution of social relations to safety is being neglected in safety education and training and ought to be more seriously considered.

The present study examined the perceived contribution of general organizational and social conditions and specific safety measures to the evaluations of hazards which are typical for an oil and gas producing platform.

Hazards considered in this study are inherently associated with the extraction of oil and gas under adverse climatic conditions characteristic of the North Sea. Five hazard dimensions were identified: major hazards (explosions, blow-out, fire and helicopter transport), destruction of installation, weather conditions, cargo-handling and falling objects. A sixth overall dimension of general safety was also considered.

It was expected that the facilitating effects of organizational and social conditions on the control and management of these risk sources would be of a lower order than the effects of specific safety measures.

This proved to be the case only for major hazards and destruction of installation, which constitute the primary targets of the existing safety measures. For the hazards of cargo-handling, falling objects and weather conditions, the contribution of organizational and social conditions is relatively much stronger. Specific safety measures are at present clearly less oriented towards the control of these hazards.

The methodological approach which this study illustrates allows a decomposition of 'safety climate' of an enterprise into constituent operational measures. As such its application is of general interest.

Further, the approach allows those concerned with safety to assess whether the above effects (and/or other effects established on the basis of similar studies) satisfy the initial intentions of existing safety measures, and whether the existing safety measures should be complemented or revised.

ACKNOWLEDGEMENT

This is a shortened version of the main report, which can be obtained from

Julius Marek, Dept. of Social Psychology, University of Bergen, Øisteinsgate 3, N-5000 Bergen, Norway.

The authors wish to thank Mobil Exploration Norway Inc. and the Royal Norwegian Council for Scientific and Industrial Research, whose financial support made this study possible.

The study was undertaken in cooperation between the Research Center for Occupational Health and Safety, and the Department of Social Psychology, both at the University of Bergen, Norway.

We wish to thank all concerned whose effort and support made this study possible.

To Dr Gordon O'Brien of Flinders University of South Australia we are indebted for giving us the benefit of his wisdom and experience in the field of labour studies, and for his permission to use his questionnaire concerning the organizational and social aspects of work. Last, but not least, our thanks to Dr Tamara Kotler of the University of Melbourne, for her insightful discussions.

REFERENCES

Axelrod, R. (1984). *The Evolution of Cooperation*. New York: Basic Books Inc.

Chapanis, A. (1976). 'Engineering psychology', in Dunette, M. D. (Ed.), *Handbook of Industrial and Organizational Psychology*. Chicago: Rand McNally.

Drexler, J. A., Jr. (1977). 'Organizational climate: its homogeneity within organizations', *Journal of Applied Psychology*, **62**, 38–42.

Dunn, J. G. 'Subjective and objective risk distribution. (1972). A comparison and its implication for accident prevention', *Occupational Psychology*, **46**, 183–187.

Døderlein, J. M. (1978). *Akseptabel Risiko. (Acceptable Risk)*. Oslo: NTNFs Utvalg for risikoforskning, 1978.

Glendon, I. (1986). Chapter 6 in this book.

Hale, A. R. (1984). 'Is safety training worthwhile?', *Journal of Occupational Accidents*, **6**, 17–33.

Hellesøy, O. H. (1984) (Ed.). *Arbeidsplass Statfjord*. Bergen: Universitetsforlaget.

Hellesøy, O. H. (1985) (Ed.). *Work Environment Statfjord Field*. Bergen: Universitetsforlaget.

Hellesøy, O. H. and Gogstad, A. Chr. (1979). 'Working environment. Health and safety at the Statfjord field.' Provisional Report. Bergen: Mobil Exploration Norway Inc.

Hovden, J. (1979). *Vurdering av ulykkesrisiko. (Evaluation of Accident Risk)*. Trondheim: Tapir.

James, L. R. and Jones, A. P. (1974). 'Organizational climate: a review of theory and research', *Psychological Bulletin*, **81**, 1096–1112.

Joyce, W., Slocum, J. W. and von Glinow, M. A. (1982). 'Person-situation interaction: competing models of fit', *Journal of Occupational Behaviour*, **4**, 265–280.

Kahneman, D. and Tversky, A. (1982). 'Variants of uncertainty', *Cognition*, **11**, 143–157.

Lowrance, W. W. (1976). *On Acceptable Risk*. Los Altos. California: Kaufmann.

MacCrimmon, K. R. and Taylor, R. N. (1976). 'Decision-making and problem solving', in Dunnette, M. D. (Ed.), *Handbook of Industrial and Organizational Psychology*. Chicago: Rand McNally.

Marek, J. (1985a). 'Evaluation of one's own existence: problems, concepts, methods', *in* Hellesøy, O. H. (Ed.), *Work Environment Statfjord Field*. Bergen: Universitets-forlaget.

Marek, J. (1985b). 'Evaluations of work environment: survey design, analysis, and presentation of results', Appendix B, *in* Hellesøy, O. H. (Ed.), *Work Environment Statfjord Field*. Bergen: Universitetsforlaget.

Marek, J., Tangenes, B. and Hellesøy, O. H. (1985a) 'Experience of risk and safety', *in* Hellesøy, O. H. (Ed.), *Work Environment Statfjord Field*. Bergen: Universitetsfor-laget.

Marek, J., Tangenes, B. and Hellesøy, O. H. (1985b). 'Organizational and social aspects of jobs', *in* Hellesøy, O. H. (Ed.), *Work Environment Statfjord Field*. Bergen: Universitetsforlaget.

Milcarek, B. I., Hellesøy, O. H., Marek, J. and Tangenes, B. (1985). 'The employees and the work they do', *in* Hellesøy, O. H. (Ed.), *Work Environment Statfjord Field*. Bergen: Universitetsforlaget.

Mowday, R. T., Stone, E. F. and Porter, L. W. (1979). 'The interaction of personality and job scope in predicting turnover', *Journal of Vocational Behaviour*, **15**, 78–89.

O'Brien, G. E. (1980). 'The centrality of skill-utilization for job design', *in* Duncan, K. D., Gruneberg, M. and Wallis, D. (Eds), *Changes in Working Life*. New York: John Wiley & Sons.

O'Brien, G. E., Dowling, P. and Kabanoff, B. (1977). *Work, Health and Leisure*. Report No. 1. to the Dept. of Social Security. Labour and Social Activity Project. Adelaide, South Australia: Flinders University. National Institute of Labour Studies.

Otway, H. J. (1977). *A Review of Research on the Identification of Factors influencing the Social Response to Technological Risks*. Salzburg: International Atom Energy Agency.

Rasmussen, J. (1982). 'Human factors in high risk technology', *in* Green, A. E. (Ed.), *High Risk Safety Technology*. Chichester: John Wiley & Sons.

Rasmussen, J. (1983). 'Skills, rules and knowledge: Signals, signs and symbols and other distinctions in human performance models', *IEEE Transactions on Systems, Man and Cybernetics*, **SMC-13**, 257–266.

Rowe, W. D. (1977). *An Anatomy of Risk*. New York: John Wiley & Sons.

Schwing, R. C. and Albers, W. A. (Eds) (1980). *Societal Risk Assessment: How Safe is Safe Enough?* New York: Plenum.

Singleton, W. T. (1986). Chapter 11 in this book.

Singleton, W. T., Fox, J. G. and Whitfield, D. (1973). *Measurement of Man at Work*. London: Taylor & Francis.

Starr, C., Rudman, R. and Whipple, C. (1976). 'Philosophical basis for risk analysis', *Annual Review of Energy*, **1**, 629–662.

Tangenes, B., Marek, J. and Hellesøy, O. H., (1985). 'The physical work environ-ment', *in* Hellesøy, O. H. (Ed.). *Work Environment Statfjord Field*. Bergen: Universitetsforlaget.

Zohar, D. (1980). 'Safety climate in industrial organizations: Theoretical and applied implications', *Journal of Applied Psychology*, **65**, 96–102.

Risk and Decisions
Edited by W. T. Singleton and J. Hovden
© 1987 John Wiley & Sons Ltd.

Chapter 9

Major Hazards and Behaviour

ALAN HEDGE
Department of Applied Psychology, Aston University, U.K.

INTRODUCTION

'Hazards are a special kind of environmental event that pose threats to humans and to the things that humans value' (Cvetkovitch and Earle, 1985)

The earth is not still. Natural events such as earthquakes, volcanic eruptions, floods, cyclones, tornadoes, droughts and so forth, ravage the earth and serve as constant reminders to us that we are the precarious and ephemeral residents of a dynamic biosphere. Our reactions to such natural phenomena are varied. Sometimes people behave eutropistically, being attracted to viewing the spectacle of awesome natural forces at work, such as when tourists visit an active volcano. More typically, our reactions are more cautious, even fearful, especially when we are likely to be directly adversely affected by the occurrence of the event. An environmental event that constitutes a major hazard:

— arises with little or no warning,
— poses a serious disruption to community life,
— causes or threatens serious injury or death,
— renders many people homeless,
— demands the special mobilization of emergency services.

Over a decade ago it was estimated that at a global level around 30 to 40 natural events occur each year in which more than 100 lives are lost and for which damage costs exceed one million dollars (Dworkin, 1973), and this pattern of natural phenomena probably has not changed significantly (other than in terms of cost). Superimposed against this backcloth of natural devastation is the potential impact of a growing variety of man-made major hazards, particularly those associated with the growth of technology in the industrialized countries. Societal concern has been stimulated by a number of disastrous accidents in recent years. For example, the contamination of the town of Seveso in Italy in 1976, when highly toxic chemicals including dioxin escaped from a trichlorophenol production plant, the accidental release of radioactive gases at the Three Mile Island nuclear power plant in Harrisburg in the U.S.A. in 1979, and the devastating escape of methyl isocyanate gas from a pesticides factory in Bhopal in India in 1984 where some 2,500 people died and where many thousands remain debilitated, are just three of the numerous incidents which have received considerable public and political attention (Lewis, 1985). In an attempt to safeguard communities against the impact of potential major hazards, both natural and man-made, many countries have established professional emergency planning organizations charged with the responsibility of formulating contingency plans to mitigate the effects of major hazards. However, the task of formulating such plans and coordinating their execution, should a major emergency arise, is a complex undertaking requiring knowledge of a diverse array of topics. The topics include:

— factors influencing people's perceptions of hazards and judgements of relative risk,
— knowledge of the characteristics of the hazard itself,
— knowledge of people's behaviour in emergency situations,
— knowledge of the likely outcomes for a variety of possible major hazard scenarios.

TAXONOMIES OF RISK AND THE PERCEPTION OF MAJOR HAZARDS

'Classification systems improve communication, aid in the generalization of research findings, are useful in identifying lacunae in the scientific and practical body of knowledge about hazards, and, most importantly, can be valuable tools for improving analytical thinking and the practical management of hazards.' (Cvetkovitch and Earle, 1985.)

By their very nature hazardous events are dynamic and any model of the hazard process needs to capture its dynamic nature. Unfortunately most studies of the relative risks of particular hazards have resulted in the formulation of static models of hazards. A transaction model of hazardous events which attempts to incorporate a temporal dimension has been formulated by Cvetkovitch and Earle (1985). The model distinguishes between three major stages in the life history of any hazard (see Fig. 9.1) and this serves the particularly useful function of providing an organizing framework for

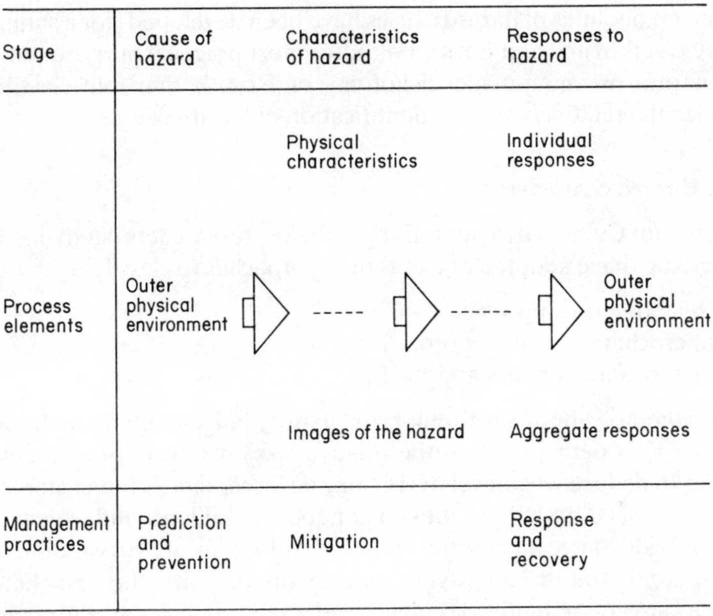

Stage	Cause of hazard	Characteristics of hazard	Responses to hazard
		Physical characteristics	Individual responses
Process elements	Outer physical environment		Outer physical environment
		Images of the hazard	Aggregate responses
Management practices	Prediction and prevention	Mitigation	Response and recovery

Fig. 9.1. A transactional model of hazard process (from Cvetkovitch and Earle, 1985).

research on hazards. Although the model is actually generalizable to any hazardous situation, the description of its three stages which follows is deliberately biased towards research on major hazards.

Stage 1: Hazard causes

Historically, the most common classification of hazard causes has been the dichotomy between natural and man-made or technological hazards. This simple distinction holds intuitive appeal for many because it serves to separate those extreme geophysical events over which mankind has little or no control but which can often be predicted from those extreme environmental events dependent on the failure of a technological system, and therefore implicitly controllable, but which usually cannot be predicted. Rowe (1977) has argued for an extension of this dichotomy into a four-fold distinction between events which clarifies the degree of human involvement by separating unavoidable natural disasters such as volcanic eruptions from avoidable natural disasters such as floods where avoidance or control can mitigate the impact, and by separating man-originated disasters such as the failure of a dam because of a natural event such as an earthquake, from man-caused disasters such as the failure of a chemical process plant because of human error. Although more

142

RISK AND DECISIONSRISK AND DECISIONS

elaborate taxonomies of hazard causes have been developed (for a summary of these see Cvetkovitch and Earle, 1985), for most practical purposes either the simple natural *vs.* man-made dichotomy or Rowe's four-fold classification suffices for the relatively simple identification of hazard causes.

Stage 2: Hazard characteristics

According to Cvetkovitch and Earle (1985), researchers studying hazard characteristics have adopted one of three approaches to classifying these:

— the psychometric approach,
— the microcharacteristics approach,
— the macrocharacteristics approach.

The psychometric approach attempts to quantify judgements about hazards by scaling people's perceptions of the relative risks of a variety of events, and often tries to deduce what level of risk may be 'acceptable'. For example, Vlek and Stallen (1980, 1981) have looked at people's similarity judgements of the risks of a wide range of hazards. Their results indicate a two-dimensional cognitive configuration underlying judgements or risks, the first dimension being the 'size of potential accident' and the second being the 'degree of organized safety'. For most of their subjects, judgements of risk increased as accident size increased whereas conflicting effects of organized safety were found. For around half of the subjects, increased organized safety decreased judged risk whereas for the others it actually increased this. Findings such as these highlight the problem of individual differences in psychometric studies of risk. Many other limitations of this approach are described by Cvetkovitch and Earle (1985) and they are also discussed in Glendon's chapter. The microcharacteristics approach involves analysing people's physical, biological and social descriptors of hazards and then the grouping of these hazards by their common characteristics. A recent example of this approach is the work of Litea, Lanning and Rasmussen (1983). From an extensive review of the literature on perceived risk, they propose that just nine characteristics can be identified that influence people's willingness to accept risk (see Table 9.1). Each of these characteristics can be represented as a dichotomous scale thus giving 512 possible combinations of characteristics. However, when Litea, Lanning and Rasmussen (1983) grouped what they claim to be all known risks on the basis of these combinations of characteristics only, 40 combinations had entries and in fact they found that most 'common' risks could be classified along only four dimensions:

— whether the risk is natural or man-made,
— whether the associated event is ordinary or catastrophic,
— whether exposure to this is voluntary or involuntary,
— whether its impact is immediate or delayed (see Figure 9.2).

Table 9.1. Characteristics affecting risk acceptability (from Litea, Lanning and Rasmussen, 1983).

Risk characteristic	Risk scale	
Volition	Voluntary	— Involuntary
Severity	Ordinary	— Catastrophic
Origin	Natural	— Man-made
Effect manifestation	Immediate	— Delayed
Exposure pattern	Continuous	— Occasional
Controllability	Controllable	— Uncontrollable
Familiarity	Old	— New
Benefit	Clear	— Unclear
Necessity	Necessary	— Luxury

From other research work the dimension of controllable–uncontrollable emerges as being particularly salient (see chapter 5 by Hale), indeed Fischhoff, Slovic and Lichtenstein (1983) state that 'People's investment in problems is determined by their feelings of personal efficacy. That is, they do not get involved unless they feel that they can make a difference personally or collectively ... people will deliberately ignore major problems if they see no possibility of effective action.' However, while the microcharacteristics approach may shed some light on the complexities of the dimensions that underly human judgement of risk it fails to capture the dynamic and labile nature of these and it also fails to specify the underlying mental processes.

The macrocharacteristics approach is based on sociological studies of collective responses to disasters and here hazards are classified in terms of both their physical characteristics and their impact (Perry, Lindell and Greene, 1980; Kreps, 1984). Unlike the former two approaches which aim to estimate the judged characteristics and perceived risks of a broad range of hazards, and also define what is and what is not acceptable, the macrocharacteristics approach examines similarities and differences between various characteristics of disasters. Perry, Lindell and Greene (1980) developed a taxonomy based on just five characteristics of disaster namely:

— the scope of impact,
— the speed of onset,
— the duration of impact,
— the degree of social preparedness,
— any secondary impact.

This approach essentially ignores any role of individual judgements of risk in determining individual responses and focuses instead on actual case studies of collective behaviour in disasters. It recognizes the role of other dimensions such as political allegiance which, at the societal level, will influence

		Voluntary		Involuntary	
		Immediate	Delayed	Immediate	Delayed
M A N M A D E	Catastrophic	Aviation		Dam failures Gas release Nuclear energy	Some industrial pollution
	Ordinary	Occupational risks Sport Surgery Driving	Smoking Saccharin Occupational risks	Aviation— people on ground	Food additives Pesticides Nuclear energy (cancer) Coal energy Industrial pollution
N A T U R A L	Catastrophic			Earthquakes Hurricanes Epidemics	
	Ordinary			Lightning Animal bites Acute diseases	Various diseases

Fig. 9.2. Preliminary classification of some 'common' risks (from Litea, Lanning and Rasmussen, 1983).

decision-making about hazards. Also, from this perspective controversial concepts such as that of 'acceptable' risk become irrelevant since this approach emphasizes the fact that societal judgements actually are made about technologies and activities rather than directly about risks. Consequently, such an approach proves rather more relevant to describing the context in which people actually take decisions and behave in real-life major emergencies. Because of this emphasis on societal and community responses to disaster the macrocharacteristics approach tends to be that which is most useful to those involved in formulating community emergency plans.

In addition to these three approaches researchers have shown that there are strong temporal effects on hazard perception. The relative infrequency of major disasters often results in individuals applying various kinds of threat minimization strategies in appraising the hazard. Various effects have been noted here and these include the crisis effect which describes how the perception of hazard is greatest during and immediately after the occurrence of an event but quickly dissipates between events, and the levee effect which describes the way that people tend to congregate around any protective measures that have been taken (Bell, Fisher and Loomis, 1978). The psychological processes that appear to underly these effects include adaptation whereby people habituate to conditions that may objectively be changing, such as people failing to attend to increased smoke emissions from a volcano or people failing to attend to signs of increased air pollution such as the presence of increasing levels of photochemical smog (Evans, Jacobs and Frager, 1982). Adaptation may also occur indirectly via cognitive dissonance which, in the context of major hazards, manifests itself by people overemphasizing consonant attitudes about an area and underemphasizing dissonant concerns (Burton, 1972; Burton, Kates and White, 1978). Thus residents of California can readily point out the many benefits of living there which clearly offset any costs because this is an earthquake zone.

Stage 3: Hazard responses

The major cost of any disaster is usually property damage (Rossi, Wright and Weber-Burdin, 1982) followed by death and physical injury. However, researchers are increasingly turning their attention to other factors such as the impact of hazards on the psychological impairment of individuals and to the resulting social disruption to the affected community.

At the individual level most of the research to date has focused on assessing the behavioural impact of disasters in terms of the levels of stress in survivors and any subsequent adverse effects on their mental health. Many of these studies of the impact of disasters on individuals have been conducted in the U.S.A. and most of these have investigated events whose impacts were relatively modest and short term, though a few studies of longer-term impact have been reported (for example, see Gleser, Green and Winget, 1981). The evidence which has been collected to date paints quite a complex and sometimes conflicting picture. In a study of the 1974 Xenia tornado, Taylor, Ross and Quarantelli (1976) showed that while this resulted in stress reactions and subsequent stress-related problems in some survivors, in others it actually induced highly-positive reactions and some survivors showed greater resilience and adaptiveness. In studies of the survivors of Cyclone Tracy which struck Darwin, Australia in 1974, Milne (1977a, b) showed that the resulting psychological stress was actually lowest for those who did not evacuate the devastated city but who stayed and helped with reconstruction work. The levels of stress were markedly higher for those who evacuated the city after the event and then returned at a later time, and highest for those who had evacuated and did not return.

More clear-cut data on postdisaster stress have been collected for the victims of the Mount Saint Helens's ashfall in 1980 (Adams and Adams, 1984) where an 'extensive stress-reaction effect on the community of Othello and its surrounding area' was documented. Comparisons of pre- and post-disaster data showed that, even after seasonal adjustments, there were substantial increases in illness, alcohol abuse, family stress, violence and aggression. The particularly interesting feature of this disaster is that it appears to illustrate an inverse relationship between the direct risk to individuals of the ashfall (invariably not a life-threatening situation to the individuals involved) and the subsequent deterioration in the mental health of the community. In fact, one of the prime determinants of the subsequent stress reaction appears to have been community bewilderment as to how to deal with the ash and the impact of this on the agricultural economic base of the community.

Other evidence has been collected on the psychosocial impact of man-made hazards such as the Three Mile Island incident. Some studies apparently have shown strong evidence of acute stress amongst Harrisburg residents living close to the nuclear plant throughout the year following the incident (Baum, Gatchel and Schaeffer, 1983). Stress levels in the high–normal, subclinical range were recorded, but 20 per cent of people studied showed no stress symptoms whatsoever. However, as earlier work has pointed out, since there are no baseline data for stress levels for the community studied the validity of such a conclusion must be treated cautiously (Baum, Fleming and Singer, 1982). A study of the actual utilization of medical care following the incident shows only minor increases compared with the preincident baseline (Houts, Hu, Henderson, Cleary and Tokuhata, 1984). The apparent lack of any serious, adverse psychological impact on local residents is probably attributable to the lack of any immediate and tangible evidence of related health problems among the surrounding populace. More clearcut evidence of changes in stress levels has been found by Fleming and Baum (1984) in a comparative study of residents living near to a hazardous toxic waste dump and those in a matched safe control area. For those living near the site they found greater concern about the hazard, elevated levels of urinary catecholamines, greater symptom distress, and poorer performance of tasks requiring motivation and concentration. This chronic stress was also strongly linked with feelings of helplessness.

Longer-term stress data have also been collected following the Buffalo Creek disaster of 1972 where a slag dam collapsed unleashing 132 million gallons of black slag, debris-filled mud and water which then flooded a river valley and killed 125 people, injured many hundreds and left many thousands homeless. A longitudinal study of a cross section of the survivors showed that for several years afterwards they continued to display a variety of symptoms of emotional distress such as anxiety, depression, belligerence, agitation and social isolation, all of which were interpreted as evidence of severe and chronic psychological distress (Gleser, Green and Winget, 1981). However, not all survivors suffered these problems in the same way or to the same degree. Those most affected were people who had been in contact with the flood waters and whose lives had thus been directly threatened, and people who had lost family members, relatives, or friends were more adversely affected than those who had only lost material possessions. Two years after the disaster 88 per cent of the sample continued to suffer from these debilitating symptoms and over 30 per cent were still suffering these some five years later.

At the social level, studies of major hazards and behaviour emphasize that the link between perceived risk and subsequent behaviour is typically weak until the point at which people recognize that danger is imminent and personally threatening, then their behaviour is generally adaptive and they will seek safety or escape (Quarantelli, 1978). In normal times, many social factors will influence people's perceptions of hazards. Cost/benefit factors are undoubtedly of major importance because areas which may be hazardous may also offer residents some comparative economic advantage and this is true regardless of whether or not the hazard is natural or man-made. For example, living nearby a river that periodically floods may ensure fertile land for agriculture, may provide access to a transportation route, may provide a dependable water supply, may provide a sewerage system and so on. Similarly, living near to a chemical plant may provide a person with a convenient workplace, reduced transportation costs, etc. In addition to these considerations, society may perpetuate the status quo by establishing institutional regimes that often compensate survivors of disasters only if they return to the same locale to repair or rebuild property (Burton, Kates and White, 1978).

Should a disaster occur then its impact on individuals appears to be more a function of the magnitude of the social disruption to a community than to either the magnitude of the physical disruption or the prior level of perceived risk. The extent of social disruption also relates to the cohesiveness of the community and the degree of societal support on which the affected community can rely. At this level, Barton (1970) has introduced an interesting concept of the 'therapeutic community' which describes the observation that many communities that have suffered a disaster appear to help themselves to heal their wounds by reinforcing activities to rebuild both their physical and social fabric. In addition to this phenomenon, Kreps (1984) points out that in a country like the USA 'communities ... recover rapidly from disasters because:

— they improvise after the disaster has struck,
— they rely on formal and informal disaster assistance,
— disaster impacts, large though they are sometimes, pale in comparison to remaining societal resources.'

Furthermore, to appreciate the full extent of social disruption it is clear that consideration has to extend far beyond the timescale of short-term recovery to include some measure of longer-term impact. Again as Kreps (1984) emphasizes 'disasters must be interpreted not only in terms of immediate damage and disruption but also of the degree to which they change already existing trends'.

MAJOR HAZARDS AND EMERGENCY DECISION-MAKING

'... there is solid experimental evidence that people avoid thinking about events whose probability is below some threshold ... This does not mean that people deny or do not fear the threat of disaster. Rather it suggests that they are necessarily preoccupied with the immediate problems and concerns of daily living.' (Kreps, 1984.)

Thus far, research into factors influencing the perception of major hazards and into their psychosocial impact has briefly been reviewed. While this work is clearly of relevance to those involved in emergency planning, it is only one facet of the many considerations that must be taken into account when formulating emergency plans to safeguard a community, for this activity often rests on a different set of assumptions from those of researchers. To illustrate this, let us briefly consider the implications of the most recent statutory requirements placed on local authority Emergency Planning departments in the U.K. Under the 1984 Control of Industrial Major Accident Hazards Regulations (C.I.M.A.H.), local authorities responsible for emergency planning are notified by the Health and Safety Executive (H.S.E.) of the location of hazardous installations for which they are required to prepare adequate off-site emergency plans for a possible major accident by January 1986 and then to keep these updated (Turner, 1985). These hazardous installations are identified by the H.S.E. according to set criteria such as the quantities of particular chemical substances stored at that site. What this means for those producing these emergency plans is that they must assume that, once notified that an installation is a potential hazard, it may only be a question of time before a major emergency occurs. In other words, measures of perceived risk among local inhabitants, emergency planning personnel, local politicians, or even company officials play no part in determining planning priorities. The fact that local authorities are empowered only to prepare off-site emergency plans means that they must direct their attention to preparing the community response rather than preventing the incident. Finally, the fact that plans must be prepared on relatively short timescales and that these must be regularly updated means that the planners tend to adopt what Simon (1976) has termed a strategy of satisficing, whereby courses of action are sought that are 'good enough' and that meet some minimal set of requirements.

In this context, the traditional concept of risk as being some function of the probability of occurrence of an event and the magnitude of its consequences is of only limited utility. A more useful concept is that of vulnerability which is operationally defined as 'the Total Vulnerability (V) of an area is ... a function of the reciprocal multiplicative relationship between Risk (R) and Preparedness (P)' (Gabor and Pelanda, 1983). The resulting equation is simply written as:

$$V = R(1/P) = (R/P).$$

Hence, it follows that a community is most vulnerable when risk is high and preparedness is low and least vulnerable when risk is low and preparedness is high. Given that emergency planners in local authorities can do nothing to alter the actual risk level, they can at least reduce the vulnerability of a community by increasing its preparedness in a variety of ways. The concept of preparedness at the community level is itself multidimensional, being a function of many factors including:

— the available knowledge-base (expert information on how to cope with the hazard),
— prevailing community beliefs (lay 'knowledge'),
— the degree of actual or perceived control over both the event or subsequent actions, e.g. evacuation,
— the predominant decision-strategy adopted in the event of a crisis,
— the sophistication of the emergency plan given the resources available in the community. Effort to improve any or all of these factors raises preparedness and consequently reduces vulnerability.

Given that it is possible to prepare a community beforehand for a major hazard by issuing warnings, providing education on protective measures, advising on strategies such as evacuation, and so forth, how one chooses the most appropriate course of action has received considerable attention. Several theories of decision-making under conditions of uncertainty have been developed (for an overview of these, see Wright, 1984) but of these, Conflict Theory seems at present to most adequately describe decision-making in emergency situations (Janis and Mann, 1977). This theory assumes that whenever we have to make important decisions between alternatives, each of which carries unpleasant consequences, then intense conflicts are likely to arise from our simultaneous desire to both accept and reject unwanted courses of action. The resulting decisional conflicts become increasingly acute the more we become aware of the risks of suffering serious losses from the possible alternative courses of action. The subjective impact of these decisional conflicts is acute emotional stress which may manifest itself as hesitancy, vacillation, feelings of uncertainty and inability to take rational decisions. In an attempt to cope with these decisional conflicts it is suggested that at any one time people typically display one of the five patterns of behaviour. These patterns of behaviour are as follows:

— *Unconflicted inertia*—a person continues with routine activities in the belief that in the event of an incident he/she will suffer no serious consequences.

— *Unconflicted change*—a person accepts the threat as real and takes the greatest available protective measures which may even mean evacuation.
— *Defensive avoidance*—a person becomes selectively inattentive to threat cues, avoids thinking about imminent danger, and absolves responsibility for decisions. Three typical patterns have been described, these being procrastination—postponement of decisions, buck-passing—placing the responsibility for a decision with someone else, and bolstering—minimizing the unfavourable consequences of a decision while exaggerating the favourable consequences.
— *Hypervigilance*—a person becomes agitated, emotionally excited and shows greater vigilance than normal in the belief that danger is imminent. Extreme hypervigilance shows itself as panic.
— *Vigilance*—a person carefully appraises alternative courses of action in the belief that there is adequate time to choose the optimal response to threat. In a pre-emergency situation this is the most common behaviour pattern.

Janis and Mann apply their theory to decision-making in an emergency situation and emphasize the important role of antecedent conditions which primarily involve communicating information to the individual, although they recognize that personality and social factors are also important antecedents to decision-making as well.

Empirical research has provided some support for Janis and Mann's theory. Perry, Lindell and Greene (1982) studied residents' perceptions of the risks associated with the volcanic activity of Mount St Helens which erupted in 1980. They interviewed residents of eight towns at varying distances from the volcano but all within the areas likely to suffer the impact of an eruption. After the first week of volcanic activity almost 50 per cent of residents thought that the likelihood of serious threat to themselves and their families or their property was 'even/odds' or greater. This view did not vary significantly as a function of distance from the volcano as might have been generally expected. Among these residents, the level of unconflicted inertia was low and most people behaved in a vigilant manner rather than a hypervigilant manner, and they carefully monitored information on volcanic activity. Some 55 per cent of residents sought volcanic hazard information four or more times per day, 35 per cent sought this two or three times per day, and only 10 per cent heard such information as little as once per day. Given the uncertainty about the consequences of alternative courses of action, Conflict Theory predicts that vigilance rather than unconflicted change (including evacuation) should have predominated and clearly it did. Similarly, in a survey of public action to hazard warnings in the urban environment, Hedge (1985) has also found that people report that they would behave in a vigilant manner requesting further information about hazards rather than adopting other patterns such as a defensive avoidance posture to minimize perceived risk if they lived in the close vicinity of a potential major hazard. However, in a study of information-seeking about environmental cancer, Weinstein (1979) found that people tended to select messages consistent with their own viewpoint about whether or not a hazard exists, and also that information-seeking about a familiar issue was dependent on their assessment of risk whereas information-seeking about an unfamiliar topic depended on their interest in it. Conflict Theory does not adequately account for these results. Whether this is because of the nature of the particular hazard being investigated or whether it highlights general inadequacies in Conflict Theory remains to be elucidated.

CONCLUSION

'In the face of uncertainty, man may be an intellectual cripple, whose intuitive judgements and decisions violate many of the fundamental principles of optimal behaviour. These intellectual deficiencies underscore the need for decision-aiding techniques.' (Slovic, 1984, cited in Wright, 1984.)

From the selection of empirical studies of behavioural responses to major hazards that has briefly been reviewed what appears to be a fairly consistent observation is that a person's perception of the associated risk beforehand is not a straightforward estimate of the probability of occurrence of the event alone and that the person's actual behaviour likewise is only loosely connected with any probabilistic risk judgement.

While there is quite good evidence to suggest that, at an individual level, the perception of imminent danger may change a person's predisaster behaviour, in the context of major hazards the risk from that event must be a function of the impact which it could have on the physical, psychological and social resources available. To describe the risk associated with any particular major hazard solely in terms of measures of physical impact such as statistics on estimated deaths, injuries and property damage or losses, is usually a relatively straightforward exercise but the resulting picture is incomplete because consideration of the psychological and social impact is absent. Measures of psychological and social impact are not well developed but in the context of major hazards they are probably the most crucial measures because they directly assess the problems that may be experienced by survivors over time. To emphasize this point, we have already seen how, in the case of Cyclone Tracy, the mobilization of societal resources to help alleviate the physical impact of the disaster actually exacerbated the social disruption being suffered by certain groups of survivors. Consequently, in the absence of techniques for estimating psycho-social disruption our ability to select appropriate strategies for action must inevitably be constrained. But by themselves, better measures of the impact of major hazards will not necessarily guarantee either better planning or a better response in the event of an actual incident. There is therefore a clear need also to further refine models of decision-making which encapsulate both the human judgemental processes and the situational factors influencing these in an emergency, and to develop improved aids to such decision-making thereby enabling better planning prior to a disaster. Only in this way can we ensure that a vigilant community can properly prepare itself for a variety of potential disasters, thereby reducing its overall vulnerability and safeguarding the lives and livelihood of inhabitants.

REFERENCES

Adams, P. R. and Adams, G. R. (1984). Mount Saint Helens's ashfall: evidence for a disaster stress reaction, *Amer. Psych.* **39**(3), 252–260.

Barton, A. H. (1970). *Communities in Disaster*. Garden City, N.Y.: Anchor, Doubleday.

Baum, A., Fleming, R. and Singer, J. E. (1982). 'Stress at Three Mile Island: applying psychological impact analysis', *Ann. App. Soc. Psych.* **3**, 217–248.

Baum, A., Gatchel, R. J. and Schaeffer, M. A. (1983). 'Emotional, behavioural and psychological effects of chronic stress at Three Mile Island', *J. Consul. Clin. Psych.* **51**, 565–572.

Bell, P. A., Fisher, J. D. and Loomis, R. J. (1978). *Environmental Psychology*. London: W. B. Saunders Co.

Burton, I. (1972). 'Cultural and personality variables in the perception of natural hazards', *in* Wohlwill, J. F. and Carson, D. H. (Eds), *Environment and the Social Sciences: Perspectives and Applications*, pp. 184–195. Washington, D.C.: Amer. Psych. Assoc.

Burton, I., Kates, R. W. and White, G. F. (1978). *The Environment as Hazard*. New York: Oxford University Press.

Cvetkovitch, G. and Earle, T. C. (1985). 'Classifying hazardous events', *J. Env. Psych.* **5**, 5–35.

Dworkin, J. (1973). 'Global trends in natural disasters 1947–1973', *Natural Hazards Research Working Paper 26*. Toronto: University of Toronto.

Evans, G. W., Jacobs, S. V. and Frager, N. B. (1982). 'Adaptation to air pollution, *J. Env. Psych.* **2**, 99–108.

Fischhoff, B., Slovic, P. and Lichtenstein, S. (1983). 'The Public' *vs.* 'The Experts': Perceived *vs.* Actual disagreements about risks of nuclear power, *in* Covello, V. T., Flamm, W. G., Rodricks, J. V. and Tradiff, R. B. (Eds), *The Analysis of Actual versus Perceived Risks*, pp. 235–249. London: Plenum Press.

Fleming, I. and Baum, A. (1984). 'Chronic stress and toxic waste: the role of uncertainty and helplessness', Paper presented at 91st Congress, Amer. Psych. Assoc., 24–28th August, Toronto, Canada.

Gabor, T. and Pelanda, C. (1983). Assessing differences in chemical disaster proneness: the community chemical hazard vulnerability inventory', *Emerg. Plan. Digest*, July–September, 9–16.

Gleser, G. C., Green, B. L. and Winget, C. (1981). *Prolonged Psychosocial Effects of Disaster: A Study of Buffalo Creek*. New York: Academic Press.

Hedge, A. (1985). 'A Questionnaire Survey of Public Reactions to Hazard Warnings', Unpublished Research Report, Applied Psychology Department. Birmingham, U.K.: Aston University.

Houts, P. S., Hu, T. W., Henderson, R. A., Cleary, P. D. and Tokuhata, G. (1984). 'Utilization of medical care following the Three Mile Island crisis', *Amer. J. Pub. Health*, **74**(2), 140–142.

Janis, I. L. and Mann, L. (1977). *Decision Making: A Psychological Analysis of Conflict, Choice, and Commitment*. New York: The Free Press.

Kreps, G. A. (1984). 'Sociological inquiry and disaster research', *Ann. Rev. Sociol.* **10**, 309–330.

Lewis, D. J. (1985). 'Case Histories of past major accidents', *in Lessening the effects of Major Accident Hazards*. Proc. Assoc. Civ. Def. Emerg. Plan. Officers/Soc. Ind. Emerg. Serv. Officers (W. Mid. Branches) Joint Conf., pp. 5–20, 19 March Birmingham, U.K.: Aston University.

Litea, D., Lanning, D. D. and Rasmussen, N. C. (1983). 'The public perception of risk', *in* Covello, V. T., Flamm, W. G., Rodricks, J. V. and Tradiff, R. B. (Eds), *The Analysis of Actual versus Perceived Risks*, pp. 213–224. London: Plenum Press.

Milne, G. (1977a). 'Cyclone Tracy: I. Some consequences for the evacuation of adult victims', *Aus. Psych.* **12**(1), 39–54.

Milne, G. (1977b). 'Cyclone Tracy: II. The effects on Darwin children', *Aus. Psych.* **12**(1), 55–62.

Perry, R. W., Lindell, M. K. and Greene, M. R. (1980). *The Implications of Natural Hazard Evacuation Warning for Crisis Relocation Planning*. Seattle, Washington: Battelle Human Affairs Res. Center.

Perry, R. W., Lindell, M. K. and Greene, M. R. (1982). 'Threat perception and public response to volcano hazard', *J. Soc. Psych.* **116**, 199–204.

Quarantelli, E. L. (1978). *Disasters: Theory and Research*. London: Sage.

Rossi, P. H., Wright, J. D., Weber-Burdin, E. (1982). *Natural Hazards and Public Choice: The State and Local Politics of Hazards Mitigation*. New York: Academic Press.

Rowe, W. D. (1977). *An Anatomy of Risk*. New York: Wiley.

Simon, H. A. (1976). *Administrative Behaviour: A Study of Decision-making Processes in Administrative Organization*. 3rd. Ed. New York: Free Press.

Taylor, V. A., Ross, G. A. and Quarantelli, E. L. (1976). 'Delivery of mental health services in disasters: the Xenia tornado and some implications', *Disas. Res. Cen. Mono. Ser.*, **11**, Columbus: Ohio State University.

Turner, M. J. (1985). 'Control of major accident hazards regulations 1984 (CIMAH)' *in Lessening the effects of Major Accident Hazards*. Proc. Assoc. Civ. Def. Emerg. Plan. Officers/Soc. Ind. Emerg. Serv. Officers (W. Mid. Branches) Joint Conf., pp. 21–32, 19 March. Birmingham, U.K.: Aston University.

Vlek, C. and Stallen, P. J. (1980). 'Rational and personal aspects of risk', *Acta Psych.* **45**, 273–300.

Vlek, C. and Stallen, P. J. (1981). 'Judging risks and benefits in the small and in the large', *Org. Behav. and Human Perform.* **28**, 235–271.

Weinstein, N. D. (1979). 'Seeking reassuring or threatening information about environmental cancer', *J. Behav. Med.* **2**, 125–139.

Wright, G. (1984). *Behavioural Decision Theory: An Introduction*. Harmondsworth: Penguin Books.

Whittow, J (1980). *Disasters: The Anatomy of Environmental Hazards*. London: Penguin Books.

Discussion: Risk and Behaviour

Hale agrees with Brehmer that subjective and objective probabilities are usually both estimates, in the former case by observation, in the latter by experts. Risk estimation by an observer includes many factors:

— who the victims are,
— whether the situation can be assumed to be under control,
— whether or not the potential victim enters the situation voluntarily,
— the time-scale in which harm may occur,
— uncertainty about future states of the system,
— the plausibility of relevant combinations of circumstances,
— the vividness of imagined consequences.

It seems that, in decision-making, the negative aspects of risk decisions are not separated from the benefits except when the negative aspects are suffered by people other than those who gain the benefits. To simplify decisions, individuals will work within boundaries of possibilities from which other possibilities have been excluded as intolerable. Risk after an event is perceived very differently from what are objectively the same risks before the event. Although risk is clearly a multidimensional concept, probability does not represent any one of the dimensions. From this behavioural viewpoint the frequency measure of risk seems to be an inappropriate level of abstraction.

Glendon separates the concept of risk into three categories:

— the physical sciences view which depends on concepts such as probabilities, cost/benefit ratios and risk analysis,
— the behavioural sciences view which depends on factors involved in perception and cognition,
— the culture which involves sociology, politics and power.

Putting it another way, we can think of risk as a one-dimensional concept, add a second dimension to incorporate the context and add a third dimension to incorporate the culture. Behaviourally, he develops the interesting concept of the individual moving from one risk environment to another and having to change his cognitive dimensions/structure as he makes such a transition. Danger will be greater if the individual's cognitive structure is not appropriate for the particular environment, and in the developmental phase the individual is at risk while he is creating his new matching cognitive structure. He distinguishes between the individual functioning in an environment where the decisions and risks are his own and are indeed idiosyncratic, and the power situation where policy-makers make decisions which involve risks for others. In the latter case risk as a concept is even less likely to be used than in the former case.

Rasmussen examines risk in the context of high technology industries where centralization and rapid design changes have resulted in increasing the consequences of errors without a corresponding increase in the experiential evidence needed to provide adequate control. Untoward events with serious consequences are less predictable and controllable. Attempts have been made to fill this gap by increasing use of risk analysis. Again, however, lack of experience led to a disappointing contribution because of lack of customer acceptance of the results. Lack of success was due partly to inability to separate risks from other value judgements in reaching opinions and decisions, and partly to the assumptions and values within the risk analyses not being clearly spelled out. A controller in one of these systems has less routine work but a greater influence in rare situations demanding elaborate diagnosis where the concept of an error becomes even less definitive. The skills of the controller involve an elaborate process of attempting a match between top-down reasoning and bottom-up symptoms. Within this process an error is no more than an 'unsuccessful experiment in an unfriendly environment'. There is a dilemma in that to enjoy his job and increase his skill the controller must explore the limits of control, but in doing so he is increasing the risk that he will go outside these limits. Looking at the team performance, the performer, monitor and adviser roles are shifting radically. One reasonable objective is more error-tolerant systems not only in technology but also in management. Error-tolerant management systems depend on a knowledge of values and intentions which are important not only to 'quality of working life' but also to effectiveness and reliability. These more social issues were taken up in the next chapter.

Marek and his colleagues distinguish between the control of specific risk sources and the more general effects of organizational and social aspects of work. For both it emerges that in the opinion of the operators effects are selective, some risks are better countered than others. In this particular study job management, reward systems and housekeeping were regarded as more important to safety than job variation, job pressure, overall job satisfaction and social relations. Emergency training and equipment and escape possibilities were consistently regarded as contributors to control of risk. Specific safety measures were oriented towards control of major hazards and protection of the installation.

Hedge takes up the problem of risk to the community which underlies much of the anxiety and interest in decisions to do with high technology. In this context, the judgement of risk incorporates a new factor, the preparedness or degree of organization to cope with the disaster after it has happened. It is important to recognize that the management of risk is not confined to prediction and prevention, it extends also to mitigation and to the organization of recovery. Such manifest precautions may increase or decrease as individual's perception of risk, although they decrease vulnerability. It emerges that there are large individual differences, not only in perceptions but also in reactions. There can be long-term social and psychological reactions which are not directly related to the degree of risk or even of physical damage. It seems that social disruption of a community has a greater impact than physical damage, and that an individual's recognition that he can or has coped has its own therapeutic value. Detailed consideration of behaviour, both in the laboratory and in real situations, confirms that the probability-based models are not adequate to explain what happens. The recondite question of the logical soundness of the model is superseded by the pragmatic question of whether or not the real world behaves according to the model. Rationality is not confined to the absolute standard of deductive logic, at the other extreme is the diffuse influence of the total social–cultural context. Somewhere between is the concept of satisficing, the situation is coped with as seems most appropriate given the resources available and the conflicting demands of other problems. Probabilities have some limited usefulness as a parameter of abstract problems and as a communication vehicle. That is, they may be used by managers dealing with large problems, by experts providing advice, or, just possibly, by individuals in unitary situations involving risks to oneself and others.

Consider, for example, a climber whose companions are injured in a fall. Does he try to conduct a rescue himself or does he go for help? Going for help may reduce the risk for himself but increase the short-term risk for the casualties. In a particular real case, there was an experienced climber whose two companions were seriously injured, his decision was complicated by guilt feelings—he was the leader and he felt that he should not have allowed the accident to happen. He decided that he could not leave his companions because they would freeze to death, but equally he could not possibly get them both back to safety. Thus he compromised, by superhuman effort he moved the casualties to a more sheltered region and then went for help. Having reached safety, his first feeling was relief that he personally would survive, immediately followed by further guilt that this reaction had given his own position precedence over that of his companions. The rescue party returned up the mountain, in darkness, and retrieved the two injured climbers (sadly they both died). This anecdotal evidence illustrates several points:

— a decision-maker begins by excluding certain options as not feasible because the probability of success is negligible,
— without assessing the probabilities very precisely a decision-maker will often take action to polarize the risks by changing the situation, thus making his basic decision easier,
— risky situations are often made even more complex by rational or irrational guilt feelings in participants,
— given an objective such as a rescue, skilled individuals will readily accept tremendous hazards, e.g., climbing in darkness in winter, presumably on

two grounds—the clear potential benefits, and their confidence in their own high levels of skill.

More generally, it seems that when faced with a risky situation an individual does not begin by quantifying risks, rather he tries to reduce them and also reduce the number of possibilities. Options are eliminated because the probability of success is negligible. This reduces the number of possibilities, perhaps in several stages so that decision emerges as the output of a smooth process rather than a grand selection between a range of alternatives each with a different attached risk.

It might even be more appropriate to consider risk as a relevant postdecision characteristic rather than a predecision one. Certainly new risks emerge as a consequence of decisions and in high technology they are often risks to others rather than to the decision-makers. The risky situation is invariably changed rather than eliminated. In safety engineering it is recognized that any attempt to remove a hazard by design results in the creation of new hazards which are not always foreseen. Hopefully, the new hazards are not as serious as the old ones.

This re-emphasizes the point that each individual should, as far as possible, have the freedom to choose his own pattern of risks. Human operators are not automatic devices, they seek variety of activity and risk patterns accompany variety. Even within an occupational situation it is desirable to leave some flexibility with the operator. Inevitably there are risks for the system and if not for the operator then for others. Flexibility in good design requires that errors should be recoverable although they are not always reversible.

If risks are evenly balanced there is a case for random choice although people are not good intuitive randomizers. In most such situations where there is no possibility of acquiring further evidence any decision is better than no decision, and people invent mystical strategies which result in a choice. For example, it has been reported that, for a primitive tribe of hunters, a decision about which direction in the forest to initiate each hunt was made by the medicine man. He heated the shoulder blade from an animal and observed where cracks appeared as it cooled—this indicated the direction to follow. As the anthropologist pointed out, this is an excellent randomizing device which, in the long run, would provide an adaptive balanced sequence of hunts.

The expert, immersed in his technology with estimates of costs and benefits, inevitably finds it difficult to communicate with the public who approach risky situations with holistic, intuitive, prejudiced, even mystical attitudes. It is not surprising that the expert despairs of the layman as irrational and it is easy for the layman to suspect that the expert is either a fool or a knave.

Section C

Risk and Public Policy

Risk and Decisions
Edited by W. T. Singleton and J. Hovden
© 1987 John Wiley & Sons Ltd.

Chapter 10

Risk: National Policy-making

JAN HOVDEN

SINTEF, Division of Safety and Reliability, Trondheim, Norway

INTRODUCTION

How our society generates and copes with risk is reflected in the national policy-making. An outline of the macroperspectives of risk is obtained for example by looking at the rising tide of public concern (Raiffa, 1982):

— popular/populistic movements,
— media publicity,
— risk as an issue in political debates,
— legislative and agency activities,
— the growth of safety institutions.

National policy-making moulds together science, facts and value judgements in risk-handling or risk-management involving risk-identification, estimation, assessment, monitoring, evaluation, the use of reactive and preventive safety measures, and control of risks. A great number of institutions, professions and disciplines are involved in this activity—the term 'risk' and the conceptual models of risk are used differently among them, which leads us directly to the main concern of this book, e.g., problems of communication and a lack of trust in one another among politicians, the public and different groups of experts.

Whether safety is viewed from an individual or a social and political perspective, the external conditions and the factual account of risks is only one of the main input factors for policy-making. Handling risks is also based on values, conceptions and beliefs (see chapter 4 'Risk: Culture and Concepts'). Knowledge of these subjective aspects of safety helps us in

161

understanding public policy and decision-making processes encompassing safety issues. Without such a broad frame of what risk-handling really means, it is difficult or even impossible to identify and attain effective implementation of remedial actions and other safety initiatives. Effective safety efforts are dependent on the framework of the social, economic and political reality around us (NTNF Risk Research Committee, 1983, 1985). This viewpoint leads to the conclusion that the dominant role of one profession, e.g., the engineers, as experts in safety work, may be dangerous for safety.

THE MEANING OF POLITICS

There is high consensus in the field of political science on the meaning of 'politics'. There is more to politics than simply party politics, politics embraces all issues and societal processes concerning the means and ends in relation to which society disburses benefits and burdens among its people. The results of the political processes are usually explained in terms of power, resources, or some related term.

In our eagerness to create goods and benefits and to distribute them, we have not become aware, until recently, of the negative side effects following in the wake of these benefits. It is easy to forget the negative side of the 'game' (Rowe, 1979). Burdens must be distributed as well as benefits. Accident risks and injuries to persons are one of these. It is the responsibility of national policy-making to determine the size and distribution of this burden and weigh it against the advantages accruing from hazardous activities (Hovden, 1980).

National policy-making which strikes a balance between advantages and disadvantages accruing from technological developments has evolved into an important activity. This is particularly true of technological developments introducing new and unknown risks and/or having a considerable potential for harm, but in respect of which the estimates of the probability of an accident occurring is small. Such decision-making processes can hardly be explained through the 'simple' logical and rational decision models of economics and utility theory. It is necessary to turn to decision models based on behavioural sciences, for example replace the 'economic man' with the 'administrative man' (Simon, 1965), using decision models like Lindblom's 'muddling through' and Olsen's 'garbage can' (March and Olsen, 1976). These decision models allow for political, and apparently irrational, elements which correspond to real policy processes dealing with safety matters (Hovden et al., 1979; Hovden et al., 1985a).

Human beings and decision-making bodies do not function irrationally, but their rationality is confined to a somewhat random problem-oriented seeking centred on crises, accidents and disasters. Instead of aiming for the 'best solution', we look for satisficing solutions which we make sure do not fall below certain tolerable limits.

The characteristic features of official decisions are the following (Hovden, 1980; 1982):

— problems that are given attention are restricted to a policy framework which is closely akin to the existing one,
— instead of matching available means to the goals it is desired to achieve, goals are chosen which match available means,
— problems are rarely solved once and for all, but have to be tackled over and over again,
— decisions tend to be a flight from diverse evils rather than an attempt to attain specific goals,
— of all the possible consequences of any given decision, only a few can really be assessed.

It may be assumed that something of the same sort applies to risk decisions. Such a way of working in safety policy-making does not conform with the ideals of rational decisions but, even so, it is capable of producing solutions for adequate risk-handling.

VALUE CONFLICTS AND PARTIES

In matters relating to accident risks, executives in government, authorities and other organizations, are faced with complex and in many cases confused decision situations. They often have to deal with seemingly insoluble assessments of hazards and benefits, balancing incommensurable values and different parties.

An unacceptable risk to one person may represent positive prospects for another. A particular consequence may be assessed very differently, depending on who is making the evaluation. The perspective on the consequences also varies, depending on whether we are discussing individual risk, group risk or population risk. Classifications of parties or interest groups use the individual's relationship to the benefits of the activity as the main criteria:

— First party—manufacturers, workers,
— Second party—consumers,
— Third party—outsiders—the public, society as a whole,

or the individual's relationship to the risk source, e.g., risk exposure by him/herself or by others:

— voluntary, self-controlled, mostly dependent on the individual's coping with the risk,
— involuntary, imposed, the individual as victim.

The various parties will raise different questions and have different judgements of risk level and consequences. Acceptability is not something a risk has, but something it gets through decision-making by individuals, organizations and society.

Safety is only one of several objectives for national policy-making. As an aim for political engagement, safety may be in conflict with other aims and basic values: individual freedom of choice, profit as the legitimate ultimate objective for industry and business, and the development of new large scale industrial projects as a means of solving the crisis of unemployment. The individual's need for physical and psychological challenges, the experience of excitement and performance may result in unsafe acts, risk taking—and happiness. This dilemma reveals fundamental philosophical, ethical and political questions on the functions and roles of a modern welfare state in protecting people against risks.

Consider, as an example, the Scandinavian risk debate: in all risk sectors of society, Sweden has significantly smaller figures on fatal accidents than the other Nordic countries. This triggered the discussions of the last Nordic Accident Research Seminar, August 1985 (see Hovden *et al.* 1985b). Is the price we have to pay for increased safety; more rules, supervision, control, discipline and boredom ('the Swedish model'), or can we find an alternative national policy for risk-handling?

The choice of economic criteria and principles for evaluating effects of risk-handling by society is another controversy in policy-making. The task of establishing acceptable safety levels is closely related to the question of how the desired reductions in risks can be achieved. Reducing risk usually means spending money. This is generally based on one or two more or less fundamentally different means of utilizing the resources at our disposal; means which have to be combined one way or the other (see J. M. Døderlein's 'Introduction').

One of these means rests on the principle that we should even out the risk between individual members of society, i.e., adopt the philosophy of risk equity. Application of this principle would, in many cases, result in poor utilization of resources in the sense that there would be little reduction in risk for the money and effort invested.

Another principle is that we should bring our resources to bear at the point of the highest return measured in terms of risk reduction for the whole population, i.e., where we are assured of achieving the greatest total reduction in risk for our investment. But then we have to forget about some small high-risk groups and individuals. Mass media's focus on accident risks promotes the principle of equity, whereas the national accident statistics promote the cost-effectiveness means as a basis for national policy-making. The mixture of these means is a question of values.

Perhaps the greatest paradox in national policy-making on safety is that accidents and disasters contribute to growth in G.N.P. Is something wrong with the traditional concept of 'growth' in economics? For a discussion, see

Mesarovic and Peste (1974).

Decisions and policy-making may be difficult for a number of reasons: for example, because the considerations on different sides are very evenly balanced; because the facts are uncertain; because the probability of different outcomes of the possible courses of action is unknown. A problem which is often forgotten in decision analysis is that the timing of decisions and actions can be more important than the alternative chosen.

There can also be cases where, even if we are fairly sure about the outcome of alternative courses of action, or about their probability distribution, and even though we know how to distinguish the pros and cons, we are nevertheless unable to bring them together in a single evaluative judgement. According to Nagel (1979), the strongest cases of conflict are genuine dilemmas, where there is decisive support for two or more incompatible courses of action or inaction. In that case a decision will still be necessary, but it will seem arbitrary.

MEANS AND INSTITUTIONS FOR A POLICY OF RISK-HANDLING BY SOCIETY

As in all areas of community life, the authorities possess several sets of means which may be put into action in the effort to reduce accident risk:

— legislation,
— roles, competence and resources of the inspection authorities,
— allocations for training, education and research,
— information and campaigns to shape certain attitudes and behaviour,
— allocations for the safety efforts of voluntary organizations for special safety measures,
— subsidy schemes for industry and for emergency preparedness measures.

All societies have some sort of institution for the preservation of safety (using the sociological meaning of 'institution'). This institution functions partly on the basis of custom, partly by legislation and regulations, and partly through organized parties and voluntary organizations established to promote special interests. There is also a system of public inspectorates, directorates and a large number of governmental and public agencies with some partial responsibility for safety.

How this system functions as a whole is more uncertain. In Norway, for example, nobody performs the overall coordination and prioritization of safety activities between the various sectors of society and the agencies involved. Responsibility and authority are distributed in a way that may cause confusion and hamper both safety efforts made within different sectors and coordinated safety efforts (NTNF Risk Research Committee, 1983; 1985).

Legislation provides a documentation of society's commitment to and system for preservation of safety. Legislation is one of society's primary means of handling accident risk. The prevailing philosophy of safety may be derived from legislative texts and the preparatory work for them.

Legislation and technological development do not always keep pace with one another. In some cases, the legislation sets goals for the enterprise requiring technology that will take a long time to develop, e.g., in the sector of environmental legislation. On the other hand, many Acts, regulations and provisions are formulated in such a way that they are already outdated before they are adopted and brought into force. More and more Norwegian Legislation tries to solve this problem by making requirements concerning the objective rather than by requiring specific details for solving safety problems.

A number of new Acts and regulations in Norway allow for the use of predictive methods such as risk analysis and consequence analysis in order to determine whether society's safety criteria have been satisfied. This is often combined with a change in the role of safety authorities. Instead of traditional inspections and controls they delegate the task to the industry when the industry can demonstrate that they have acceptable qualifications and organizational resources for internal control. This new safety policy of control in Norway is rather different from the main trends in safety policies of the Common Market countries of Europe.

THE ROLES OF MASS MEDIA

Risks in society are perceived and experienced. This determines attitudes and yields information which is channelled back to society's decision-making bodies. Media, therefore, constitute an important part of the base on which decisions are made at any given time. What information gets through, what is filtered out as uninteresting or irrelevant and what is either not grasped or not passed on, are of vital importance in formulating acceptance criteria and in allocating funds in this field.

The hunger of the mass media for 'news', for what is unique, out of the ordinary and even bizarre may well give the receiver a distorted impression of the true accident risk picture. The impact on politicians and policy-making is perhaps even greater than on the general opinion:

— politicians have to be sensitive to opinions if they want to be re-elected,
— disasters and major hazards also represent a political risk where they can be blamed for responsibility. On the other hand, the great numbers of single-casualty accidents in traffic, homes, etc., are seldom a political risk.

By describing the newspaper coverage of the 'Alexander L. Kielland' accident Hovden and Vinje (1983) in the report *Disaster Journalism* aimed to make a contribution to the debate on the function of the press in the dissemination of information and knowledge in connection with catastrophic events. On March 27, 1980, at 06.30 p.m., the 'Alexander L. Kielland' platform capsized in heavy seas in the Ekofisk oil field. The most disastrous accident in the North Sea to date and one of the most disastrous in recent Norwegian history was a fact. After a couple of days of confusion as to the extent of the damage, the mass media established that there were 123 dead and 89 survivors.

In the study of Hovden and Vinje (1983), all Norwegian newspaper articles on the 'Alexander L. Kielland' disaster published between March 28 and April 15, 1980, were subjected to a systematic content analysis (2,459 articles). Briefly, the method consists of counting how many times particular issues, opinions and items of information concerning the 'Alexander L. Kielland' accident appeared in the newspaper articles. Some of the main trends of this content analysis are shown in Table 10.1.

When the drilling rig 'Ocean Ranger' capsized with 84 people off the Coast of Newfoundland in 1982, we got the opportunity to compare the media coverage of two very similar disasters, e.g., empirical evidence for the effects of geographical and cultural distance of a disaster on the amount and content of media coverage (Hovden and Vinje, 1983). The 'Ocean Ranger' accident was given only 1/10 of the attention accorded to the 'Alexander L. Kielland' disaster (attention measured as number of articles) in Norwegian newspapers. No Norwegian reporter was sent to Newfoundland.

Most of the coverage of the 'Ocean Ranger' accident in the Norwegian newspapers was about its relevance to Norwegian oil actitivies and society policy and not the event itself. In contrast to the coverage of the 'Alexander L. Kielland' accident, little attention was given to the 'Ocean Ranger' victims and their relatives.

THE ROLES OF RISK ANALYSIS AND EXPERTS

Formal risk analysis as a tool for policy-making has been considered as the solution to uncertain irrational decision-making about accident risks by many politicians, managers, society executives and engineers. Risk-analysis became 'big business' in many industries faced by major hazards, but the use of results from these analyses and other formal methods in decision-making processes has been disappointing to the enthusiasts.

This has resulted in some thinking about the practical use of risk analysis in policy-making and risk-handling. There is, for example, concern about the false precision that comes with the use of numbers like probabilities, and what to do about them. On the other hand, we get a false sense of imprecision when using qualitative reporting with terms like seldom, not unthinkable, not so often and sometimes.

Only rarely do scientific facts speak for themselves. They have to be synthesized and made comprehensible for use in the policy-making process. Raiffa (1982) summarizes the criteria for good reporting as follows:

Table 10.1. Some trends of the content in the articles on the Alexander L. Kielland disaster March 27th 1980.

	3.28–3.29 Period of discovery	3.31–4.5 Period of clarification	4.8–4.15 Period of reflection
1. *Amount of space:*			
Number of articles	+	O	−
Article length	−	O	+
Size of headlines	+	O	−
Size of picture	+	O	−
2. *Subject:*			
Account of the accident	+	O	−
Cause/blame	−	O	+
Individual's situation after the accident	O	+	−
Assessment of consequences	−	O	+
Assessment of other media forms coverage of accident	+	O	−
Personification phase	O	+	−
Politicization phase	−	O	+
3. *Some central assessments:*			
Risk level unacceptable	−	O	+
Risk level acceptable	+	O	−
Re-evaluation of the oil activity	−	O	+
Oil activity should continue as before, as planned	O	+	−
The probability of the accident:			
Shocking, inconceivable, incomprehensible	+	O	−
Not inconceivable	−	O	+

The symbol + means a lot, large, central, etc. More than average for all three periods.
The symbol O means in between, close to the average for all three periods.
The symbol − means little, not central, etc. Less than the average.
The symbols show increasing or decreasing trends for:
1. The amount of space.
2. The attention accorded the different subject-categories.
3. The frequency of some assessments.

'— inclusive—should synthesize relevant information (theory, experimental data, epidemiological data, etc.),
— free from values, the report should not prejudge policy conclusions: values appropriate to policy evaluation should not influence assessments of uncertainties,
— comprehensive and meaningful to clients—informative and relevant,
— useful in the decision process—use of proxy variables

— honesty and prudence',

and the roles of risk analysis summarized as follows (Raiffa, 1982):

'— should keep in mind complex, socio-economic–political interactive processes for coping with risk,
— most decisions based on commonsense 'ordinary' knowledge, with little formal analysis,
— analysis can help with incremental choices,
— analyses are often multipurpose for multiple audiences
— analysis cannot eliminate judgements about uncertainties and values,
— analysis can raise the level of discourse,
— analysis can generate creative alternatives,
— poor analysis may be worse than none,
— analysis should be iterative, it should improve over time,
— analysis can be used or misused as a political weapon,
— analysis can be used or misused in the adversarial process,
— need for peer review,
— need for more and better analysts.'

These lists are compatible with the ten rules on 'do's' and 'don'ts' for risk analysis developed by NTNF Risk Research Committee (Vinnem, 1983; 1985):

1. Any risk analysis and associated safety recommendation must be based on complete knowledge of the operating system.
2. A risk-analysis in itself cannot define the acceptable level of society, nor is it possible to place responsibility for accidents by means of a risk-analysis.
3. Risk-analysis by itself cannot improve safety. It must be part of the safety management system of the project.
4. Successful application of risk-analysis requires proper knowledge of the methods involved, and the ability to plan and carry out the analysis. The ability to interpret the results correctly is also required.
5. The risk-analysis must match the needs of the decision-maker and the associated criteria laid down for the particular system.
6. The information on which a risk-analysis is based must be adequate to ensure that the analysis matches the real system.
7. It is essential to ensure that assumptions and limitations of a risk-analysis are systematically checked and verified.
8. Collection, analysis and presentation of data must be based on insight and carried out with care.
9. The area of application of a risk-analysis must be clearly stated in order to ensure that the results are used only where appropriate.
10. When presenting the results of a risk-analysis, great care must be taken to ensure that they cannot be misinterpreted.'

Experts often disagree on risk assessments, even reputable scientists can give opposite answers, and furthermore, they may not even agree on what they disagree about. This is a problem which experts and scientists cannot avoid. If they want to work with real-world problems they have to face and handle the problems of mixed facts, judgement and values. In order to keep their integrity and trust they must analyse what is what, and may be helped by the lists and rules mentioned.

Politicians and executives responsible for safety may want to delegate uncomfortable, unpopular decisions on risk issues to scientists and other experts, even to computers. It is important to keep in mind that all fundamental risk issues are political and/or moral in their nature, and should be solved by the experts on politics, e.g., the politicians and risk managers themselves.

AN APPROACH FOR RESEARCH ON SAFETY POLICY ISSUES

A tiny part of the whole activity of empirical safety and risk research has been the topic of this chapter. It seems to be a common misunderstanding that real world decision-making and politics are out of the range of scientific discovery and systematic empirical research. However, there are good examples of such research, and I would specially mention the comparative studies of Kunreuther and Linnerooth (1983) on decision-making on liquid gas transportation in different countries.

A similar, but more elaborate research design is used in an ongoing Norwegian project (Hovden *et al.*, 1985a). The project consists of a number of case studies of decision-making processes in which risk acceptance is the main question or an integrated part of more general decisions.

The project encompasses all main actors in policy-making, but focuses on the following decision-making bodies:

— government—political institutions,
— authorities—public administration,
— industries—companies.

We are using an analytical criteria which states that the sum of cases should cover all main risk arenas in our society. First we wanted cases with a learning effect on the handling of future decision-making situations.

Based on the individual's viewpoint, we ranged the cases on an ordinal scale using the 'distance' of the risk from the individual's everyday life. We have four groups:

(1) Near, familiar risks in everyday life with case studies on:
    — consumer's product safety,
    — handling accident risks of children,
    — road traffic accidents,
    — occupational accidents,

(2) Traditional major hazards onshore with case studies on:
  — water dams in mountains and valleys,
  — transportation of liquid gas in a narrow fjord.
(3) Major hazards offshore in the oil industry, especially examples where formal risk analysis has been used in the decision-making process, e.g., on risk of collision between platforms and flotels.
(4) Abstract and remote risks: documents from governmental committees on questions like nuclear power and an analysis of the sensitivity of a modern society.

We try to get a brief overview of the decision-making process by using PERT-diagrams and identifying key events and the main stages into which the process can be divided. Within the most interesting stages of the process we do in-depth studies of interactions between the actors, content analysis of the information in the documents and evaluations based on operational definitions of the elements in lists of rules mentioned earlier in this chapter.

As a starting point for the analysis of the processes we don't use any specific model of decision-making. We would rather look at how reality fits different models.

With this approach, we hope to produce empirical evidence for risk-handling and policy-making of relevance for recommendations on the coping of future risk issues in all main risk contexts of society.

CONCLUSION

National policy-making moulds together facts and value judgements in risk-handling. Formal decision theory is of little help in explaining policy-making involving risk issues.

Risk-handling is often just an integrated part of more general decisions, and/or a step-wise or even a continuous decision-making process. Risk issues are not solved once and for all. The complex properties of policy-making show that approaches for empirical research in this field need to be very elaborate and sophisticated.

We have theories of accidents and theories of risk, but no theory of risk-handling by the individual, by organizations, or by political institutions. The development of a theory of risk-handling would be of great utility in improving policy-making and safety work.

Risk analysis can be very useful in technology related risk decisions if the analysts and the users of such methods keep in mind the lists of 'do's and don'ts' presented in this chapter.

REFERENCES

Hovden, J. (1980). *Accident Risks in Norway. How Do We Perceive and Handle Risks.* Oslo: NTNF's Risk Research Committee.

Hovden, J. (1982). 'Noen tanker om beslutningstakere og bruken av bedriftsinterne informasjonssystemer om ulykker', *in* Hovden, J. and Kjellen, U. (Eds), *Nordiskt forskningsseminarium om skyddsinformationssystem—arbetsolycksfall.* Trondheim/Stockholm: SINTEF/KTH.

Hovden, J. and Vinje, K. E. A. (1983). *Disaster Journalism.* Oslo: Yrkeslitteratur.

Hovden, J. *et al.* (1979). *Vurdering av ulykkesrisiko.* Trondheim: Tapir.

Hovden, J. *et al.* (1985a). *Akseptering av riskio. Forslag til en eksempelsamling.* Trondheim: SINTEF.

Hovden, J. *et al.* (Eds) (1985b). 'Ulykker og sikkerhet—individ og samfunn', *Report from the Fifth Nordic Seminar for Risk Researchers.* Trondheim/Oslo: SINTEF/ SFT/SIFF.

Kunreuther, H. and Linnerooth, J. (1983). *Risk Analysis and Decision Process.* Berlin: Springer-Verlag.

March, J. G. and Olsen, J. P. (1976). *Ambiguity and Choice in Organizations.* Bergen: Universitetsforlaget.

Mesarovic, M. and Peste, E. (1974). *Mankind at the turning point. The Second Report to the Club of Rome,* Norwegian Edition (1975). Oslo: Cappelen.

Nagel, T. (1979). *Mortal Questions.* Cambridge: University Press.

NTNF's Risk Research Committee (1983). *Perspektiv pa sikkerhets forskning i Norge.* Oslo: NTNF. Draft in English (1985). *Perspectives on Safety Research in Norway.*

Raiffa, H. (1982). 'Science and policy: their separation and integration in risk decisions', *in* Kunreuther, H. C. and Ley, E. V. (Eds), *Risk Analysis Controversy.* Berlin: Springer-Verlag.

Rowe, W. D. (1979). 'What is an acceptable risk and how can it be determined?' *in* Goodman, G. T. and Rowe, W. D. (Eds), *Energy Risk Management.* London: Academic Press.

Simon, H. (1965). *Administrative Behavior.* New York: The Free Press.

Vinnem, J. E. (1983). *Vaer varsom regler for risikoanalyse.* Draft in English (1985), *'Think Twice' Rules for Risk Analysis.* Oslo: NTNF's Risk Research Committee/ Forlagsservice.

Risk and Decisions
Edited by W. T. Singleton and J. Hovden
© 1987 John Wiley & Sons Ltd.

Chapter 11

Risk-Handling by Institutions

W. T. SINGLETON
Aston University, Birmingham, U.K.

INTRODUCTION

This paper is positioned between policy-making considerations and more specialist papers on Industry, Defence and Medicine. It therefore seems appropriate to concentrate on risk in the context of the larger national institutions which act in support of the population as a whole, or, if you like, in the service of the state.

Such institutions include the legislature, the Health and Safety organizations, and the industries which supply the basic needs of water, food, and fuel.

RISK AND THE LAW

Risk policy at the national level is related to law but legislators in every country have difficulty in deciding how far an individual should be responsible for his own actions and their consequences and how far individuals should be protected from their own and other people's risk taking.

The difficulty is compounded by the inadequacy of risk theory and safety theory. This is a nice illustration of the way in which good law depends on sound academic theory. If the scientists have not defined the terms and their relationship then the lawyers also cannot use them with any precision. To take an example from another field, consider the difficulty of defining insanity. Lawyers were not satisfied with the guidance from the clinicians and made their own attempts which were equally unsatisfactory. Table 11.1

Table 11.1. The pursuit of occupational safety as defined in various countries.

NORWAY 1977	WORKER PROTECTION AND WORKING ENVIRONMENT 'The work-place shall be arranged so that the working environment is fully satisfactory as regards the safety, health and welfare of the employees.'
SWEDEN 1978	WORK ENVIRONMENT BILL 'Work must be planned and arranged in such a way that it can be carried out in healthy and safe surroundings.'
SWITZERLAND 1977	LAW CONCERNING WORK 'To protect the life and health of workers ... the employer must take all measures which are shown by experience to be necessary.'
U.K. 1974	HEALTH AND SAFETY AT WORK ACT 'It shall be the duty of every employer to ensure, so far as is reasonably practical, the health, safety and welfare at work of all his employees.'
U.S.A. 1970	OCCUPATIONAL SAFETY AND HEALTH ACT 'To ensure as far as possible every working man and woman in the nation safe and healthful working conditions.'

illustrates the way in which legislators in different countries have struggled with the problem of stating simply what they wish to do in relation to occupational risk.

In Norway and Sweden there is an implicit assumption that safety depends on the environment rather than the worker. The Swiss retreat to reliance on past experience. In the U.K. and the U.S.A. there is a cautious belief that we can only move towards the goal of safety and health rather than insist on attaining it. There is acknowledgement that unfortunate outcomes are bound to occur sometimes, hence the emphasis on phrases such as 'reasonably practicable' and 'reasonably possible'. The difference between these two is that 'practicable' takes into account economic limitations whereas 'possible' does not.

One such difficulty is that all senior persons from legislators to managers, have to assume that they and others are responsible for their actions and yet we also know that everyone makes mistakes. Hence the use of the phrase 'reasonable care'. This leads to a second problem which legislation in every country tends to avoid—after an unfortunate incident does an individual have to prove that he took reasonable care or is it up to his prosecutor to prove that he did not take reasonable care? On the one hand, we have the principle of 'innocent until proven guilty' and on the other hand, it is easy to assume that because an accident happened someone did not take reasonable care unless he can prove otherwise.

Fortunately, as Green (1980) points out, laws are not immutable. There is always flexibility in the way the police administer the law, the way the courts interpret it and the way parliaments devise it and change it. Individuals engaged in all these activities are sensitive to the climate of the times and what they do is governed by what are understood to be the current attitudes in society generally. These attitude changes are related to other changes in society, in particular technology and wealth, so that administrators and engineers find themselves reluctantly becoming politicians because what they are allowed to do is governed by public opinion. Moreover, this public opinion is not swayed entirely by rational argument such as the comparison of known risks or the prediction of particular gains. The principle here seems to be that a layman will not trust technology for the very good reason that he does not understand it. However, he will, if need be, trust a particular technologist or user of technology. For example, he will fly in an aeroplane because he knows by experience that crashes are rare and that pilots are well trained and responsible individuals.

RISK AND OCCUPATIONAL SAFETY AND HEALTH

A few years ago, at the instigation of the International Labour Office, I attempted to compare Occupational Safety and Health Legislation and organization in three countries (Singleton, 1983). The three countries, Switzerland, U.K. and the U.S.A. were selected to provide a size range but it emerged that this was not an important variable. Switzerland and the U.S.A. were highly decentralized whilst the U.K. was more centrally controlled. This affects not only the law but also the organization of inspectorates.

The risks per person of accidental death and work accident death were lowest for the U.K. but this raises the questions of criteria and statistics. Should the aim be to minimize injury risk or death risk? How important are risks per unit of product as opposed to risks per person? How important are the total numbers of injuries and deaths as opposed to the exposure risks? Incidentally, as technology improves, the risk per unit of product always seems to diminish although the risk per person may stay more or less constant, if the risk per person also decreases there may be a reduced risk of minor accidents but an increased risk of major ones. The collection and presentation of statistics depends on the needs of the user, in the case of accident statistics this may be the government, the inspectorate, the employers or may be the research worker. The U.S.A. introduced two useful principles in relation to statistics: firstly, the returns provided by employers must be made available to the workers and secondly the organization responsible for statistics is independent of the organizations responsible for safety and health.

Swiss statistics support the phenomenon, noted also in other countries, that whilst accidents at work are decreasing, accidents whilst not at work are increasing. This might be seen as evidence for the risk homeostasis theory but a more prosaic explanation would be that both trends are related to an increased standard of living rather than related to each other (see Fig. 11.1).

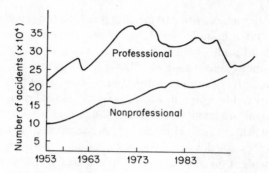

Fig. 11.1. Reported accidents in Switzerland.
(Source: 66th annual report, SUVA.)

The U.K. system has an interesting separation between policy execution (Health and Safety Executive—H.S.E.) and policy making (Health and Safety Commission—H.S.C.) These are guidelines for policy-making and research priorities which centre on risk but in a rather complex way (Table 11.2). For example, in policy changes the change in social acceptability of risks is recognized and in research priorities international and public pressures are recognized.

Table 11.2. Guidelines used by the U.K. Health and Safety Commission.

Policy Changes
   New risks from new technology.
   New risks identified in current processes.
   Changes in socially acceptable risks.

Priorities for Research
   Risk level and exposed population.
   Seriousness of consequences.
   Feasibility.
   International and public pressure.

By contrast, the U.S.A. system separates the administration of principles of safety and health including the inspectorate (Occupational Safety and Health Administration—O.S.H.A.) from the supporting research (National Institute of Occupational Health—N.I.O.S.H.) This would seem to be a useful way of concentrating attention in the two different areas but in practice it leads to difficulties of communication between them.

Looking at what the three countries have in common there are a number of outstanding features.

1. A reliance on the same hierarchy of acts, standards and codes with increasing flexibility and specificity going down the hierarchy.
2. An inspectorate as the basic means of execution but problems of how to distinguish between national and local inspectors, whether to specialize in functions or industries and the criteria by which to arrange inspections.
3. A problem of how to separate but simultaneously maintain contact between the three essential activities of administration, research and inspection.
4. Difficulties in collecting and using relevant statistics.
5. A tendency to proliferation in the committee structure.
6. How to determine whether or not the system is cost effective.

It is also possible to detect important differences between the three systems.

1. The Swiss system separates Prevention, Legal affairs and Finance with a considerable emphasis on Finance. Economic sanctions in the form of changes in safety and health levy on firms with comparatively poor safety records is a major way of enforcing compliance.
2. The U.K. system relies heavily on the concept of duties and tries to avoid using the courts; for example by the use of improvement and prevention notices served on companies rather than legal prosecutions.
3. The U.S.A. system relies on the courts to deal with non compliance, difference of opinion and the interpretation of standards.

In general, acceptable risks and other social norms diminish as economic standards increase and legislation parallels the social style of the particular country. Both these features negate the possibility of a world standard of safety and health legislation and emphasize the importance of dynamic cultural/economic factors. Europe since 1970 is an excellent example of these influences. Almost every country developed more stringent safety and health laws at this time. Usually, the reason given was that a new awareness of risks had arisen and there was a public demand that managers and others should be required to take these things more seriously. More prosaically it seems likely that, having reached a generally satisfactory state of economic development, governments felt able to meet the costs of the new bureaucracies and research institutes which were created by the new laws (Singleton, 1984).

RISK AND THE BASIC INDUSTRIES

There are two kinds of basic industry. Those which are too complex to organize nationally; for example, food production and distribution and those where it is possible to arrange national systems; for example, provision of water and energy.

AGRICULTURE

Market-controlled industries such as agriculture and fishing are difficult to include within a risk framework because collection of data, monitoring of activities and enforcement of hours and standards are all extremely difficult. Not surprisingly these are dangerous industries. No country or political system has so far solved the problem of how to allow them the freedom which seems to go with productivity and simultaneously impose standards so that risks are minimized. Inappropriate risk-taking is an important feature and the general principle that accidents relate to energy sources applies here as it does elsewhere. So also does the feature that it is easier to write scenarios of common kinds of accidents than it is to try to identify specific causes (Table 11.3).

Table 11.3. U.K. fatal incidents involving tractor drivers over 15 years.

	No. of cases
He tuns off a track and tractor turns over	129
He is driving in a field over a steep slope and the tractor turns over	126
He falls off a tractor or trailer	91
He is hit by a tractor or trailer	59
He gets too near a rotating shaft	50
He tries to get on/off a moving tractor	40
He gets underneath to make an adjustment	36
The tractor falls over when towing	27
He tries to stop/start the tractor when not in seat	17

ELECTRIC POWER

By contrast the nationally-based industries such as power generation are perhaps too readily accessible to control by government and public opinion. This can result in considerable delays in implementation, e.g., whilst awaiting the results of public enquiries, and to policy changes by the industry or by the government which with hindsight seem detrimental to costs and efficiency. A power station may take ten years from conception to power production and yet the power requirements in ten years time cannot be predicted very precisely. Thus an energy policy is very much in the risk business in both economic and safety contexts. The leaders of such an industry have difficulties in formulating policy and even greater difficulties in ensuring that the policy is acceptable to public opinion. They conduct elaborate scientific and economic analysis of the cost, efficiency and risks of generating power in particular ways (basically by using different energy sources: nuclear, hydro, coal, oil, wind and tides). They conclude with a distribution of sources defined by their criteria and they then have the task of communicating with their lay masters; politicians and the public who rely on the mass media for impressions which form their opinions and set their attitudes. The interfaces where responsibilities meet (see Døderlein in the Introduction) are not easily defined. The experts may well develop a sense of mission and may resort to their own public relations campaigns but the lay people will be tempted to question the technical opinions if too strong a component of 'selling the case' is detected. The situation may well become one of mutual distrust where politicians dislike having to make decisions which will probably satisfy no-one. There is some analogy with the traditional management/trade union discussion where there is great difficulty in agreeing on the relevant evidence and even when this is possible, the objective of the two parties are not necessarily coincident. This problem is normally resolved by 'free collective bargaining' in which the two sides recognize that they have a mutual long-term interest in maintaining the work and the work force. In the electric power case, the long-term interest of the public is the availability of power but this may be too remote to affect the formation of current attitudes. Obviously people are more likely to accept risks if they can perceive the potential gains and thus they might accept the location of a power station in their neighbourhood because it generates jobs as well as power. On the other hand, there are few jobs associated with nuclear waste sites and it is correspondingly more difficult to get anyone to accept such sites in their neighbourhood.

On the whole, it would seem wiser for the technical specialists to confine their criticisms strictly to their technical role, although this may impede communication. Lawyers are often used in this role of communication in that they are required to conduct enquiries, that is to receive representations from the concerned public and from the experts and put these together with opinions for the benefit of policy-makers and the community generally. The communication problem is particularly acute in nuclear power which is at the frontier of technological advance. Calculating risk levels such as megawatts per life lost which favours nuclear power seems to have very little impact on public opinion which still regards anything 'nuclear' as dangerously suspect. It is instructive to try to evaluate the reasons for this (Table 11.4). They seem to have little to do with calculable risks. The result is that if we regard a country as having a limited resource to expend on safety and health it may well be that too large a proportion of this resource is used in high-technology industries. Thompson (1981) puts it graphically 'my personal conclusion is that our time and money would be better expended by trying to make the highways more safe and perhaps not quite as much effort to get the last gnats eyebrow of safety from the nuclear power industry'. In the U.K., there is a Minister for Energy whose job presumably is to interpret the attitudes of society and more particularly the policy of the current government in terms of national level decisions about energy policy. During a discussion about nuclear power recently, he pointed out that people's attitudes to risks are very much a function of long-term familiarity. As an illustration he quoted gas—a substance which is both explosive and toxic and yet we pipe it across the country, down streets and into homes without protests because we have been doing so for almost a century. Each year there are several explosions, some resulting in deaths, but there is never any suggestion that gas should be abandoned as a fuel.

Table 11.4. Risk-independent objections to high technology.

Unfamiliarity—dread of the unknown.
Inexperience of gain—have managed so far without it.
Mass-media controversy generation.
Ignorance—prejudice and dogma.
Hindsight—accidents imply unreasonable risks.
Frail public—workers are paid to take risks.
Further generations—genetic effects (legacies).

CONCLUSION

Large institutions are, by their nature, prudent and cautious in the way they operate. Such inertia is admirable in moderation but if it becomes excessive, then the cost to the country concerned can be high in terms of lost wealth and lost opportunities.

Public opinion plays a considerable part in restricting or at least slowing policy-making. One of the reasons is that there is a discrepancy between the weight which professionals and laymen attach to technical evidence. Both sides may have valid viewpoints which are not easily communicated because the concepts involved are not easily defined. Central to these concepts is the interpretation of risk as something much more complex than a calculable probability. People with or without a particular expertise do seem to be capable of sophisticated trade-offs involving many factors. If it were possible to express these trade-offs in an acceptable language then there would be much better communication and much less frustration.

REFERENCES

Green, H. P. (1980). 'The role of law in determining acceptability of risk', in Schwing, R. C. and Albers, W. A. (Eds), Social Risk Assessment. New York: Plenum.

Singleton, W. T. (1983). 'Occupational safety and health systems: a three country comparison', *International Labour Review* 122(2) 155–168.
Singleton, W. T. (1984). 'Future trends in accident research in European countries', *Journal of Occupational Accidents* 6, 3–12.
Thompson, W. A. (1981). 'Some probabilistic aspects of safety assessment', *in* Berg, G. G. and Maillie, H. D. (Eds), *Measurement of Risks*. New York: Plenum.

Risk and Decisions
Edited by W. T. Singleton and J. Hovden
© 1987 John Wiley & Sons Ltd.

Chapter 12

Risk in Industry

TORVALD SANDE
A/S Norske Shell, Tananger, Norway

INTRODUCTION

In industry, as in all other sectors of society, the most effective facilitator of safety is communication. The process of communication must be based on mutual understanding of ends and means for achieving safety and the basic driving force for the process should be a real feeling of positive motivation. One problem of communication on safety is that it is most effectively done by using the complementary factor: risk. To share one's experience on negative issues is rather difficult.

One branch of industry is far ahead of others, the aviation industry. Aviation deals with a difficult environment, has catastrophic potentials, and a public that needs to be convinced of safe performance. A general public feeling of 'fear of flying' would destroy the whole business. The aviation industry secures safety, in order to stay in business, by frank and unrestricted exchange of safety information between competitors, and between users and producers of components and systems. They have a systematic approach to the man/ machine interface and they have reporting systems for 'near misses' ('reportable occurrences') based on strict anonymity control, presented in generic terms, structured to suit the needs of decision-makers.

Most people believe that cross-fertilization of safety thinking between different sectors of the industry is beneficial. In order to understand better what to learn and how to apply our new knowledge we have to systematize and define the content of our problem area.

WHAT IS 'SAFETY?'

The communication problem exists, not only amongst safety specialists, but for the public at large. A surprisingly high percentage of our fellow citizens have the following attitude to safety: 'What can I get away with before somebody makes enough fuss to insist on calling a halt.' To other people 'Safety' is absolute, unquestionable and therefore sacred. Even if the majority of us fall in between these extremes, all aspects must be taken into account when building up systematic communication on safety problems.

Laurence S. Edwards defines safety as follows: 'Safety is a means to reduce the probability of premature death, injury or disturbing circumstances to an acceptable level and to maintain that level.' It is also important to underline that safety must never be treated as a separate issue. Safety is connected to activities—production, transport, etc.—as one of several boundary conditions.

I will further underline the above broad definition of safety by looking at it from three different viewpoints: industry and commerce, society and government.

Industry and commerce

In all 'profit-and-loss' calculations/evaluations, safety is one of the many factors which must be taken into account. The provision of safety costs money and that money can only be provided by the buyer of goods and services. The management have to balance all aspects of the cost/benefit scene. Their direct responsibility is with the employees and the shareholders. Too much as well as too little can destroy a business. After some time, the only information management can get is whether they have got it wrong or have not got it wrong. There is no optimal solution, and furthermore, there is no direct way of judging whether they have got it right. However, there is a learning process tending to give decremental expenses and decremental uncertainty. A good, controlled learning process will decline to an optimal solution for the questions raised. The uncertainty lies in the possible risk problems never formulated.

Society

Individuals, pressure groups and media all express various opinions. Many individuals and some groups have a surprisingly pragmatic attitude to safety problems. But some groups of well-meaning, uninformed enthusiasts can add to the problems rather than solving them. However, I regard this as a positive challenge. They contribute in the process of getting an optimal/acceptable solution for the whole society. Truth, as Francis Bacon once put it, can arise more readily from error than confusion.

Government and associated executive bodies

The regulation of safety has to reflect on short-term wishes of citizens, the need for commercial flexibility for industry, and the long-term public good.

DEVELOPMENT OF SAFETY CONTROL IN INDUSTRY

General

In his lecture on 'Determining Optimum Reliability Programs' in the 1969 Annual Symposium on Reliability, Mr Irving Doshay illustrated the reliability control in the following steps:

— Fly-and-Fix,
— Test, Fly-and-Fix.
— Analyse, Test, Fly-and-Fix.
— Simulate, Fly-and-Fix.

These steps illustrate the development of the safety control in aviation. The first step, the Fly-and-Fix approach, has a long tradition in technical development. Even today, this may be the most cost effective way of developing simple equipment. The concept of simulation, based on mathematical modelling is not new. However, the application to safety and reliability control has rapidly developed through the last two decades, not only for aviation but for all industry. What is unique to aviation is the number of reliability, maintainability and failure figures and the quality of those figures, and hence the quality of the results of the simulations.

Regulation of safety

All industry in industrialized countries has to comply with Government regulations. Communication on safety with Government Agencies and Inspectors is as important as other aspects of safety communication. The ways and means of communication must be carefully structured.

In industry, as well as in Government, there are various views of how safety regulation should be structured and how achievement of safety should be monitored. The philosophy of the basic principles has two extremes: specification criteria and functional criteria. Different countries have different traditions of how to apply these principles. In general, all have a mixture of the two. The pace of change also varies. The tradition of safety regulation in the

U.K. goes back to the 'First Factory Act' of 1802. Norway has more than 100 years of tradition in safety and health regulation.

Even so, aviation can be used as an example, not because of a long tradition, but because of the rate of change. The comprehensive and detailed code of regulations in aviation started around the First World War. Already towards the Second World War the detail had grown and, at the same time, the development was so rapid that innovation tended to stagnate. In 1943, the aviation industry recommended that codes be stated in terms of objectives rather than specifications. That is, the code should spell out what is to be achieved and leave to the regulated to choose the means of achievement. The monitoring consists largely of examining and sample testing what is being achieved. The British aviation regulation adapted this philosophy more quickly than that in the U.S.A. In addition, in the U.S.A., about 35 Government agencies are enforcing regulations affecting aviation. For Norwegian offshore business, the number of agencies is 52. Even so, the development of aviation industry in the U.S.A. and the offshore industry in Norway seems to be as strong as anywhere else. This leads to the following conclusion: safety and hence communication on safety is not the driving force of industrial development. If economy and market potential is strong enough industry will overcome the problems of safety communication.

An interesting development has been initiated by the authorities in Norway. This is demonstrated by the new petroleum law which came into force on 1 July, 1985. This law fully recognizes the philosophy of objectives and functional criteria and channels all the 52 agencies through one: the Norwegian Petroleum Directorate. This opens up a new opportunity for the offshore industry. I will come back to this later.

THE COST OF SAFETY

The overall cost of accidents (personnel and property) in society is in the order of magnitude of 2 per cent of G.N.P. Some sectors of the industry, like the pharmaceutical industry, spend 30–50 per cent of their gross earnings on safety problems. In the U.S.A., another cost factor has shown up on the safety market—product liability. This 'Lawyers Paradise', for some parts of industry, consumes more than 10 per cent of the gross earnings.

For all industry the cost of providing safety must be weighed against its counterpart, the cost of not providing safety. The element of judgement is essential for all decision-makers. The cost/benefit ratio cannot be calculated with any precision. However, the refinement of the calculation tools and the quality of input data is crucial. The driving force of the further development of the cost/benefit area must come from industry—providing the Government agencies are prepared to accept this approach.

HOW DOES INDUSTRY MONITOR SAFETY?

There are two main ways of making industry take safety actions: reactive and inductive:

— reactive action is based upon pure commercial interest of balancing cost/benefit questions in the current market situation,
— inductive actions are based on market predictions and technical research.

Based on the objective of staying in business, again aviation is leading the way. Aviation has developed systems of incident/accident data recording and analysis far beyond what is required by law. These have been refined to become management tools. The monitoring of safety is only one of the side benefits of the data recording system. Refinement of maintenance and areas of possible simplifications both have resulting economies, in addition to motivating effects, on the personnel in charge.

A useful data-recording system must first serve to highlight trends, and the trends must be based on a level of detail beyond the recording of accidents. All maintenance and incidents data must be recorded together with performance data. From all this recorded data the presentation must be given as 'rates of occurrence'. Change in performance and change in boundary conditions are important to monitor. Time and cost are vital parameters. By measuring past achievement at this level of detail, we can be specific in assessing acceptability of performance and setting goals for the future.

A good example is a recording programme under the British Civil Aviation Authority—the C.A.A.D.R.P. (Civil Aircraft Airworthiness Data Recording Programme). Under this programme, all mandatory flight-data recorder capability is considerably extended to include a large number of parameters. After removal from the aircraft, the tapes from these recorders are processed. This processing is designed to protect the identity of the flight crew concerned. However, a limited time is allowed for possible further investigation of the flight crew under strict anonymity control. After that time limit the record is permanently cleared of any identifying capability. Exceptions are made in cases where the tape will form a part of a formal accident investigation. The further processing of data identifies trends and exceeding of limits. The result of this information is a much clearer perception of the way pilots fly aeroplanes. The programme has produced a vast amount of information which probably could not have been made available in any other way.

Any effective safety programme can only be based on an orderly and organized collection of data, knowledgeable analysis and interpretation of results and finally well balanced corrective actions.

THE OFFSHORE INDUSTRY IN NORWAY

The offshore petroleum industry handles considerable amounts of flammable materials. The environment is harsh. The units are large and associated investments are high. The number of people on board varies from one hundred to several hundreds.

How do we comply with safety? Many factors can be given:

— offshore industry has a reasonably good system for accident statistics for personnel injuries,
— special training courses for preventive safety and emergency are given to every offshore employee,
— risk analyses are performed and gradually refined,
— mathematical modelling and simulation techniques are used to test reliability and perform accelerated component testing.

The above examples are not given as a complete list, but rather to illustrate that the offshore industry in Norway is developing away from the 'Fly-and-Fix' concept.

What is lacking to catch up with the 'Simulate, Fly-and-Fix' concept is data on performance, maintenance and failures. However, a promising development has emerged: The OREDA-Handbook was issued in February 1985 (Offshore Reliability Data). This handbook is the result of cooperation between eight companies, pooling maintenance and performance data. This forms the first milestone of reliability data gathering in the offshore business. I am sure that further steps will be taken.

The industry is lagging behind aviation in the understanding and follow-up of the man-machine interface. However, simulators for drilling and production purposes are being constructed and research projects have been initiated.

Concerning the communication with the Government agencies the following is emphasized:

— NPD and industry cooperate on the structuring and issuing of personnel accident statistics,
— the Norwegian Government way of thinking on safety aspects is close to that of the British Aviation Authority,
— the Department of Labour and Local Government (KAD) initiated and funded a four-year research programme on preventive safety and contingency. Projects like OREDA and the NPD Guidelines for Concept Evaluation originate from that programme.

FUTURE TRENDS

As mentioned earlier, the new law of petroleum will soon come into force. This law will not only coordinate the 52 agencies through one (NPD), it also clearly states the principle of functional criteria for performance and safety. However, industry itself has to take initiatives and lead the way towards the complete build up of functional criteria.

In addition the Norwegian Government has issued 'Regelverksinstruksen' of 17 December 1982. This 'Rule for Making Government Rules and Government Decisions' clearly spells out the need for Government agencies to base all decisions, including issuing of new Rules and Guidelines on cost/benefit evaluations. However, the refinement of the tools and the quality of the input data have to be created by industry.

We are invited to go ahead.

Risk and Decisions
Edited by W. T. Singleton and J. Hovden
© 1987 John Wiley & Sons Ltd.

Chapter 13

Risk in Defence

MICHAEL PAGE
Captain, Royal Navy (Retired)

RISK IN DEFENCE THINKING

The concept of risk is not often discussed in military circles because the technology of defence has generated a whole culture which handles this aspect of the defence establishment's work. Conventional military wisdom deals with risk by a process of appreciating the situation as it is seen from the stylized perspective of the staff college. This has generated a reliable and valued framework for identifying those dimensions which contribute to handling the uncertainty of military operations. The concept has been buttressed by scientific applications which became known as operations analysis during the Second World War. This operations research gave a different perspective to many of the longer-term aspects of risk. In particular, it enabled military decision-makers to alter the time frame in which different sorts of risk were examined.

The way the whole concept of risk is seen in military thinking reflects the stages through which military leaders go as they rise in the service and as they mature.

— in the first stage, military leaders are close to their men and are trained to react rather than to think,
— in the second stage they are taught to analyse and make recommendations entirely dependent on the evidence as presented giving clear and unequivocal argument,
— in the third politico–military phase of a military leader's career, he makes

decisions in the mode which is encapsulated by 'don't confuse me with facts my mind is made up'.

It is this third mode where the flair of the great leader—the military decision-maker who is successful—will shine through. He takes all the advice given but doesn't necessarily act upon it. He has an additional 'feel' for any given situation. It is this last dimension which allows even a General who has failed to say in good faith; 'I acted in the best interests of my country and my service as I saw the situation at the time.'

International debate of the significance of risk in Defence is very variable. In Europe, the process of debate and the freedom of the press to explore the concepts of risk in its many dimensions allows the differences to be examined and for some consensus to be reached. The price that is paid is apparent indecision. To the military mind this is anathema. The alternative is to shroud the arguments under cloaks of security and to present predigested analysis backed up by statements of military judgement.

It is this process by which the super powers tend to negotiate for arms reduction. Because of the nonavailability of a true balance of risk the uninformed have to make their judgement on the credibility of each of the protagonists. In the context of negotiations the balance tends to be difficult to strike because of the very deeply felt social pressures and psychological insights which play a part on both sides. There can be no doubt that the Russian military concept of risk is deeply imbedded in the corporate memory of the price they paid for defence in the early 1940s. However intellectually penetrating the military planner might be, the individual facing any decision of a military nature in Russia must be affected in a similar direction by the recollection of that catastrophe. It is difficult to see how any negotiator could make too big an allowance for this factor in deciding on a line to take when negotiating with the Russian team. On the American side of such negotiations there is a deep-seated and well-founded distrust of the Russian negotiating technique.

There is, however, a very different corporate concept of risk in the American population at large. The U.S. military tradition views the management function as a series of pigeon holes and each individual is expected to optimize his own activity. There would appear to be a positive disincentive applied where an individual tends to seek a wider perspective. This results in a different mechanism of checks and balances in the formulation of policy when compared with a European organization.

The American approach produces tremendous successes. The space programme is perhaps the most easily comprehended example of what a group can undertake. A less well-organized people would see it as an impossible task and would entirely reject it because of the risks involved. However, by superb organization and by immaculate attention to detail the brave people involved demonstrated that every risk could be dissected and (provided the political will and finance was unstinting in its support) that the achievement in prospect could be assured. The increase in national self-confidence from this series of achievements, combined with the trauma of the Vietnam experience, has produced a perception of risk which is unitary in nature and creates barriers at the negotiating tables.

There are three levels at which risks are assessed and accepted or rejected:

— Politico–military level.
— Military command level.
— Military obedience level.

The Political Leader when deciding whether to take a military course of action must assess the chances of success against the risks implied. There are many risks:

— Total failure.
— Stalemate.
— Winning the battle but achieving an outcome as bad or worse than before the start.
— Being so internationally unpopular that it is not worth winning.
— Casualties.
— Winning but being so weakened in the attempt that defeat follows later.
— Loss of credibility if you do not act.

The assessment is obviously much easier in a defensive action than an offensive. 'Being a dead last ditch defending hero is easier to live with than being a live aggressive winner.' (Anon.) This has been recognized in the 'Just War' theory since Augustine of Hippo in A.D. 300.

The politician takes military advice on the chances of success, but must then judge and decide. He can minimize the risks by following a policy of achieving security without actually having to fight. Today this is called Deterrence: 'A show of determination to resist and beat the hell out of any aggressor.' The Swiss do it alone. NATO does it through a strong alliance.

Risk when viewed by the High Command is more complex again. Examples today would be the group in the Ministry of Defence in the U.K. headed by the Chief of the Defence Staff or those led by General Rogers as Supreme Commander of NATO in Europe. Here, the balance of risk will have been analysed very carefully indeed with many models and much staff-work examining the full range of consequences. However, when the moment comes for a major decision there will be little opportunity to take counsel and to decide in an analytical way what is to be done. In these circumstances, there are other pressures on the policy-makers (the politicians) and these will be closely related to what would be possible. Therefore, at this level, the High Command must take decisions about risk where the concept has been formalized into the price that the military is prepared to pay for credibility and continued contribution to the society which they serve. The politicians and the High Command together provide the politico–military view of risk.

At the Military Command level, the leader—the General, the Admiral or the Air Marshall—has an extremely mature view of risk. In this position the man is benefiting from good advice, probably the best available. It will never be adequate and tremendous time pressures are a big factor. Mr Healey, when he was Secretary of State for Defence, said that in these circumstances the only way to make a correct decision was to separate the elements; the facts from the opinions; and those decisions which must be made immediately from those which may be delayed. In this way, he claimed, the decisions may be taken piecemeal. There is much truth in this but in the case of a General, it is frequently impossible to undertake such a systematic analysis. In a dynamic situation where communications are almost certainly interfered with, there must be a large element of flair and reliance on sixth sense. It is this highly-tuned and integrated perception of risk which enables the best leader in such circumstances to reject what would seem to the Staff Officer to be excellent advice and to go straight to a different decision.

For those who are on the staff, the general staff or in a Ministry of Defence, there is a different concept of risk. Here, risk is abstracted by examining the likely outcome of any course of action. It is at this level that every conceivable aspect of a situation must be extracted. Due balance is given to the information about own forces, which is firm and certain, against information about the enemy which is uncertain and almost certainly suspect. This concept of risk requires a very highly trained awareness if a correct balance is to be struck between overoptimism on the one hand and sheer paralysing pessimism on the other. There are many examples of the good and bad Staff Officer. The most criticized have been those responsible for the conduct of the First World War in the trenches of France. A walk around the memorials, even today, especially in the spring, brings into sharp relief the tremendous price paid for that strange conception of risk held by Staff Officers in 1914.

As an aside, there is a nice definition of the difference between management and leadership which refers to that period. 'Management in the military is the process of getting your battalion back from the front line after a particularly bloody period in the mud and filth of a winter campaign. Leadership is taking your men forward, back into their trenches after this period of rest and recuperation is over.'

At the Command Level, the balance of risk will always give a very considerable weight to the quality of the individual fighting man. He is called 'the greatest single factor'. This person, at the military obedience level, has little power of decision over the risks taken but is always ultimately responsible for his actions. Such individuals are the people in those units which are considered to be the teeth of the fighting organization. In the case of the Army, it would include those officers who live and work with their men. In the Air

Force, it would embrace the aircrew and those who provide the aircraft with first line support. In the Navy, it includes all those who go to sea in ships. In this group, the handling of the concept of risk is dealt with by a very formal process. The foundation is instilled at every level by training courses and enshrined through the attitudes generated by the approach that the group is encouraged to take. In this process, a very real element is the dulling of the critical faculties. This is encouraged to ensure that in moments of high danger the individual will subjugate his own interest to that of the group. There are many examples of how this self-discipline operates. In peacetime it can be seen most clearly in group activities employing the martial arts like the Royal Tournament at Earls Court. This is a military pageant where there is a competitive element, one field-gun team racing against another trained to a peak of efficiency. Teams have been known to equate with success to the extent that a man, in the heat of the moment, will put his finger in the place of a cotter pin which he has dropped by mistake. He does of course lose his finger. Risk has no meaning.

The task of training the fighting man to accept the concept of risk is built around familiarity with the dangers involved and a mental attitude which says that 'we will succeed; disasters will only happen to the other man'. This is not to say that the fighting man is trained to take risks. The attitude is that risk is an inherent part of daily life. It must be accepted and balanced and a sensible judgement made. But when the moment of facing risk arrives minimum energy must be spent in considering the unpleasant aspects of a negative outcome. There are many examples of how this process is integrated into the training of military men but the most stark example is probably in those individuals who are required to cope on their own such as the Special Air Services. Here, the training given takes this line to the ultimate of logic, and possibly beyond.

Discussion at the seminar brought out the observation that those who face the greatest risks spend least time evaluating them. It was agreed that the military were at one end of a spectrum while the medical world was at the other in considering the risks from drugs and hazards from smoking.

APPRECIATION OF RISK

The military have stylized risk by developing a technique called the Standard Appreciation. This has evolved as a logical method for appreciating the situation. It is claimed that it gives excellent training in clear thinking and logical reasoning and facilitates sound and rapid decision-making in an emergency. There are five distinct steps in this process.

— Studying the existing situation by a review.
— Deciding on the aim to be attained by examining the factors affecting the selection of the aim.
— Reasoning out all the factors affecting the attainment of the aim.

— Considering all possible ways of attaining the aim.
— Deciding the best course of action to attain the aim.

It is significant that in the guidance notes the aim must be expressed in positive and vigorous terms. Negative verbs such as 'prevent', 'stop' and 'delay' should be avoided. Nowhere does risk get a mention. It follows that in military terms, there is a real dilemma for people who are involved with plans and policy when balancing risk in any decision-making process. Its utility is rarely proven. Staff officers are rarely court-martialled.

This balancing can be considered as a discounting process to examine risks in the future against risks in the present. These, in turn, are often of a different fundamental nature. Examining the likelihood of having an acceptable level of force that would be available to defend the nation in ten to twenty years time calls for the need to examine the threat at that stage. This then relates directly to an estimate of the operational risk of deploying a proposed force against that threat and, assuming that the required parameters of that force are met, judging the likely outcome. For example, the case for a warship could be stated as: If the ship was there under those circumstances would the ship win? This can be looked at as a balance of risk depending on a number of interrelated factors to do with the military leadership at the time and the skills and numbers of the sailors who are available to fight. There is another risk to be assessed which can be put in the form of a question 'will the ship actually be there when it is required to fight, giving it a chance of winning?' This, in turn, is dependent upon the number of ships planned to be in service at that time and the political decision on the use to which these ships might be put in addition to their prime task. There is the risk to the military that for one reason or another there would be a political embargo on using that particular ship. An immediate example comes to mind—the attitude adopted by the New Zealand people in not wishing nuclear powered vessels to enter their waters.

Even assuming that all these factors are favourable, the operational risk still contains an element for the uncertainties of inaccurate assessment. This embraces both the performance of that ship and the enemy and also environmental factors which although assessed with the best information available will prove to be in error (Fig. 13.1).

Over and above all these factors is the indisputable uncertainty of the quality of the potential enemies' cunning. Clearly, if there is the prospect of confrontation there is another (probably equally talented) group trying to decide themselves how they would balance the risk, so that they can win.

In parallel with this operational balance, there must be a similar analysis of the procurement 'project risks'. These are intrinsic in any rolling programme which needs to keep abreast of the general level of armament. These costs and engineering uncertainties are well understood by project management who must attempt to answer the questions: Can it be produced in the timescale

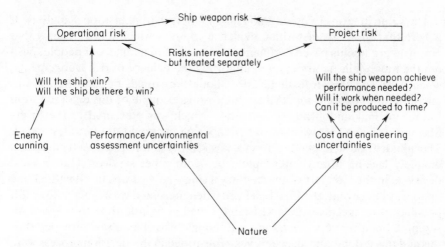

Fig. 13.1. Analysis allows a balance sheet to be drawn up and this diagram shows one method. The difficulty is in focussing the attention of decision-makers on the relative importance of the constituent parts.

needed? Will it work in a reliable manner when it is needed? Will that particular ship/weapon combination achieve the performance that is required to match the operational need?

The physical laws of nature, the political will and the organizational arrangements of the nations will interact upon this balance. These risks are very closely related to the operational scenario upon which the whole intellectual exercise is built. This interrelation seeks a balance between the procurement process now and the risk of defeat in the future. It is very complex and rarely are the two considered as interrelated nor is a risk analysis attempted. The more usual process is that project assumptions are made and a political judgement reached in the light of the credibility of the proposing team. Unhappy experience indicates that projects rarely meet their claims. However, intelligence gathering about the other side almost always exaggerates the achievements of the enemy. Thus the resulting balance is usually found to be acceptable.

These concepts and definitions are justified in two directions. The experience of many military campaigns is distilled and then preserved in the staff colleges and in service tradition. It is also refuted or confirmed by scientific studies. The difficulty with the latter is that the assumptions are very often not discussed as openly as the results. This is particularly true in sensitive areas where security requires a very limited dissemination of the debate because of 'the need to know' factor. This can be extremely dangerous by not preventing the fallacious argument, which sometimes emerges, from gaining credence.

The value in terms of operational utility emerges from historical analysis. It is here that the most disturbing evidence emerges which tends to show that powerful arguments based on finance, timescale and numbers of people, push out the more delicate arguments supporting the balance of risk. Judgements, when based on this difficult balance should be sound, but so often fail to measure up to expectation. A very interesting example of this emerged from the recent Falklands war. The situation which was presented to the Prime Minister was one that was not of her choosing but could not be sidestepped. The military option depended upon a naval contribution which was central and uniquely lacking in any interdependence with other services. Unlike most decisions in the late part of this century a single service was faced with all the options. In the event, the First Sea Lord when presented with the question 'is it possible to retake the Falkland Islands?' had very little time to prepare his response but after very few minutes of thought was able to say 'provided this, this and this is done, the answer is yes'. Enshrined in this decision process were many years of specialized training, thinking and acting which allowed a man under considerable stress (he knew that the consequences of the wrong judgement could be catastrophic) to analyse the risks involved and reach a decision. This turned out to be a very good decision because the political will, the mood of the country, the circumstances of the ensuing battle, all came together in a way which resulted in a military success. This was overshadowed by the importance of the political success in the wider scenario. It was also a good decision because having balanced the risk, the decision was taken unequivocally and action followed. It has been said that the biggest risk in military affairs comes from indecision. In subaltern's training this is brought out by the instructor shouting across the parade ground 'for goodness sake say something, even if it is only goodbye'.

When preparing for a decision like that made to proceed with the retaking of the Falklands, the Staff papers had been prepared by a group of military planners who do paper exercises over and over again with different assumptions. To this group of the military fraternity the concept of risk is far more abstract, and here the operational researcher would find a community of interest. Risks are viewed statistically, as time dependent, and as just one more element within the equation. Very often the equation is treated mathematically. Unfortunately, it has not been easy for the military to become numerate and there has been much heart searching over the last decade in attempting to use these techniques to make good military decisions at the planning stage. The worst consequences of this have been in the financial sphere where budgets have overrun in an impossible manner and where the numerical assessment of the threat against the response always seems to be loaded against defence. Simple soldiers' stories are always about 9-ft-tall Russians. The same numerical exaggeration is seen in every aspect of military planning in all services and all nations.

The balance as seen by all individuals before the fighting starts will be different and more complex than the perception of risk after the catastrophe of the first shot fired in anger. The transition is difficult to study and like all transients is particularly sensitive to the starting position. However, it is the author's view that it is this transient which is the most important feature in examining the utility of risk in any of these situations. The constancy displayed across this watershed and its relation to the perceived response before the event can be absolutely crucial. An example of this phenomenon is well documented in the military view taken in Germany before the outbreak of the 1939–45 war. The military planners and German policy-makers misjudged statements made in the abstract by the young men of the British universities. They said in their liberal way they would not fight. The statements were belied by the behaviour of some of them who were fighting in the Spanish Civil War but these signals were missed. Subsequently, Allied leaders found that they were able to marshall the youth of the nation in facing hostilities when the decisions based on these false assumptions made it necessary.

OPERATIONAL UTILITY AND DETERRENCE

The utility of the military way of handling risk in defence must be judged on the results achieved:

— It is claimed that it is the duty of the Government and Allies to maintain adequate forces to guard against nuclear blackmail and non-nuclear aggressors.
— Deterrence is built on fear and it is the prospect of escalation that deters.
— It is important that the risk of escalation must not be allowed to inhibit all resistance to an aggressor.
— A churchman states 'a ruthless adversary must be met by resolution no less adamant whatever the risks'.

All easily said.

The concept of deterrence and the position of the fighting man has always presented an interlocking dilemma. This has been seen in recent times in the conflict between the tank and the antitank weapon, between the aircraft and the antiaircraft gun, and now we see it in the missile, especially the ballistic intercontinental missile and the antimissile system. The offensive system is always perceived as a war winning tool. It would be claimed by the owner therefore, as a deterrent weapon. It should deter the weaker nation from attacking the stronger whatever the provocation. Even when the nuclear debate brings the meaning of deterrence into sharp relief via the ultimate price of failure to deter, the arguments for and against weapon systems are never resolved. For this reason, endeavours to control armaments by the League of Nations and later by the United Nations appear doomed to failure. The concept of deterrence and its corollary, disarmament, deserve greater examination. The risks are enormous.

The utility of 'risk' to military decision-making is dependent upon the time frame and the purpose of the decision. This is shown when examining the very lengthy and complex process of choosing the next generation of a weapon system. There are many counter arguments for each element of the decision process which will finally result in an order being placed. Some of these will be judgements based on quite nebulous reports. Others will be bureaucratic decisions made because of previous errors. A most clearcut example comes from personal experience. Operations analysis showed that certain equipment was essential for the survival of a particular design of warship. The process of installing this equipment in that particular hull encroached upon the standard safety margins included in all warship design. In all other design matters involving choice, the process would be a trade-off. However, in this particular case there was a predisposing inhibition. This was the result of a tragedy when *H.M.S. Captain*, a new design, commissioned and built in the last century foundered on her maiden voyage; a similar story to that of the *Vasa* in Stockholm. As a result of the trauma, a board of enquiry recommended that in future the professional head of the Royal Corps of Naval Constructors would give a personal guarantee that each new ship design was sound. Over one hundred years later, this same personal guarantee to the Admiralty Board meant that the risk of a ship foundering under extreme conditions because of an increase of top weight through icing, was more unacceptable than the certainty of being unable to defend herself against attack. Despite heated debate the concept of 'balance of risk' was not seen as an acceptable methodology. However, this represents a debate within a very abstract world. It is rare for such decision-makers to be called to account.

Since this chapter is examining the place of risk in the context of national security, it is important to identify the role played by technical change in the security posture of a nation. This subject has been well documented in the recent past and high points in the last fifty years are clearly identifiable. The introduction of the tank, the airplane, the submarine, the guided missile and the nuclear weapon, each in its turn made the need for a new strategy clearly apparent. Each brought in its wake a different perspective for the attainment of national security. For example, the fluid land battle implicit in tank warfare with air support made the Maginot Line obsolete. Today, the command and control arrangements made possible by modern communication methods mean that powerful weapons can be deployed worldwide, yet remain under the control of a central leader. Technology in this way gives adversaries the ability to outmode the opponent's investment. Unless one adversary sees an opportunity for a clear victory, both sides at some point will seek ways to moderate the rate of technical change, so that technology will not degrade their own security *vis-à-vis* their opponents. One way in which this moderation can be achieved is through the formal process of arms control reducing perceived risk.

Technology has always been an essential ingredient of any attempt at arms control by mutual agreement. Many examples can be given demonstrating arms control successes and failures caused by the level of the technological art at the time when the control was sought. The cause of a fresh initiative for arms control can sometimes be observed in a technological acceleration which has outstripped the economic and social competence of the adversaries. A recent example of these pressures can be seen in the concentration of Russian inventiveness which led to Sputnik 1 and the subsequent space race. The potential for conflict was recognized and outer space demilitarized by treaty.

On a different plane, the U.S. demonstrates a remarkable propensity to produce the volume of equipment required for achieving military superiority but in times of peace suffers from an inability to man this equipment at a sufficiently high level. This makes negotiation based on steady-state numbers more difficult. Differences in national attitudes highlight the dubious utility of seeking sheer volume in warlike materials. They bring into sharp focus the desirability of formal limitations providing both sides with a 'top line' for planning purposes.

Where there is a political will to achieve military superiority over a potential adversary, it is natural for the military hierarchy to develop this perceived need to the limit of the existing technology. In that case, the restriction on military growth will emerge from economic pressures. These economic pressures are second-order effects from the political point of view but have a considerable impact upon the rate of change of military preparedness. They are particularly significant when political attitudes undergo marked and rapid change.

The major differences between the military and the political perspective of technology is most apparent in the time frame in which each discipline operates. Military strategy lays down the broad guidelines for the policy of material procurement which supports that strategy. This material will be designed to the then current technology but will not be available to either the political leader or the tactical commander until some ten years later. This imposes a very rarely understood inertia upon the possible tactics of the adversaries. Occasionally, the significance of a procurement policy is not understood on either side until the material is in position. Then a rare overturning of traditional tactics sometimes occurs. Such an occurrence was seen following the procurement and deployment of the SS-20 system in Eastern Europe over the last few years. More normally, the transition from a procurement programme which is built upon strategy, followed by deployment and resulting in technical evaluation, is a ponderous and closely documented procedure followed by military analysts on both sides.

Arms control encapsulates the idea of ensuring that parties to an agreement obey the spirit and letter of some legal documents. This agreement may embrace strategy or philosophy, but more likely will talk numbers and technology. Technology is an essential ingredient because arms control seeks to limit the capability of subject nations to prosecute a warlike aim. This can be attractive from three points of view:

— by seeking to diminish the risk of war,
— helping to minimize the global costs of war,
— by reducing the cost of preparing for war.

A further attractive aim is to reduce the consequence of war, should it unfortunately occur. All these aspects contain an element of technical assessment which requires the accurate identification of technological achievements.

A major part of the technical responsibility within arms control is in verification and enforcement. Technical advance in weapon development can nullify policing methods. This implies a requirement for some form of international verification which could be seen to be technically sound. It must also, of course, be politically acceptable. For example, because national technical means have reached a limit in supporting the SALT negotiations, some form of verification is required on the ground. However, this means that nations must relinquish some of their sovereignty for this to happen. If they are unwilling to do so, an alternative technical solution must be sought. Treaties without soundly based verification are most dangerous.

Security, as explained earlier, is a state of mind based upon the complex evaluation of military material, the political will to deploy this equipment and the capability it has against the adversary's military power. Without arms control, technology provides each adversary, in isolation, with the opportunity to perceive that he has achieved superiority over his opponent. In such circumstances, it is conceivable that optimistic evaluations could make hostilities appear attractive. Arms control, using advanced technical means, is able to provide the mechanism by which each side can evaluate its forces against those of the adversary in a formal and objective way. Thus, the opportunity for misunderstanding is significantly reduced. For this reason alone, technology has a central part to play in supporting the role of arms control as a source of Alliance security. Reducing uncertainty must always reduce risk.

It is not sensible to expect all endeavours in this direction to be successful. Indeed, some arms-control measures have had almost the opposite effect to that which was intended. A frequently quoted example was in the 1927 Washington Agreement which was intended to limit the size and construction of world naval forces. The wording of the agreement was such that it permitted those nations who wished to rearm to achieve it with greater success because it unwittingly gave an advantage to a nation building new classes of ships. Similarly, it is possible to argue that SALT I gave the Soviets the opportunity to increase their military capability, in terms of nuclear weapons, by carefully examining the wording of the treaty to suit their particular military aim.

It is the real risk of this being repeated which is so very plain to Western negotiators today. Fortunately, these risks appear equally real to both sides and to the public at large. This must create a more hopeful climate for balancing risk in so vital an area.

SUMMARY AND CONCLUSIONS

Risk from a military standpoint has been under close scrutiny on the fortieth anniversary of the first use of the atomic bomb. Listening to the discussion with the wisdom acquired at this seminar in Oslo has reinforced some of the key issues that were raised there. While certain perspectives in the military concept of risk can be identified, they appear to be at variance with those held by the population at large. Leaders are trained to react rather than to think, to analyse and decide according to factual evidence and to trust powerful arguments. Only later does the military leader use an intuition, born of experience, to make decisions in spite of the presented evidence.

There are three levels at which risks are accepted or rejected after critical assessment. At the politico–military level, the politician aims to minimize risk, this follows a pattern described as the art of the possible. The session on risk and behaviour highlighted some of the reasons why performance in this field is so often less than satisfactory.

The military High Command balances risk according to how it judges the price that society is prepared to pay for the continued credibility of the military establishment. Direct parallels emerged in discussion of the balance of risk in the nuclear power industry. The link with the offshore industry was less clear because the people do not perceive any direct risks and only count the benefits.

At the military command level, correct decisions depend on skills in separating the elements of the risk equation. The addition of flair or sixth sense, acquired through long experience, is then applied to reduce the risks to an acceptable level. There are direct parallels here with the work of the Safety Executive and consultants in Risk Analysis. The striking difference is that these civilian specialists are normally advisers. The military commander carries the responsibility for the execution of the plan.

At the military obedience level, a dulling of the critical faculties is vital, allowing the individual, in moments of high danger, to subjugate his own interests to those of the group. The mental attitude is one of 'we will succeed' and minimal thought is given to the unpleasant aspects of the outcome of failure. This same behaviour pattern is seen in professional divers and construction workers. It can be most counterproductive in those carrying responsibility for enforcing safety measures. Programmes of instruction to raise the level of awareness to real risk are vital but difficult to structure.

In military planning and policy-making, it is possible to identify a discounting process measuring risks in the future against risks now. Evidence emerges from historical analysis which suggests that arguments based on finance, timescale and numbers tend to overshadow the less easily measured concept of risk. However, it has been said that the biggest risk in military affairs comes from indecision. The community experience in many fields indicates that it is probable that the reverse is true.

In military preparation for the decision-making process, risks are viewed statistically, as time dependent, and as just one element in the equation. This is a very similar process to that in trade and industry. Dr Spjotvoll made it clear though that statistical competence is rare and that the mathematical underpinning of many decisions is suspect.

The defence establishment view of risk before the fighting starts is very different from that held when the battle is in full swing. The changing perception of risk as the odds change was touched upon in a number of different contexts. It was most clearly seen in a description of role playing by the operators of offshore support ships in the evaluation of procedures to avert disaster to the rigs.

It is claimed to be the duty of government to maintain adequate forces and to guard against nuclear blackmail and non-nuclear aggressors. Deterrence is built on fear. The offensive system is perceived as a war-winning tool and hence as a deterrent. Technical advances give adversaries the ability to outclass the investment in arms of the other side. Because of this, it is likely that both sides will seek to moderate the rate of technical change so that their own security systems do not become too rapidly outmoded. Economic factors have a great, though indirect, effect on the rate of change of technology. Arms control is attractive for three main reasons—it diminishes the risk of war, it minimizes the global cost of war and it reduces the costs of preparing for war. The risks implicit in this philosophy are badly handled at the political level and always have been. The necessary process for educating a society to face risk was identified as an essential but difficult duty of government.

It is concluded that while risk plays a central part in the daily life of the military person, the whole training and operational perspective reduces its impact. Risk is not a concept which is easily recognized by the military establishment and as a word, is not often used. Yet, despite this cultural aberration, risk is at the heart of military affairs. It is the balance of risk in a complex world, which will determine the future prospects of our civilization.

FURTHER READING

Adamson, A. (1970). *The Effective Leader*. London: Pitman.

Baynes, J. C. M. (1969). 'The influence on the army of change in the British Society', *Defence Fellowship Report*, Edinburgh: University of Edinburgh.

Bensham-Booth, D. F. (1968). 'The sociological problems of integrating the military and civil communities in the U.K.', *Defence Fellowship Report*. London: University College.

Bellini, J. (1981). *Rule Britannia. A Progress Report for Doomsday 1986*. London: Jonathan Cape.

Eberle, J. H. F. (1971). 'A study of politics—military aspects of Operational Command', *Defence Fellowship Report*.

Geraghty, T. (1981). *Who Dares Wins. The Story of the S.A.S. 1950–80*. London: Collins.

Harries, R. (1982). *What Hope in an Armed World*. London: Pickering and Inglis.

Heseltine, M. (1983). 'Don't gamble with defence', *Sunday Times*, 13 March, 1983.

Langford, D. (1979). *War in 2080. The Future of Military Technology*. London: David Chambers.

Mitchell, V. F. (1970). 'Need satisfaction of military commanders', *Journal of Applied Psychology* 24(3), 282–287.

Page, M. R. H. (1981). 'Automation and manning studies for the 1980's', *Naval Electrical Review* 34(3), 13.

Page, M. R. H. (1982). 'Human factors and the procurement cycle in naval computer-based systems', *Journal of Naval Science* 8(4), 261–267.

Prior, P. J. (1977). *Leadership is Not a Bowler Hat*. Newton Abbot, UK: David & Charles.

Rusbridger, J. (1985). Sinking of the Automedon. New Light on two Intelligence Disasters in World War II. *Encounter*,64, 8–14 May.

Risk and Decisions
Edited by W. T. Singleton and J. Hovden
© 1987 John Wiley & Sons Ltd.

Chapter 14

Cancer Risks from Food and Drugs

FRANCIS J. C. ROE
Independent Consultant in Toxicology and Cancer Research, London

INTRODUCTION

Cancer is an unfair disease. It attacks the abstemious almost as often as the profligate and the poor even more than the rich. The victim's question 'Why me?' compels man to try to find something to blame. Irrespective of the facts, intuition steers attention towards environmental factors which are either unnatural, e.g., artificial colourants in food or unpleasant, e.g., diesel fumes. In this chapter, I attempt to narrow the present gulf between perceived and actual cancer risk factors.

THE TWO-STAGE THEORY OF CARCINOGENESIS

Cancer constitutes a large group of different diseases which share the common property that body cells of one or more types proliferate (grow autonomously) when there is no call for them to do so. Not only do the cells concerned proliferate but they invade and destroy surrounding normal tissues and spread (metastasize) to distant sites in the body where they continue to proliferate.

It is naturally tempting to assume that the cancerous process begins as a mutation in the DNA of a previously normal cell, and that the mutation confers a proliferative advantage on the mutant cell. Given this proliferative advantage, the cell becomes the progenitor of a clone of mutant cells which, when big enough, is called tumour or cancer. Going on from this simple concept, there emerged during the 1940's the so-called two-stage theory of carcinogenesis. According to this theory, the first stage, tumour initiation, is the mutation and the second stage, tumour promotion, is the period of proliferation from a single mutant cell to a tumour-sized clone. Agents which bring about the first stage are, thus, called tumour-initiators and those that hasten the second stage are called tumour-promoters.

This simple paradigm for carcinogenesis was based on the results of certain rather contrived skin-painting experiments in rabbits and mice, and from the start, it was clear that the theory was oversimplistic. In particular, most of the skin tumours produced in response to the sequential exposure to an initiator and a promoter were benign warts and not malignant cancers. Moreover, many of these benign warts regressed when exposure to the promoter ceased or even while exposure to it continued. Nevertheless, the simple theory had a compelling charisma, and was soon applied uncritically to carcinogenesis at all tissue sites. The two-stage theory has now held sway for over quarter of a century and still dominates much thinking.

Irrespective of the validity of the theory itself, there are two further problems. First, most investigators have tacitly assumed that the initiating stage is more important than the promoting stage, and, therefore, that initiators are more dangerous than promoters. Secondly, until relatively recently, it has been widely assumed that the only important initiators are man-made chemicals and that no naturally-occurring substances possess mutagenic activity.

The assumption that initiators are more dangerous than promoters led to the development of sensitive tests for mutagenic activity, including tests in which naked, mutation-prone bacterial DNA is brought directly into contact with test substances or with mixtures of test substances and enzymes that might be capable of converting them to electrophilic metabolites with DNA-damaging potential. For a period, some investigators really believed that the demonstration of mutagenicity in a bacterium was equivalent to the demonstration of carcinogenic potential in a laboratory animal or man. For various reasons, most investigators no longer fully believe this. However, even today, bacterial mutagens tend to be regarded as guilty of potential carcinogenicity until proved innocent.

At the same time, relatively little attention has been paid to agents that favour the proliferation of cells or to the mechanisms whereby cellular proliferation is switched on and off. Thus, it is only in the past year or so that the possibly major importance of hormones and regulatory peptides in the carcinogenesis process has begun to be widely entertained.

GENETIC VERSUS ENVIRONMENTAL

Both genetic and environmental factors contribute to the aetiology of virtually all diseases. For a few diseases, e.g., mongolism, xeroderma pigmentosum, familial polyposis coli, the genetic contribution is virtually a total explanation. For others, e.g., alpha$_1$-antitrypsin-deficiency-associated emphysema, obesity, gout, the contributions of genetic and environmental factors may be more equal. And yet for others, e.g., most infectious diseases, asbestosis, the genetic contribution is negligible.

It is generally agreed that, overall, environmental factors contribute far more to the causation of most human cancers than genetic ones. Notable exceptions are cancer of the colon in subjects with the rare disease familial polyposis coli and of skin cancer in subjects with xeroderma pigmentosum. However, environmental factors are considered to be 80–90 per cent to blame for most common human cancers (e.g., stomach, colon, breast, cervix, uteri, lung). The evidence, which is necessarily circumstantial, includes the fact that when persons migrate from one geographical area and culture to another, the spectrum of cancers to which they and their children is prone becomes progressively more like that of the area and culture which they have newly adopted and progressively less like that of the area and culture which they abandoned. This is strikingly true for migrants from Japan, where stomach cancer incidence is high and colon cancer incidence is low, to the United States, where the opposite is true.

CANCER RISKS FROM FOOD AND DRUGS

The need to exclude poisons from food and to ensure that drugs are safe has long been recognized, but the specific need to test food additives and drugs for possible carcinogenic activity goes back only about 50 years. Four perceptions conspired to focus attention on food additives and drugs as possibly important environmental carcinogens:

— the increasing popularity of the two-stage theory of carcinogenesis,
— the growing belief that all mutagens are carcinogens,
— the mounting evidence that environmental factors are much more important than genetic ones in the causation of cancer,
— a widespread belief that all environmental carcinogens must be man-made chemicals since Mother Nature is benign.

These perceptions, rather than any evidence of cancer risk in humans from food additives, have led national and international regulatory authorities to demand more and more evidence of lack of mutagenicity and carcinogenicity before sanctioning the addition of chemicals to food. The position is a little different in the case of drugs in so far as increased cancer risk in man has been demonstrated for a minority of pharmaceutical agents, e.g., leukaemia from chloramphenicol. Also, benefit can be weighed against toxic risk in the case of a drug since the person at risk is one and the same as the potential beneficiary, whereas, in the case of a food additive, the potential benefit may be no more than trivial and the beneficiary may be the person selling the food rather than the person eating it.

In any event, huge resources are presently devoted worldwide to the testing of food additives and drugs for carcinogenicity. And it is against this background that three developments of major importance have occurred during the past few years:

— a paper by Sir Richard Doll and Richard Peto,
— a paper by Bruce Ames,
— the recognition that laboratory animals used in conventionally-designed carcinogenicity tests are overfed and that overfeeding causes major disturbances of hormonal status and alarming increases in cancer risk.

THE CAUSATION OF HUMAN CANCER ACCORDING TO DOLL AND PETO

Some five years ago, Doll and Peto (1981) were commissioned by the Office of Technology Assessment of the United States Congress to provide background material relevant to the assessment of environmental cancer risks of all kinds. They tackled the monumental task by first dividing environmental factors into 12 different categories and then, in the light of evidence, estimating the percentage of current cancer mortality in the United States caused by each category. In reaching their estimates, they attached far more weight to epidemiological data than to evidence from animal and other laboratory studies because they felt that the latter 'cannot provide reliable risk assessments'. Their best estimates of the contributions to cancer deaths by the 12 categories of factors, are summarized in Table 14.1.

This brilliant paper was attacked vigorously from many sides. Lawyers advising trade unions and environmentalists were dismayed that Doll and Peto considered so few cancer deaths to be due to factors which they were making so much fuss about. At the same time, 'back-to-Nature-healthnics' did not want to believe that foodstuffs and how much people eat are probably 35 times more important than either food additives or drugs as causes of cancer. Indeed, the idea that food additives, particularly antioxidants and preservatives, might actually protect against cancer rather than increase the risk of it was anathema to them. Despite all the emotion and argument, Doll and Peto's paper has stood its ground and there has been no scientifically sound challenge to their 'best estimates'.

DIETARY CARCINOGENS AND ANTICARCINOGENS

Bruce Ames (1983) attacked contemporary dogma with quite brutal force. Ames, from a deep knowledge of bacterial genetics and biochemistry, had earlier given his name to a sensitive test for mutagenicity based on the use of a number of different strains of salmonella typhimurium. It is this test system, more than any other, which researchers concerned with the safety of exposure

Table 14.1. Proportions of cancer deaths attributable to different factors (after Doll and Peto, 1981).

No.	Factor	Best estimate (%)	Range of acceptable estimates (%)
1	Tobacco	30	25 to 40
2	Alcohol	3	2 to 4
3	Diet	35	10 to 70
4	Food additives	<1	−5 to −2*
5	Reproductive and sexual behaviour†	7	1 to 13
6	Occupation	4	2 to 8
7	Pollution	2	<1 to 5
8	Industrial products	<1	<1 to 2
9	Medicines and medical procedures	1	0.5 to 3
10	Geophysical factors‡	3	2 to 4
11	Infection	?10	1 to ?
12	Unknown	?	?

* Allowing for protective effects of antioxidants and other preservatives.
† Multiplicity of sexual partners predisposes to cancer of the uterine cervix.
‡ In addition to the small percentage of sunlight-induced skin cancers that are fatal, there is a much larger number of nonfatal cancers of similar origin.

to man-made chemicals have used to distinguish potential human 'initiating' carcinogens from substances without such potential. It thus came as a great surprise when Ames listed the enormous number and variety of natural food constituents that are mutagens according to the Ames test and other tests for mutagenicity. Included in the long list of foods that contain mutagens are root beer, black pepper, various species of edible mushroom, celery, parsnips, figs, parsley, potatoes, broad beans, and mustard. To this list must be added a further wide range of mutagens that are formed in food during heating or cooking. However, Ames' purpose in publishing his paper was not to frighten us all to death nor to suggest that testing for mutagenesis is pointless because we simply cannot hope to avoid exposure to mutagens. On the contrary, it was to provide a new perspective and to float a new theory concerning the relationships between food, diet and cancer risk.

Ames groups cancers with the degenerative diseases associated with ageing. He writes: 'A plausible theory of ageing holds that the major cause is damage to DNA and other macromolecules and that a major source of this damage is oxygen radicals and lipid peroxidation. Cancer and other degenerative diseases, such as heart disease, are likely to be due in good part to this same fundamental destructive process.'

Something which has intrigued cancer researchers for decades is that rats and mice begin to exhibit ageing-related diseases, including cancers, after only two years of life while humans take 60 years to reach the same condition. And yet, under the microscope, it is difficult to distinguish rat and mouse cells of a particular tissue from human cells of the same tissue. Ames suggests that a major determinant of the rate at which a species ages and its longevity is the basal metabolic rate. This is much higher in small rodents than in man. The basal metabolic rate in turn determines the rate at which oxygen radicals capable of damaging DNA are produced endogenously within cells in the course of their normal metabolic processes. In effect, Ames is suggesting that DNA damaging mutagens are constantly being produced during the quite ordinary and necessary metabolic processes which cells have to carry out as a part of the life process. In other words, even if we abolished mutagens from the external environment and from food we would still be at risk of developing cancers because of the unavoidable endogenous production of mutagens.

Tangential to this concept is the current interest in the protective effect of antioxidants—both the naturally occurring ones (vitamin A, vitamin E) and the synthetic ones (e.g., butylated hydroxyanisole, BHA). There is plenty of evidence from laboratory studies that, under defined conditions, vitamin A deficiency (or deficiency of β-carotene, a precursor of vitamin A) enhances cancer risk. There is also some evidence, both from laboratory studies and from epidemiological surveys, that high dietary intake of vitamin A protects against cancer, e.g., lung cancer in smokers. However, there are two flies in this ointment. The first is that excessive intakes of vitamin A are toxic. Secondly, excessive intake of BHA has recently been shown in Japan by Ito and his colleagues (1983) actually to cause cancer of the forestomach in rats. The mechanism for this latter effect is a puzzle in so far as BHA gives clearly negative results when tested for mutagenicity. Could it be that BHA stimulates an epithelial growth factor in forestomach epithelium or that, as is known to happen with other antioxidants, at high concentrations it acts as a pro-oxidant? The answers to these questions lie in the future. In the meantime, Ames proposes that the antioxidant, uric acid, which is present in the blood of humans in much higher concentration than in other mammalian species, might have evolved to enable a marked increase in life span.

OVERNUTRITION, ENDOCRINE STATUS AND CANCER RISK

It has been known since the 1940's that, in rodents, restriction of food intake protects against the development of cancers both spontaneously and in response exposure to known carcinogens. Until recently, it was believed that, in the case of rodents, 'diet-restriction' is equivalent to 'undernutrition' and that anything short of maximum body weight gain is to be regarded as abnormal. In other words, it did not seem to occur to most toxicologists or animal nutritionists that obesity is just as much a disease in laboratory animals as it is in man. During recent years the major extent to which overfeeding can increase cancer risk in untreated rats and mice has become evident from a number of publications (Tucker, 1979; Conybeare, 1980; Ross et al., 1982). I (Roe, 1981) pointed out that many of the excess tumours in overfed rats were of endocrine glands, e.g., pituitary, thyroid, adrenal, or of hormone-dependent tissues, e.g., mammary gland, uterus, gonads, and furthermore, that serious disturbances of endocrine status always precede the onset of tumours at the affected sites. I next realized that the natural history of endocrine tumours is quite the opposite of that to be expected if the previously discussed two-stage theory of carcinogenesis operated. According to that theory, DNA change comes first and cell proliferation second. But in hormonal carcinogenesis the reverse order seems to be true. First, there is hyperplasia of seemingly normal cells—which is entirely reversible—and only later, if the cause of the hyperplasia continues, do nodules (?clones) of abnormal (?mutant) cells appear. Characteristically, there is a sequence of changes from hyperplasia to benign neoplasia to malignant neoplasia with only the last of these changes being characterised by invasion and metastasis. Does this progressive process, which was called 'tumour progression' by Foulds (Foulds, 1958), represent a sequence of mutations? And is the risk of mutation increased because the rate of generation of oxygen radicals increases *pari passu* with hyperplasia? These important questions clearly merit urgent consideration because some of the commonest cancers of man are of hormone-dependent tissues (e.g., breast, ovary and uterus in women, prostate in men) and it is already clear that overeating and obesity are associated with high risks of cancers of some of these sites. Furthermore, it is quite possible that the risk of cancers of other sites is influenced by hormones or regulatory peptides. It is known, for example, that raw soya flour exhibits potent trypsin-inhibitory activity. When fed in a high concentration in the food to rats, raw soya flour causes hyperplasia of the exocrine part of the pancreas. If the feeding of the soya continues, hyperplasia progresses to benign neoplasia and eventually to malignant cancer (McGuinness et al., 1981). The trigger for the initial hyperplasia is known to be the regulatory peptide, cholecystokinin, which is released in the duodenal wall in response to the presence of proteins in the gut lumen. This suggests that, in the rat, pancreatic cancer may be, in the broadest sense, a hormonally-mediated disease. Is the same true for pancreatic cancer in man?

DISCUSSION

With very few exceptions, e.g., arsenic-containing compounds, all chemicals and physical factors known to be carcinogenic for man have also been found to be carcinogenic for animals. However, for various reasons, the reverse is very far from true. In some cases, the demonstration of carcinogenicity in animals has been dependent on their exposure to very much higher doses than those to which man is ever likely to be exposed. Also, if carcinogenicity tests in animals give positive results, there may never be comparable data for humans since it would be unethical to see whether man would mimic the rat merely to establish the predictive value of the animal test. Another reason for apparent discrepancies between animal and human data may be that it is too early to be sure whether or not a particular compound, e.g., a drug, causes cancer in man because 20 or more years may have to elapse before cancers begin to arise as a consequence of exposure of humans to a carcinogen, whereas only 12–18 months is needed in the case of rats and mice.

If rats or mice develop significantly more cancers following exposure to a test chemical in a carcinogenicity test, it is important to look at the context in which the positive result occurred. Faced with an apparently positive result, I ask a whole series of questions: Were the dose level and the route of administration realistic? Is the test substance absorbed, distributed, metabolized and excreted in the same way in the animals used for the test as in man? Was the apparent excessive cancer risk an artefact associated with a beneficial effect of exposure on survival? Was excessive cancer risk seen only after exposure to toxic levels which led to tissue destruction and regeneration? Was the apparent effect of exposure on cancer risk manifest as an increased incidence of neoplasms that arose commonly or only rarely in contemporary controls? Is the test substance genotoxic? Is the positive response peculiar to one sex or to one species? Does the test compound obviously disturb endocrine or regulatory peptide status?

In the absence of relevant clinical and epidemiological data, laboratory data can provide useful clues as to whether particular foods, drugs or other chemicals are likely to be safe or to constitute cancer risks for man. However, extrapolation across the gulf between the laboratory and man should not be left to persons such as statisticians or lawyers who have no grounding in the complexities of biology. In a qualitative sense, different animal species tend to react similarly to environmental stimuli, but quantitatively they vary widely. An understanding of mechanisms helps to explain species differences in response and improves the precision of prediction as does a full review of the context of positive laboratory results. There are, in fact, five levels òf research in carcinogenesis: epidemiological, whole body, tissue, cellular and subcellular (including molecular biological). All are important. All can provide insights into mechanisms, but only sound epidemiology can pinpoint actual risk for man. Extrapolation from studies on populations of animals to populations of humans can be useful provided common sense is exercised, but extrapolation from some other level of investigative research in the laboratory to prediction of cancer risk for human populations, e.g., solely from investigations at the tissue, cellular or subcellular levels is very unreliable.

REFERENCES

Ames, B. N. (1983). 'Dietary carcinogens and anticarcinogens', *Science* **221**, 1256–1264.

Conybeare, G. (1980). 'Effect of quality and quantity of diet on survival and tumour incidence in outbred swiss mice', *Fd. Cosmet. Toxicol.* **18**, 65–75.

Doll, R. and Peto, R. (1981). *The Causes of Cancer: Quantitative Estimates of Avoidable Risks of Cancer in the United States Today*. Oxford University Press.

Foulds, L. (1958). 'The natural history of cancer', *J. Chronic Diseases* **8**, 2–37.

Ito, N., Fukushima, S., Hagiwara, A., Shibata, M. and Ogiso, T. (1983). 'Carcinogenicity of butylated hydroxyanisole in F344 rats', *J. Natl. Cancer Inst.*, **70**, 343–352.

McGuinness, E. E., Morgan, R. G. H., Levison, D. A., Hopwood, D. and Wormsley, K. G. (1981). 'Interaction of azaserine and raw soya flour on the rat pancreas', *Scand. J. Gastroent.*, **15**, 497–502.

Roe, F. J. C. (1981). 'Are nutritionists worried about the epidemic of tumours in laboratory animals?', *Proc. Nutr. Soc.*, **40**, 57.

Ross, M. H., Lustbader, E. D. and Bras, G. (1982). 'Body weight, dietary practices, and tumor susceptibility in the rat', *JNCI*, **71**, 1041–1046.

Tucker, M. J. (1979). 'The effect of long-term food restriction on tumours in rodents', *Int. J. Cancer* **23**, 803–807.

APPENDIX—PREMATURE DEATH

This term surfaced during Conference discussions and although it is not directly relevant to the above paper, it seemed worthy of comment in a medical context.

'Premature death' is commonly bandied about by those seeking to clean up the environment or persuade their fellows to live simpler, purer lives. For instance, it was used in a 1971 Report by the Royal College of Physicians, London entitled 'Smoking and Health Now'. Death rate data were available for certain smoking-associated diseases among doctors who smoked and doctors who didn't smoke. The assumption was then made that if the smoking doctors had not smoked their death rates from the same diseases would have been the same as those for nonsmoking doctors. On this basis, the number of premature deaths among doctors attributable to smoking was calculated. The further assumption was then made that doctors are representative of the whole population of the United Kingdom. On this assumption the number of premature deaths among the U.K. population was computed.

Although there may be some validity in the two assumptions made, they are obviously far from completely justified. Smokers tend to differ from nonsmokers, both in personality and the extent to which they expose themselves to other environmental factors that are potentially harmful to health. Death rates from all sorts of diseases differ between the social classes. Doctors fall mainly into Social Class II whereas the bulk of the population fall into Classes III to V. For these reasons little reliance can or should be put on calculated actual numbers of 'premature deaths' such as those presented in the Royal College of Physicians Report.

Similar reservations apply to calculations that have been made to the effect that the average smoker reduces his life by x minutes for every cigarette he smokes.

Whatever may be true for populations of exposed as compared with unexposed individuals, it is obvious that the concept of 'premature death' has little meaning in terms of the individual. One cannot say for any individual how long he was designed to live. To some extent, longevity is genetically determined. Therefore, if a man dies or is killed at a tenderer age than is the average for his colleagues, one cannot precisely state whether his death was actually premature and, if so, by how long.

Finally, if one glibly accepts the concept of 'premature death' should one not also conceive of 'postmature death'? Such a term might apply to living vegetables suffering from all sorts of incapacitating age-related diseases except any one that is fatal. Thus, I distrust the term 'premature death' because it presumes that we know more than we do about how long man is supposed to live and what he is designed to die from. When actual numbers are calculated their imprecision gives them a distinctly false ring.

Discussion: Risk and Public Policy

Hovden approaches the central issues of this book, which is the place of risk in decision-making affecting others. At the national level this is labelled public policy and involves politics, not in the narrow sense of manoeuvring between political parties but in the more general sense of the distribution of benefits and burdens within a community. Risk is to do with burdens as they are estimated before decisions, and also as they emerge from decisions. The emphasis again is on the continuous process of satisficing rather than the unequivocable choice of direction. Risks get mixed up with values and objectives such as profits, freedom and happiness. The variety of means at the disposal of authorities also confuses the concept of a decision in the decision theory sense and encourages further the continuous iterative nature of progress. This is now partially recognized in the way that authorities proceed with an emphasis on the distribution of responsibility rather than the enforcing of specific methods. Inevitably, the contribution of risk analysis is much more ambiguous than in a bounded technological situation. It follows that research on risk and safety should include theories of risk handling by individuals, organizations and political institutions, but the methods appropriate to such research are different from research in the physical sciences.

Singleton stresses the importance of conceptual clarity, not only as a foundation for scientific progress but also as a basis for unambiguous legislation. Fuzzy legislation can confuse the highly important question of burden of proof, for example, after an accident does management have to prove that reasonable care was taken or does the aggrieved party have to prove that reasonable care was not taken? In this, as in other areas, it seems that laws and law courts are not as rigid as those involved sometimes like to pretend, there is always flexibility and the influence of current cultural norms as expressed by public opinion is all-pervasive. These cultural norms also dominate the formulation of safety and health law, this is demonstrated by the different approaches of different countries. These are manifestations of the ways in which individuals, either the public or those in authority, respond to a change involving risk in the context of the current zeitgeist. Communication between laymen and experts is also confused by changing cultural patterns.

Sande underlines the importance of costs in considering risks: 'The provision of safety costs money and that money can only be provided by the buyers of goods and services' (p. 184). He considers that although unambiguous information about the success of a safety system is not available, nevertheless a good system will, over time, converge by increasing certainty and reducing costs. He sees the Norwegian offshore oil industry following the example set by the world aviation industry in modelling situations so as to produce extensive data which can guide self-regulation on a cost-benefit basis.

Page 193 describes the different approaches to risk and decision-making at three different levels in the military hierarchy. At the senior level of broad politico-military judgement there is little calculation but an intuitive feel for the total picture. At the intermediate level, detailed calculations involving costs and benefits are the basis of recommendations. At the junior (action) level, risks are part of the whole way of life and men are trained to ignore them at least in the sense that the possibility of failure should not intrude into thought or action. The different attitudes to risk in the preparatory phase and after the declaration of war are analogous to the effects of environmental transitions described by Glendon in Chapter 6. The same reorienting effects of transition are sometimes seen when a procurement policy reaches fruition and the new system is operationally available. It emerges that the success of mutual deterrence depends on accurate evaluations of risks, and on the balance of risk.

Roe demonstrates very clearly that risk estimation based on laboratory studies requires very careful reasoning and that at least some scientists are prone to simplistic extrapolations based on currently fashionable concepts, which may not be entirely valid. In the medical context, the combination of evidence from the laboratory and from epidemiology provides a more reliable understanding of the situation. Epidemiology alone may provide overall risk levels but the linking of causes to more specific risks requires a more theoretical understanding of processes. The nonmedical equivalents of epidemiology are studies involving accident statistics and other data-collection methods involving events relevant to the topic of interest. In these cases, it is even more difficult to move from collated data to concepts of causation. 'Premature death', in common with risk, is a term which can lead to imprecise thinking because superficially it has a straightforward meaning, but closer analysis reveals that it is complex and difficult to calculate. It appears to be relevant to an individual case but in fact it is little more than a descriptor of populations.

More generally, public policy has to be determined by politicians and currently the support they are given by scientists can be diffuse and ambiguous. Scientists also have personal political views which tempt them to unwittingly bias the evidence, rely too much on current fashionable theories which are not unchallengeable and trespass outside their remit into areas properly reserved for managers and politicians. These latter rely on realistic assessments incorporating values as well as factual evidence. It is debatable whether or not such decision-making can be improved by analysis. It becomes more and more clear that probabilistic evidence is not a useful communication vehicle. In the context of risk this means that either this term also must not be used for communication across the scientific/political interface or it must be defined more widely than probabilistically. Psychologists tend to confuse studies of risk with studies of decision-making and hence are tempted to include conse- quences in the definition of risk. In common with other social scientists they are constantly in danger of over-emphasizing the measurable.

Chapter 15

Final Discussion

W. T. SINGLETON AND J. HOVDEN

Risk is to do with exposure to danger and more specifically to mischance. It involves uncertainty as to what might happen and thus is present in situations where there is incomplete information about what will happen. The risks change as the information changes and there is constancy only when there is no more information available. Risks are not entities which can be measured in the way that physical attributes can be measured, they are abstract and dynamic but they remain interesting because they are one set of factors which human beings incorporate into their decision-making. The generic situation is one in which an individual or a group proposes to take action the consequences of which are partially unknown. A move into unknown territory always involves risk, but the move is made because there are also potential benefits. The overall risk is the probability that the outcome will not be beneficial, the downside of the gamble. There are complications in that a particular outcome may have some desirable features and some undesirable features. There may not be agreement about what is or is not desirable—the value problem.

It is inherent in a probabilistic situation that an outcome may be beneficial for a long time and then a disaster occurs because a low probability event happens. In simple situations such as throwing dice, what actually happens does not change the probabilities, but in decisions related to changing technology it does because the frequencies of real events are the best measure of the probabilities.

Management decisions are complicated by the fact that it is not only the real situation which has to be coped with, account must also be taken of relevant legislation. This adds organizational aspects to the already difficult technical aspects.

219

Political decisions incorporate social and cultural aspects from the problems of communication between the decision-makers and the experts to wider societal communication to do with expression of and agreement about values. The credibility of the expert is difficult enough to sustain in a management situation. It becomes almost impossible in a political situation where the evidence and values within an expert opinion are inextricable. When this happens we have recourse to the procedure used by the courts which involves observation of confrontation between experts who support contrasting viewpoints.

The saving grace is that managers and politicians are only making temporary decisions, these can always be reorientated, even reversed, as experience accumulates. In considering decision under risk it is important to accept the dynamic nature of every situation. Nothing is static, the risks change and the decisions change, each situation is just one within a continuous series.

Looking more closely at individuals making decisions it is useful to distinguish four categories:

— one person in a situation involving risk to himself and others,
— the expert examining a situation where he is not in danger and he does not make decisions, rather his task is to pass evidence to the decision-makers,
— the manager, not himself in danger, who is making a decision in the context of the law as well as risks to others for whom he is responsible,
— the policy-maker, again not in danger himself but concerned with very broad and changing risks usually because of the impact of new technology on his constituency.

An individual at risk seems to cope by attempting to adjust the situation so as to make his choice easier. It is difficult to think of an instance outside the laboratory where he might weigh many possibilities, estimate probabilities and consequences for each and then proceed logically on some optimal cost/benefit ratio. The individual begins by eliminating options where the consequences are intolerable and then tries to alter the remainder to bias the odds more in his favour. He then selects a temporary option and proceeds but only tentatively and with a willingness to adjust his strategy as new evidence becomes available.

The expert attempts a scientific approach by systematically considering various possible strategies and assessing the risks within them in the form of probabilities. These probabilities are based on the known history of particular mechanisms which are the same or similar to the ones used in the process under consideration. He looks for patterns and sequences of possible failure and tries to avoid particular design features which increase risks such as 'common-mode' failure. His greatest problem is to include the influence of human operators within his calculations in both the positive sense that the human operator can detect and remedy a potential failing and in the negative sense that human errors introduce new risks. His customer, the policy-maker accustomed to dealing with more concrete reports from natural scientists, medical specialists, accountants and the like, finds it difficult to accept the much more subjective evidence which is the best that a risk scientist can provide.

The manager sometimes acts directly in relation to risks but more usually works by setting up organizational systems which are intended to minimize risk and also to satisfy the legislative authorities who have their own standards of what is acceptable. In principle, the acceptable standards are based on legislation but in practice it is not possible to legislate so precisely as to avoid leaving a great deal of discretion to management and to the compliance officers. Legislation always contains phrases such as 'reasonable care' which requires discussion and even negotiation in the assessment of particular cases.

Policy-makers have the most difficult task because their decisions involve not only complex technical questions but also the incorporation of the particular societal values. There are conflicts originating in technical evidence and in the weight attached to different values. The calculus of risk is very remote from this level of decision-making.

In all these levels of risk consideration the characteristic is decisions within a continuous ongoing process. There is intuitive recoil from decisions which are irreversible, if possible the decision-maker indulges in what he most probably thinks of as a compromise thus keeping options open as long as possible. Given the uncertainties, this is a skilled strategy which nevertheless is irritating to engineers and others who prefer to operate in a world of unambiguous choices. Unfortunately, the necessary lead time and the size of required investment in particular solutions to problems of high technology exacerbates the difficulties and criticalities of such decisions. For example, a problem for every country is to determine the size and mix of particular ways of generating electricity over a decade or so when estimates of electricity demand are uncertain and the costs and risks of using the different energy sources are also uncertain. In such situations it is not surprising to find a manifest resort to satisficing rather than optimizing. Political science has a contribution to make in clarifying the contribution of risk, in concept as well as in measurement, to the complex processes behind decisions within particular societies. The inevitable fuzziness is not, of course, an excuse for relapse into vagueness and mysticism. Although clarification can never be complete it can at least be pursued intelligently and energetically. Complications to do with features such as the different approaches to decision-making within an organizational hierarchy and the very different issue of extrapolation from laboratory data to real problems can only be treated as challenges to more intensive studies. A fundamental difficulty is that most systematic methodologies of study involve analysis whereas decisions of this complexity are essentially holistic.

Although risks have their part in decisions at all levels, the formulation and acceptance of decisions is connected more with features such as credibility and confidence rather than any overall risk computation. Risks in the form of probabilities are mainly useful in systematic task analysis. They help technologists in their individual appraisals and also help communication, particularly in bounded technical systems. The more the system becomes open the smaller the role of risk. That is, risk is a part of technical methodology but has very limited use in communication across the boundaries of technical questions.

This is hardly surprising if it is acknowledged that risk is a measure of ignorance. The essential ignorance is minimal for systems of intermediate size such as technical complexes. For very large systems such as regional and national economies risks are only one minor aspect of the factors contributing to decisions. At the other extreme it is doubtful whether risks can be of much assistance to individuals or decisions about individuals because they only have meaning in relation to populations.

Risk reduction requires a continuous dialogue within and about any system. This is necessary not only because of the tentative nature of all decisions but also because implementation of decisions alters the pattern of existing risks and creates new ones. This is true for the populations exposed as well as for risk levels. All systems, from individuals through working organizations to societies move along assessing risks, adjusting them, accepting them, transferring them and generally trying to preserve and develop themselves in environments which always have some hostile features. When moving forward into unknown territory it is always useful to have a map. The more comprehensive the map the less dangerous is the journey, but functional maps incorporating risks, by definition, contain unknown and only partly known terrain. Risks are measures of the unknown expressed as uncertainty, that is, degree of ignorance.

The limited knowledge which a risk indicates can be refined if risks for subpopulations can be obtained. The opposite process of combining risks to obtain some overall value may have its uses in broad decision-making but it always entails a loss of information. Similarly, attempting to reduce a decision to a series of alternatives may be of some value in describing the process but it disguises other essential features of choice, such as determining the range of options and the range of matching strategies which are collectively called the possibilities.

It remains to try to answer the question raised in the Preface.

1. There are qualitative differences in the meaning of the term risk. The simplest meaning is a probability obtained by logical inference about the behaviour of one part of the physical world, a particular event within this part does not change the risk because events of any level of probability can happen. If the course of events does not match the probabilities then the world is wrong,

e.g., the coin is biased 'do not adjust the controls, there is a fault in reality'. For the statistician, this simple view is extended by various elegant methods of incorporating new evidence into preliminary predictions. For the actuary, risks are based on counts of events which have occurred and have been recorded. Arithmetic only is required, the records are assumed to be correct and the future is assumed to be a linear extrapolation of the past. For the engineer, past data is also the basis of risk estimates, but this is obtained by systematic study and it is modified to take account of changes in technology. For the psychologist, risk is a subjective feeling based on experience of how the world seems to work generally, on what happened in similar situations in the past and on other factors such as confidence in personal skill and the availability of remedial or rescue procedures. For the lawyer, risk is a problem which must be balanced within investigations which must yield a positive (guilty/not guilty) answer from situations loaded with ambiguities. For the manager, risk is partly an ethical problem of personal responsibility and partly a legal problem imposed by the government. For the policy-maker, risk is one feature of complex decision processes on which he may obtain some guidance from technical experts who must restrict their contribution to that which is ostensibly factual—'experts should be on tap and not on top'.

2. Risk is descriptive of populations, not of individual cases. The skills required to convert a risk into a contribution about one case are based on extensive knowledge and experience, e.g., the patient consulting a doctor or the client consulting a counsellor are interested in their own case not in what happens to some overall population. It is not clear how these skills operate. There seems to be an iterative process where the consultant considers the individual as a member of various populations and gradually converges on specific advice. There is an analogy to the use of key word indices to extract a more specific answer by using several indicators. In this sense a risk is one indicator.

3. Prediction using risk data is notoriously fallible in practice and in theory. Unlikely events do happen and the fact that one has happened does not preclude the possibility of it happening again almost immediately. Thus, risks are essentially background information which have only a minor part in strategies of investigating past events and extrapolating to future events. In complex systems, the designer's problem is to try to identify paths leading to untoward events and to find ways of blocking or breaking these paths. Unfortunately, he has no way of concluding that all possible paths relevant to the avoidance or reduction of risk have been identified.

4. Experts and laymen do have qualitatively different ways of forming opinions. This goes some way towards explaining the mutual antipathy which commonly arises during a dialogue. The expert tries to stay within the scientific rules of evidence gathering which requires that he should look carefully at sources of data, their reliability and validity and their relevant populations. His

judgement depends on an understanding of the underlying processes and on detailed analysis of relevant incidents. By contrast, the layman is strongly influenced by the recency and vividness of particular incidents and by mass-media with their peculiar criteria of newsworthiness.

The validity of estimates or opinions for relatively frequent events can be assessed by comparisons of these with event frequencies obtained from records. For highly infrequent events such as the 10^{-6} commonly used in high technology, check of an estimate can only be done indirectly by independent analyses, debates and negotiations.

5. Biases in decisions by experts are often suspected because the experts are usually enthusiastic supporters or opponents of particular technology. Balanced conflict of this kind is a reasonable and democratic way of reaching compromise solutions to large scale problems. The biases in decisions, or more particularly opinions, of laymen are well documented. These are not necessarily unadaptive, there has to be some way of filling gaps in evidence and the apparently irrational procedures used by laymen may have their own relevance. For example, a decision to cancel a flight after hearing of or witnessing an aircraft crash may not be justifiable in terms of the numerical risk of accidents, but it may be quite reasonable on the grounds that continuing with the plan to fly would result in excessive personal stress. The behaviour of groups has been studied extensively in laboratory settings. For many years it was believed that groups make choices involving greater risks than do individuals—this is the 'risky shift' phenomenon which was a very popular research topic around 1970. More recently, the consensus in experimental psychology has swung back to the more commonsense view that the phenomenon is one of group polarisation in which the positions of group members shift towards the majority opinion which may happen to be adventurous or conservative. Thus, any bias will be the bias of the majority.

6. The many factors other than probabilities which individuals use in formulating opinions involving risk are discussed in detail by Brehmer (Chapter 2) and Hale (Chapter 5).

7. Life expectancy is not the ultimate criterion even when dealing with large populations or national scale problems. If it were no country would ever resort to war. At every level, from the nation to the individual, there are other ideals and objectives which are described generally as quality of life. Countries and individuals should have the freedom to select their idiosyncratic risk profiles providing that these do not unduly affect others.

Name index

Subject Index